Praise for *Business Unusual*

As we face increasingly complex challenges, this book offers a vital road map for how we might transcend old ways of doing business and charter a more resilient, purposeful and values-driven path forward. Essential reading for business leaders and educators alike. SCOTT BARRY KAUFMAN, HUMANISTIC PSYCHOLOGIST, AUTHOR AND PODCASTER

Change happens to us or because of us. It's a choice, really. As Nathalie Nahai teaches us, life and work, and possibility, are all a process of becoming. It's what we do along the way that shapes our next adventure. Be the change. BRIAN SOLIS, DIGITAL ANTHROPOLOGIST, FUTURIST AND BESTSELLING AUTHOR OF *LIFESCALE*

Through Nathalie Nahai's thoughtful application of behavioural science and the humanity of her stories, *Business Unusual* lights the way for the future of intelligent branding in a turbulent world. A highly engaging and informative read for anyone wondering how marketing can meet the moment in an authentic way. CAROLINE WEBB, BESTSELLING AUTHOR OF *HOW TO HAVE A GOOD DAY* AND SENIOR ADVISER AT MCKINSEY & COMPANY

Once again Nathalie Nahai has translated the latest findings from psychological science into an immense store of practical wisdom. RORY SUTHERLAND, VICE CHAIRMAN, OGILVY GROUP

In a world where there is no longer any such thing as 'business as usual', Nathalie Nahai's *Business Unusual* is the timely guide to the future you need. This thoughtful and deeply researched study of a wide-ranging spectrum of business challenges – from the trap of 'wokewashing' to the issues of 'Zoom culture' – arms the reader with perspectives and insights that will enable anyone to future-proof their business with confidence. CINDY GALLOP, FOUNDER AND CEO, MAKELOVENOTPORN

Business Unusual is a powerful clarion call for business leaders to see themselves and their stakeholders differently. Nathalie Nahai explains these new rules of engagement with empathy and conviction. These are new rules that we can all embrace. SHARATH JEEVAN, AUTHOR OF *INTRINSIC*

For leaders who feel as though they are bouncing from one crisis to the next, Nathalie Nahai makes sense of the tumult and helps us to feel like there is a path forward built upon resilience, empathy and creative problem solving. JOSHUA MACHT, ACTING CEO, HARVARD BUSINESS PUBLISHING

Very few thinkers, and even fewer writers, can articulate the complex nuances underlining today's biggest business challenges with the elegance, depth and eloquence of Nathalie Nahai. A rare polymath with deep expertise in tech, marketing and psychology, she has written one of the defining business books of our times. Every leader should study this book in detail – we will all be better off if they do. TOMAS CHAMORRO-PREMUZIC, AUTHOR AND PROFESSOR OF BUSINESS PSYCHOLOGY AT UNIVERSITY COLLEGE LONDON AND COLUMBIA UNIVERSITY

Nathalie Nahai richly illustrates the cultivation of bravely responsible, authentic and empathic values – those that build true resilience in this bewilderingly disruptive age. NELL WATSON, TECH ETHICIST, MACHINE INTELLIGENCE RESEARCHER AND AI FACULTY MEMBER AT SINGULARITY UNIVERSITY

In *Business Unusual*, Nathalie Nahai successfully captures changing times as reflected in changing generations. She makes clear the old ways of doing things will no longer suffice in the third decade of the 21st century, when shifting preferences and proclivities dominate business as they do politics. BARBARA KELLERMAN, AUTHOR AND JAMES MACGREGOR BURNS LECTURER IN PUBLIC LEADERSHIP AT HARVARD KENNEDY SCHOOL

A lively, practical guidebook for any business leader navigating the perils of pandemics, tech disruption and radically more judgmental expectations of customers and talent. Because the rules are changing in real time. DAVID ROWAN, FOUNDING EDITOR, *WIRED UK*

Nathalie Nahai is one of the finest minds working in the field of digital culture and consumer behaviour today. This volume is not only timely, important and wise – but clearly written from the heart of a person who values what connects us as humans in the context of the grave challenges and exciting opportunities presented to us by modern technologies. DR AARON BALICK, PSYCHOTHERAPIST, AUTHOR AND DIRECTOR OF STILLPOINT INTERNATIONAL

A powerful, practical guide to thriving in difficult times – a must-read for business leaders and change makers seeking to build a better world. NIR EYAL, BESTSELLING AUTHOR OF *HOOKED* AND *INDISTRACTABLE*

A smart, wide-ranging and wittily accessible tour of our near future, in all its strangeness and novelty. Nathalie Nahai is an expert, insightful guide to what lies ahead – and what it means to face it with hope and resilience. DR TOM CHATFIELD, TECH PHILOSOPHER AND AUTHOR OF *HOW TO THINK*

A wonderfully readable book from one of the field's sharpest thinkers. RICHARD SHOTTON, AUTHOR OF *THE CHOICE FACTORY*

Leaders, learners and lovers of life: Nathalie Nahai has crafted a survival manual for our turbulent times. Building more principled businesses, understanding our minds and crafting a conscious way to act. Business unusual for a world less ordinary. PERRY TIMMS, AUTHOR OF *TRANSFORMATIONAL HR* AND CEO OF PTHR

Business Unusual is a thought-provoking read that provides an engaging and informative road map for a business world filled with uncertainty. This title is supplemented by a series of digital resources, making it not just another business book but a standout toolkit that helps readers join the dots across a sea of complexity. CHRIS KANE, AUTHOR, ADVISER, ADVOCATE AND FOUNDER OF SIX IDEAS

Nathalie Nahai gives you the tools to be fearless in your pursuit of a new kind of business – one that'll make you and the world happier. TARA L LEMMÉY, CEO, LENS VENTURES

In *Business Unusual*, Nathalie Nahai brilliantly explores how values motivate business relationships and gives a road map for cultivating resilience in the face of uncertainty. STEPHANIE M H MOORE, LECTURER IN BUSINESS LAW AND ETHICS, INDIANA UNIVERSITY

Nathalie Nahai brings a powerful combination of business and psychological knowledge to the table to help business leaders navigate the complexities of the modern world. Packed with historical case studies that add rich context to each point, *Business Unusual* is a must-have on every executive's desk. JEREMY DALTON, AUTHOR OF *REALITY CHECK* AND HEAD OF XR AT PWC

The world around us is changing faster than ever and the COVID-19 pandemic is just one of many tectonic shifts in how we approach business, the brands we trust and how we work. In this essential book, Nathalie Nahai guides us through the psychological impact of this incredible pace of change, and most importantly helps us understand how we can be more resilient as people and businesses. MARTIN ERIKSSON, CO-FOUNDER AND CHAIRMAN, MIND THE PRODUCT

It is both a challenge and a privilege that we must rebuild our organizations around a deeper, more meaningful grounding. I'm delighted that Nathalie Nahai has contributed this book. These issues are certainly an important part of the discussion. JOHN FEATHERBY, FOUNDER, SHOREMOUNT

A book about resilience is both timely, but also urgent. Nathalie Nahai skilfully introduces the idea that in the face of adversity, and with the risk of failure at its highest, we have an opportunity to frame our context, not in terms of what went wrong, but in terms of what we could do differently. She reveals how insight and self-knowledge are our most powerful tools and how, as a society, we can choose to cultivate a culture of optimism, purpose and meaning to help guide us through one of the most extraordinary moments in human history. This is a must-read for anyone who is looking for inspiration for how to drive transformational change in the face of adversity.   TOBY DANIELS, CHIEF INNOVATION OFFICER, *ADWEEK*

This is a wonderful read. Full of insights based on rigorous psychology studies and recent technological discoveries explained in an eloquent and accessible way. It includes practical tips for business leaders that need to adapt to the challenges of an ever-changing world.   DR DIMITRIS PINOTSIS, ASSOCIATE PROFESSOR IN COMPUTATIONAL NEUROSCIENCE AND PSYCHIATRY, UNIVERSITY OF LONDON

Nathalie Nahai has written a timely book that illustrates the importance of rethinking company brands in the post-COVID-19 era as well as actionable guidance for how to do it. Based on the socio-cultural changes we have all endured for the past 14 months, Nahai clearly lays out how companies can enhance brand awareness and credibility by addressing transformed consumer values. The increasing focus on trust, authenticity, sustainability, workforce choices and changing attitudes toward interaction – both online and in person – are critical to how companies must represent their brands going forward. She artfully weaves together stories and case studies with insight from psychologists, business leaders and subject matter experts – all connected by her own deep expertise in psychology. The resulting narrative is both enlightening and engaging.   CHRISTOPHER BISHOP, CHIEF REINVENTION OFFICER, IMPROVISING CAREERS

Business Unusual

Values, uncertainty and the psychology of brand resilience

Nathalie Nahai

Kogan Page
INSPIRE

First published in Great Britain and the United States in 2022 by Kogan Page Limited

2nd Floor, 45 Gee Street
London
EC1V 3RS
United Kingdom

122 W 27th St, 10th Floor
New York, NY 10001
USA

4737/23 Ansari Road
Daryaganj
New Delhi 110002
India

www.koganpage.com

Kogan Page books are printed on paper from sustainable forests.

ISBNs

Hardback   978 1 3986 0223 6
Paperback   978 1 3986 0221 2
Ebook   978 1 3986 0222 9

British Library Cataloguing-in-Publication Data

A CIP record for this book is available from the British Library.

Library of Congress Cataloging-in-Publication Data

Names: Nahai, Nathalie, author.
Title: Business unusual: values, uncertainty and the psychology of brand resilience / Nathalie Nahai.
Description: London; New York, NY: Kogan Page, 2021. | Series: Kogan Page inspire | Includes bibliographical references and index.
Identifiers: LCCN 2021022475 (print) | LCCN 2021022476 (ebook) | ISBN 9781398602236 (hardback) | ISBN 9781398602212 (paperback) | ISBN 9781398602229 (ebook)
Subjects: LCSH: Electronic commerce–Psychological aspects. | Consumer behavior. | Internet marketing. | Business ethics.
Classification: LCC HF5548.32 .N353 2021 (print) | LCC HF5548.32 (ebook) | DDC 381/.142019–dc23
LC record available at https://lccn.loc.gov/2021022475
LC ebook record available at https://lccn.loc.gov/2021022476

Typeset by Integra Software Services Pondicherry
Print production managed by Jellyfish
Printed and bound by CPI Group (UK) Ltd, Croydon CR0 4YY

Contents

About the author

Nathalie Nahai is an international speaker, author and consultant, whose work explores the intersection between persuasive technology, ethics and the psychology behind evolving consumer behaviours. With clients including Google, Unilever, Accenture and *Harvard Business Review*, she teaches businesses how to ethically apply behavioural science principles to enhance their online presence, content marketing, product design and customer experience. A member of the BIMA Human Insights Council, she also hosts *The Hive Podcast* and speaks about the impact of emerging technologies in *The Atlantic*, *The Wall Street Journal*, *Business Insider*, *Forbes*, *Harvard Business Review*, *Stylist* and *The Telegraph*, as well as on TV and radio.

Acknowledgements

Writing a book is rarely a solitary endeavour, and this one would not have been possible without the extraordinary contributions of all the researchers, scientists, thinkers and business leaders whose work and case studies I have drawn upon in these pages. I am especially grateful for the generosity, candour and thoughtfulness of the many people who kindly agreed to be interviewed: Aaron Balick, Amy C Edmondson, Barbara Kellerman, Brian Solis, César Christoforidis, Chris Kane, Cindy Gallop, David Rowan, Gillian Isaacs Russell, Jeremy Dalton, John Featherby, Lewis Garrad, Nell Watson, Octavius Black, Perry Timms, Rita Clifton, Scott Barry Kaufman and Stephanie M H Moore. A special thank you to Tomas Chamorro-Premuzic whose insights and introductions were invaluable, and to Reece Akhtar, Tara Lemméy, Toby Daniels and Yessi Bello Perez whose ideas informed my thinking. This project would not have been nearly as joyful nor possible without the brilliance, kindness and competence of Kiki Leutner and Aled Evans, and the attentive editing and support of my editor, Géraldine Collard. My thanks to Kogan Page for believing in this project, to Sven Buechel and Udo Hahn for the use of your VAD model, and to Caro C, my producer at *The Hive Podcast*, for your skill and suggestions. Finally, a heartfelt thank you to Freddy Sánchez Guzmán, for your unwavering patience, insight and support. This project would not have been as rich without you.

Introduction

Thank you for picking up this book. Throughout its pages, you will find stories, case studies and frameworks alongside insights from psychologists, business leaders and experts, which will help you to cultivate greater resilience, whether in your organization, your brand or your team. For a richer experience, you can dive into the full-length guest interviews at *The Hive Podcast*, and discover your values archetype with The Values Map, all of which are listed in the references section at the end of the book. Whatever your goals, I hope that this ecosystem of tools will equip you to better navigate these unchartered waters, and inspire you to build a better world that future generations will be proud to inherit.

CHAPTER ONE

Times they are a-changin'

And the day came when the risk to remain tight in a bud was more painful than the risk it took to blossom. ANAÏS NIN[1]

A shift in priorities

I still remember where I was when I heard the news. It was late February 2020 and, paintbrush in hand, finishing an art sabbatical in Barcelona, the whispers arrived that within 24 hours all schools would be shut and government restrictions announced. With little time to react, I bundled all the materials I could carry into a taxi and headed home to stock up on food and water. Only a month before, as word from Italy was reaching Europe, I had travelled back to London to deliver a workshop and remember, even then, the strange sensation of walking through Heathrow airport for what I suspected would be my last flight in quite some time. Making a beeline to buy hand gel (already in short supply back in Spain), I had been struck by the eerie normality of fellow passengers milling around shops, unaware of the impending chaos, and the creeping sense of dread that would colour the weeks to come, as restrictions ricocheted from one nation to the next. Despite the warnings, few were prepared as we collectively braced for impact, watching on in stunned silence as the world slowly shuttered its doors.

So what do we do when we're knocked off our feet by a blow we never saw coming? Maybe we nurse our injuries, take stock and pick ourselves up, setting out into the world again. But when *all* of us take a hit? How do we recover from that? This question, in its various forms, is one we have had to grapple with since the birth of our species. Although we may long to walk through life unscathed, the reality is, of course, that existence is shot through with challenge, and while some of us may be luckier than others in what we must endure, we will all experience hardship of some kind, at some point. What governs the outcome of these stories, however, is our capacity to conjure **resilience** when we need it most.

What governs the outcome of these stories is our capacity to conjure resilience when we need it most.

Rather than numb ourselves to what is happening or march on with a stiff upper lip, resilience is about developing the psychological skills to cope with adversity, so as to gather ourselves and move forward without suffering long-term negative consequences. There are many ways in which we can increase resilience – from cultivating optimism and learning to regulate our emotions more skilfully, to reframing failure as a form of helpful feedback. Yet when it comes to resilience that spans the personal and the societal, there is one strategy in particular that is known to help us cope with even the hardest situations: consciously living according to our values. From reducing our cortisol levels (a powerful stress hormone) and stabilizing our heart rate,[2] to decreasing the degree to which we ruminate after failure,[3] actively affirming our values can be a powerful way of buffering against the psychological and biological effects of stress (especially if we already possess a solid self-esteem).[4]

In the face of adversity, it can be all too tempting to look for the quick fix or seek avenues of temporary respite, yet research suggests that to build real and lasting resilience, we must bring our whole selves to the task. Dr Edith H Grotberg, author and founder of the International Resilience Research Project, put it beautifully when she wrote that 'a resilient response to adversity engages the whole person, not just aspects of the person in order to face, endure, overcome and possibly be transformed'.[5] Whether we achieve this by focusing on the values we hold dear (such as our relationships, political ideals or love of beauty), or by reflecting on a cherished skill or expertise (that talent in ceramics you've been nurturing), self-affirmation can help to shore up our sense of integrity and wellbeing in very real and tangible ways.

Even amongst those who have survived truly life-shattering events, we know that there are some who will find ways to thrive despite unimaginable odds. In Viktor Frankl's powerful book *Man's Search for Meaning*, he writes of his observations while interred in a concentration camp – that those prisoners who held onto a sense of greater meaning in their lives were somehow able to 'transform a personal tragedy into a triumph, to turn one's predicament into a human achievement'.[6] Amidst the trauma and brutality of the Holocaust, Frankl witnessed the extraordinary capacity people have for resilience even under the most horrific conditions. Indeed, in the years since the book's first publication in 1946, research has come to identify what we now call *post-traumatic growth*: those positive changes we experience as a result of grappling with deeply challenging life crises. From an increased sense of personal strength and appreciation, to more meaningful relationships and a richer internal, existential life, surviving adversity can sometimes lead to greater development and deeper wisdom.[7]

So what does this have to do with business? Well, from the perspective of human resources, we know that people who develop resilience are more likely to bounce back from adversity with greater strength and resourcefulness,[8] a capacity that will only increase in value as we build out of this crisis and into new ways of working. Viewed through an organizational lens, resilience includes coping with disruptions to one's structure, supply chain and business strategy, and, for brands, how one reacts to (and recovers from) attacks against the outward-facing persona of the business. While there are many ways in which to build resilience, as we shall explore throughout this book, to play from a position of strength requires that we understand and adapt to oncoming issues before they become problematic.

For instance, in the light of the intractable challenges we face today, global studies investigating the evolution of consumer behaviours reveal that there are deep and fundamental shifts unfolding in our individual priorities, within society, in our economies and beyond.[9] From observable changes in purchasing decisions, to the ways in which people seek out and consume content they can trust, the commercial landscape is changing. It is as if someone had tapped our collective moral compass and set the needle swinging in search of a new north. Whatever is causing this sea change to arise – and there are many theories – if an organization is to thrive it must first identify the dynamics underpinning these changes, so it is better prepared to meet them.

The first great shift, as you may have sensed, is in the realm of consumer values, with firms such as EY stating that, 'Consumer-facing companies urgently need to anticipate what kind of consumer is emerging, so they can make it through the current crisis and build the capabilities that future relevance will require.' In a survey they conducted with just under 5,000 consumers across the United States, Canada, the United Kingdom, Germany and France, one-quarter of respondents said that they now pay more attention to what they consume and the impact it has, with one-third reporting they would reappraise what they value most and not take certain things for granted.[10] This shift echoes a wider trend towards conscious consumerism, which although criticized by some as a veil for greenwashing, does reflect a real and growing concern among consumers around the impact of their product and lifestyle choices, especially as it pertains to food. When it comes to diet for instance, in the United States alone, surging interest in plant-based products has seen the value of the vegan food industry boom to US $5 billion,[11] with similar shifts in the UK,[12] Australia,[13] Germany and the rest of Europe,[14] heralding a global decline in meat production and consumption.[15] This trend does not stand alone. Attributable to a plethora of causes, this dramatic departure in dietary preferences also parallels another: how we source our products.

Whether for reasons of sustainability, anti-globalization or a sense of renewed patriotism, the provenance of what we buy is becoming an increasingly hot topic. In a study canvassing over 100,000 people across 60+ markets,[16] a whopping 65 per cent of respondents expressed they were in favour of buying goods and services that were produced within their own country, with China, Italy, South Korea and Spain championing the 'buy local' mantra. A further 42 per cent reported that they now pay greater attention to a product's origin, and one in four stated they would prefer that brands bring production back to their own country (no small

Whether for reasons of sustainability, anti-globalization or a sense of renewed patriotism, the provenance of what we buy is becoming an increasingly hot topic.

feat). Not only does this reflect a growing realization of the fragility of our interconnected systems, but also an understanding that resilience (whether personal, social or economic) must be grounded in the local in order to yield greater stability and longer-term success.

At a more grassroots level, we have seen a boom in people wanting to learn about how to grow their own produce, whether in a pot on a balcony, or in a community allotment or garden. While (for most of us) it is unlikely that we would ever be able to grow enough food to claim real independence from the supermarket shop, this renewed interest in self-sufficiency does speak to a desire to reconnect more directly with our food. During the COVID-19 pandemic, urban farms and emergency gardens cropped up from the Philippines[17] to the United States,[18] with volunteers and community groups supplying fresh produce to local food banks and charities, supporting those who were hit hardest. Whether through reclaiming unused land or repurposing existing plots, these actions enabled people to meet the needs of those who were most vulnerable, ensuring greater local resilience and building social support systems that would previously have been inconceivable.

While such projects may seem innovative (especially in more capitalist and individualist societies), these approaches are not new – in response to the European food crisis that emerged during the First World War, the US government encouraged civilians to 'Sow the seeds of victory' to support agriculture across the country. In 1917 alone, 3 million new garden plots were established, with a further 5.2 million planted in 1918. By the time the Second World War was over, the cultivation of 20 million postwar Victory Gardens in the United States produced an estimated 8 million tons of food, roughly equivalent to 40 per cent of all the fresh fruits and vegetables consumed in the United States alone.[19] Far from being a small-scale endeavour, this humble patchwork of emergency gardens grew to such an extent that it was able to support the needs of nearly half the population.

These days, the allotments that flourish across towns and cities not only serve to support elders and communities below the poverty line, they also paint a picture of what can be achieved if we balance business priorities with the need for local food resilience. Although the crises we now face may be different to those encountered by our grandparents, the urge to shorten the distance from field to fork still speaks to our desire for security and reconnection with what sustains us. Yet while this is one example of a move towards greater sustainability, the broader trend need not be confined to the realm of mud and wellies: another sector beginning to respond to the tremors, is transport.

As the spectre of contagion continues to haunt travel at the time of writing, and calls to reduce carbon emissions grow louder, some car manufacturers are struggling to meet competing consumer needs. Take SUVs, for example – since 2010, the sale of these massive cars has accounted for 60 per cent of the increase in the global car fleet,[20] despite their terrible track record as the second-largest contributors to increasing global emissions since that year.[21] With reports warning about the devastating impact such trends could have on vital climate goals, it is clear that our worldwide appetite for bigger, more polluting vehicles needs to find a less damaging expression. So how are businesses responding?

Well, this is where green technology comes in. When Ford declared in 2019 that they would be developing a hybrid-SUV in preparation for the first of several fully electric vehicles, it was welcomed by many as a step in the right direction. The optimism, however, was short-lived. When, in 2020, Ford made the announcement that they would be reviving the Bronco (an off-road SUV discontinued in 1996) without so much as a hybrid version, public backlash among certain sectors was swift and fierce. Touted by *Vice* magazine as 'An Obscene Monument to Climate Denialism',[22] their article captured the growing impatience felt by many, inflaming an already heated debate centering around the US $11 billion investment expected to be made by Ford in 'green machines' by 2022.[23] Such headlines reflect and reveal something of the zeitgeist in which we are living, and when heads of state start announcing grand plans to replace hundreds of thousands of government vehicles with electric fleets (the likes of which iconic, gas-guzzling brands can throw their weight behind), you know that an epic change of gear is under way.[24]

With many such changes rippling out across sectors and industries, being sustainable (or at the very least, taking concrete steps to strive towards this goal) no longer serves as a differentiator; for many, it has become the expected norm. Where a vague nod towards corporate social responsibility (CSR) might once have been enough, consumers now expect businesses to find and enact solutions, especially when their industry is part of the problem. Take Burger King, for example, who in July 2020 released a controversial video ad featuring kids in cowboy hats, yodelling about how cow farts (or more specifically, methane) contribute towards global warming. Despite efforts to name the issue, reframe the conversation and encourage US farmers to change cow diets to reduce emissions, the #cowsmenu campaign quickly came under fire not only for its condescending depiction of cattle ranchers, but also for making the unverified claim (promoting a scientific study that was still undergoing review) that farts and not burps were to blame for the damage.[25] Although admonished by some as empty virtue signalling (which we will explore in Chapter 5), the attempt to educate consumers on the environmental impact of beef, and suggest a possible course of action, indicates the willingness to take a step – albeit a clumsy one – in the right direction.

Talking 'bout my generation

Although employees of all generations appear to be seeking out greener businesses, Millennials stand ahead of the curve, with nearly 40 per cent accepting one job offer over another due to a company's environmental credentials.[26] Given that nearly half have also spoken up publicly either in support or criticism of their employer's actions regarding key societal issues,[27] and leading brands are increasingly taking a stand on pivotal topics, it is becoming clear that traditional CSR may not be up to the task of attracting and retaining upcoming talent. In light of the youth-led climate protests of 2019, estimated to have drawn more than 7.6 million people from 185 countries,[28] the World Economic Forum (WEF) founder Klaus Schwab may have been right when he suggested the global response to COVID-19 has been a 'litmus test for *stakeholder capitalism*'.[29]

When it comes to assessing the validity of claims made by organizations about their social and environmental impact, no cohort is more savvy or critical than the Gen-Z and Millennial generations. While businesses may historically have been conscious of the cost of giving, opting instead to commit the bare minimum to charitable causes (benefitting from tax breaks in the process), this group increasingly wants their employers to put their money where their mouth is and enact their values from the inside out, especially when the going gets tough. This call for responsible business leadership is especially poignant given that the most financially impacted tend also to be those most invested in companies 'doing good',[30] and that during the COVID-19 pandemic it was precisely the younger generations that were hit the hardest.[31] While you might be forgiven for mistaking such trends as relatively new, in reality the signs of dissent have been apparent for many years to those courageous enough to look.

From students putting pressure on 'Big Law' (a nickname that refers to the world's largest, most successful law firms) to protest policies and practices,[32] to employees engaging in mass walkouts for gender equality and racial justice, younger workers are increasingly engaging in employee activism across the spectrum of industries – and some to dramatic effect. In 2021, after years of protests and walkouts by Google staff, a group of 226 employees decided they had finally had enough, and formed a union with the hope of ensuring that the company's motto, 'Don't Be Evil', would be upheld through fair and ethical work practices.[33] While this is only one example, and we are yet to see how such interventions play out in the long term, whether confronting behemoths or the business next door, this climate of accountability is changing the face of business as we know it.

Quite beyond the scope of jaded corporate responsibility, young professionals are peering deeper into the identity of the businesses they work for, and being vocal in naming and shaming unethical practices when they find them. Yet even as this strikes a death knell for some, for organizations that are leading with better environmental, social and governance (ESG) performance there are significant benefits to be gained. From attracting younger talent and eliciting greater employee engagement once hires have been made,[34] to reaping superior shareholder returns that stem from playing a positive role in society,[35] those businesses brave enough to make the change are already cashing in on the perks of doing good.

Even the finance sector, not renowned for its progressive, ethical leadership, has taken note. Prior to the Bank of England receiving a government mandate to buy 'green' bonds,[36] the UK's Financial Conduct Authority had already taken proactive steps to prevent 'greenwashing' and challenge firms making misleading claims over sustainable investments,[37] with the European Commission stating in 2019 that advisers should 'take sustainability risks into account in the selection process of the financial product presented to investors before providing advice, regardless of the sustainability preferences of the investors'.[38] That financial advice firms are integrating ESG considerations into their approach not only demonstrates a commitment to bringing this industry in line with the European Union's climate action plan, it also sends a clear message that ethical investments have gone mainstream. As consumer appetite for sustainable services materializes in a boom of green, digital-first banking products, such as Good Money and TreeCard, and with consumers born between 1981 and 2012 set to make up a whopping 72 per cent of the workforce by the year 2029,[39] it is clear that integrating ESG into one's business strategy – from supply chains and product development, to financing and human resources (HR) – will be absolutely vital if businesses are to recruit, retain and develop talent from this growing pool.

But it is not only the hiring of employees and the structuring of business that is set to change. With 87 per cent of companies citing rising customer expectations as a primary business disruptor, and conversations both public and private centring around the state of our collective future,[40] the rising affluence (and financial leverage) of younger consumers will also exert increasing pressure on companies to meet their more conscientious, values-driven needs. In the third wave of Kantar's COVID-19 Barometer, which canvassed more than 30,000 people's opinions in over 50 markets, 18–34-year-olds were found not only to hold brands to higher account for their actions, but also to carry higher expectations that brands should engage more proactively with society and its citizens[41] – yet this forecast is still to hit home. Published by the World Economic Forum, the Global Risks Report 2020 asserted that while younger people attribute a greater impact to societal and environmental risks on global prosperity, societal leaders and businesses are still lagging behind.[42] It is only a matter of time,

As the youngest come of age, this group will bring their transformative vision, values and expectations to the workplace, the store and the ballot box.

however, before they are forced to catch up. Whether our focus falls upon Millennials or Gen-Z, it is the norms and ideals of the upcoming generations that will shape the future we are yet to inhabit. As the youngest come of age, it is this group that will bring their transformative vision, values and expectations to the workplace, the store, and of course, the ballot box.

Online behaviours

While the ongoing COVID-19 lockdowns spelled disaster for countless industries across the world, sheltering-in-place also ushered in an unprecedented boom for e-commerce, social media platforms and media consumption, sending the profits of Silicon Valley's tech giants soaring. Enforced isolation not only revealed (and reinforced) the extent to which the internet scaffolds society, it also cemented the notion of tech companies as fundamental necessities for modern life. From the increased trial and adoption of online fitness, gaming and entertainment streaming, to the widespread use of grocery and restaurant delivery apps, our reliance on digital services to help us work, rest and play fundamentally changed the way in which we operate, with Gen-Z, Millennials and higher-income households driving much of the change.[43]

But it is not just the accelerated adoption of technology that birthed new trends in consumer behaviour. External pressures, such as the limited availability of products and lack of access to preferred brands, also resulted in more mutable consumer-brand relationships. With studies reporting swathes of consumers shopping online for products they had never bought on digital channels before (in this instance, 50 per cent),[44] and others finding 40–50 per cent of consumers worldwide switching stores, brands or websites in the absence of their preferred choice,[45] it fast became apparent that the holy grail of customer loyalty might be flimsier than we thought. Factor in a desire for greater convenience and control alongside this willingness to explore new, unfamiliar brands and products, and a fissure starts to widen between those businesses that can respond to these trends with agility, and those that cannot.

Where adaptive businesses stand to gain from such exploratory behaviours, there are many others that will lose. Take the movie industry, for example. With 96 per cent of global consumers reporting that they now consume more digital media since the outbreak (60 per cent watching more news, 52 per cent streaming more videos and films),[46] our embrace of the virtual has also transformed expectations around how and where we consume entertainment. When cinemas were forced to close their doors indeterminately, film studios from Disney and Universal, to Sony and Paramount took the bold (and some would say, obvious) decision to release some of their films as paid downloads for viewers to access via digital platforms, many of which were their direct competitors. Given the reluctance of many audiences to venture back into enclosed public spaces, this move was generally welcomed by film-lovers, and in some cases even wound up breaking viewership records. When Sony Pictures sold *Greyhound* (the Second World War movie starring Tom Hanks) to Apple for US $70 million, Hollywood news site Deadline declared the takings as 'commensurate with a summer theatrical box office big hit'.[47]

Despite (or perhaps due to) this success, the decision to abandon physical venues in favour of their virtual counterparts predictably incurred the wrath of many cinemas, with AMC and Cineworld declaring a ban on Universal Studios movies once theatres reopened. They probably feared what we all suspect: that new habits can be hard to break, and once we get a taste for the convenience of life-on-demand, businesses that fail to reinvent may find themselves on the shelf alongside the Blockbusters of this world (this was not AMC's fate – they ended up striking a deal with Universal to release films online at an earlier stage[48]).

Beyond the big screen, the increase in media consumption has also brought opportunities to reach and connect with customers in a different, more personalized context. With trustworthy content a high priority for many, the ability to assess and discern the appropriate environment to place an ad, for instance, can make the difference between its success or failure, and ultimately, that of the product or service behind it. Given the mass migration of consumers to e-commerce and our increasing reliance on digital advertising, it pays to ask, what makes for a persuasive context? This is exactly what Adobe and YouGov set out to discover, in a study exploring seven credibility beliefs.

Assessing how appealing, credible, trustworthy, believable and relevant video ads were perceived to be, as well as whether the video made consumers want to learn more or purchase, the research revealed that ads placed on premium channels were ranked as 20–50 per cent more credible than those placed on non-premium channels. Perhaps unexpectedly, ads on TV were also rated higher across all key performance indicators (KPIs) by respondents under age 30, and ads placed on Facebook and

Instagram outperformed ads on Twitter across all measures.[49] A similar trend was also echoed by display ads – those located on premium sites and content channels elicited better engagement, outperforming the same ads placed on UGC channels (platforms that rely on users to generate content, such as photos, videos and articles), with click-through rates 2.3 and 4.5 times higher than non-premium on mobile and desktop, respectively.

But advertising is not the only area in which trust is playing an increasingly prominent role. With global trust in societal institutions of government, business, media and non-government organizations (NGOs) at an all-time low even prior to the COVID-19 pandemic,[50] the importance of building trust throughout the entirety of one's business ecosystem cannot be overstated (as we shall see in Chapter 2). The tide has turned, and along with it, the dynamics of consumption. Frustrated with the pace of change, people are increasingly voting with their virtual feet, even in domains where friction is greatest. The canary in the coal mine, as waves of consumers finally abandon WhatsApp in favour of other, more secure messaging platforms such as Telegram and Signal, it is clear that the battle to build trust – especially as it pertains to data, privacy and the abuses of both – will be one of those most fiercely fought this decade.

A digital transformation

For most businesses, ambiguity and profit do not make great bedfellows. Unless you are in the trading industry, a volatile market is not likely to inspire confidence for decisive action, yet it is especially under such conditions that clarity of leadership, vision and purpose can lead a business to develop the capabilities required for resilience. Historically, during a downturn, most companies typically take either significant hits or fail completely, with only one in three successfully navigating disruptive shifts.[51]

In 2020, despite substantial risk to IT infrastructure and cyber-security,[52] businesses rolled out remote working capabilities at such scale and with such urgency that it betrayed the panicked realization of what might happen if they didn't. Companies that had been dragging their feet, resisting digital transformation or finding excuses not to engage with it, were suddenly confronted by a bleak vision of what might await them if they didn't.

Of course, under lockdown conditions, our reliance on technology to fulfil needs as varied as social contact, access to education and food meant that, for many, it became the fulcrum upon which the balance of our lives depended. Yet the crisis also offered a radical opportunity for digital resilience. With 75 per cent of executives regarding digital transformation as more urgent in light of the COVID-19 pandemic, and 65 per cent anticipating increasing their investments in this area,[53] the accelerated adoption of automation, data analytics and digital tools will not only deepen our dependence on technology, but also transform the future of how (and where) we do business.

Already, the rapid development of voice recognition and mixed reality (whether virtual or augmented), appear poised to change the ways in which we communicate, which, alongside an increased comfort with video calls, are causing some to question whether pre-pandemic artefacts such as call centres might soon be consigned to the past. As more advanced technologies enable us to experience richer, truly omni-channel interactions with our favoured brands, the line between digital and physical customer experiences will continue to blur. Already in China, companies have seen their

How can we create a sense of attachment and purpose in an agile but atomized workforce?

revenues increase by 10–30 per cent as a result of retail staff engaging local customers through social channels,[54] and it is only a matter of time before the blending of the virtual and the physical is no longer the exception, but the norm.

Whether you are using advanced analytics to predict daily demand for specific stock, integrating chatbots to automate customer recommendations, or investing in internet of things (IoT)-enabled operations, no aspect of business will be left untouched by this technological renaissance. Yet if businesses are to thrive in the long term, we must lift the veil on the human psyche and explore the behavioural dynamics that are shaping (and arising from) this moment in time. What do such changes mean for the culture of our organizations? What consumer trends must we understand if we are to contextualize and interpret data-driven insights? How can we create a sense of attachment and purpose in an agile but atomized workforce? In the face of such gargantuan change, it is our insight, creativity and subtle understanding of human behaviour that will enable us to truly cultivate resilience. Technology may be a great enabler, but if we are to achieve anything of real value, we must put our tools in the service of something greater: a sense of purpose and meaning in which we can find deeper fulfilment, whether as employees, stakeholders or consumers.

In the face of such gargantuan change, it is our insight, creativity and subtle understanding of human behaviour that will enable us to truly cultivate resilience.

Key takeaways

- Resilience is about developing the psychological skills to cope with adversity, and can be developed by reframing failure as feedback, cultivating optimism, learning to regulate emotions, and consciously living according to our values.
- When encountering adversity, if we can connect with a deeper sense of meaning it is possible to experience the kind of growth that enhances our appreciation for life, increases our personal strength, and leads to wisdom and development.

- The COVID-19 pandemic has accelerated many changes in consumer behaviours, from increased interest in local, sustainable goods with clear provenance, to products and services that reflect customer lifestyles and ideals.
- Gen-Z and Millennials hold brands and employers to higher account, and are a key force pushing for organizational culture change. Concerned with societal issues, they believe brands should engage proactively with society and its citizens, and prefer to work for (and buy from) businesses whose values align with their own.
- Ethical and sustainability concerns are driving big changes across industries, as organizations leave CSR behind in favour of more comprehensive ESG strategies.
- With global trust in government, business, media and NGOs at an all-time low, trust is one of the most fundamental factors vital to the long-term success of any organization.

CHAPTER TWO

We demand more

Hard times arouse an instinctive desire
for authenticity. COCO CHANEL[1]

And who, are you?

The year was 1920, and it was another grey, dreary day in London. At the sparkling Rolls-Royce showroom in Mayfair, staff were going about their business, lavishing attention on well-heeled prospects, when in walked a nondescript, almost shabby-looking man in simple clothes. Scanning the room, he spotted the Rolls-Royce Phantom II Tourer, and turned towards a young salesman to enquire about the car. With a cursory glance, the salesman dismissed him out of hand and invited the interloper to leave the premises. Undeterred, the gentleman summoned the manager and promptly announced 'I will have every one of these', pointing to the seven gleaming cars arrayed in front of him.

This was no ordinary walk-in. The collector revealed himself as the Maharaja of Alwar, and upon making his purchase, demanded that the vendor meet one condition – that the salesman who had snubbed him escort the cars personally to India. Naturally, the employee was delighted, and his friends envious. He embarked upon the long journey to the continent, and on the appointed day saw that the cars were proudly displayed in front of the great palace. When the Maharaja finally made his appearance, he gestured towards the cars and instructed that the municipality use them to collect local rubbish. Of course, news spread fast, and with the attendant 'shame' of having to sweep the streets, it is said that the Rolls-Royce fleet and reputation took a heavy hit.

Whether fact or fiction, this tale of delayed revenge illustrates not only the pain wrought by rejection and discrimination, but also the lengths to which we will go to redress the balance when we have been so callously dismissed. It also reminds us that even the most prestigious of brands are not immune from such fates, a theme I unpack when I interview Tomas Chamorro-Premuzic, author and Professor of Business Psychology at University College London and Columbia University. When I ask him about what brands can do when mistakes are made, he tells me, 'It's really difficult to repair and patch things up... Trust and credibility take ages to build. There's a reason why reputable brands have been with us for a long time. They've been consistent and they have very clear principles and a clear image.' Although few of us might share the standing or wealth of a maharaja, we do possess the power to call out and amplify stories of wrongdoing when we find them, which is why, as Tomas warns, 'one small blip can really destroy your reputation'. So what can businesses do to build reputational resilience while reducing the possibility of things going wrong? It all starts with trust.

Fundamental to happy, well-functioning relationships,[2] trust not only enables us to create more meaningful, fulfilling bonds with our friends and loved ones, it also plays a pivotal role in our relationship to organizations. From building stronger brand attachment and commitment, to increasing customer loyalty and resilience towards negative brand information, trust is vital to the consumer–brand relationship. It is also the magic ingredient that engenders forgiveness from customers when brands inevitably err.

At a moment in which the very fabric of global society is being strained, and our capacity for change tested, it is our ability to understand, prioritize and forge trusting relationships that will enable us to collaborate with deeper meaning and direction, to create a future that is more hopeful than the present we inhabit. If we are to build greater resilience, not only in our businesses, but also at societal and international levels, we need bold, creative visions that we can work towards – especially during times of upheaval, in which the distress we experience can make it all too easy to fall into apathy, fear and depression. Indeed, when I ask *New York Times* bestselling author Dan Pink what qualities he believes are key to business resilience, he responds, 'One would be tolerance for ambiguity. It's murky out there. That's always been true, but today the murkiness (and the dread that often accompanies it) is even greater. Instead of pushing for false certainty, we're better off simply accepting the ambiguity and understanding that we're always going to make choices based on insufficient information from a menu of imperfect choices.'

Without the comfort of a clear path forward, in the face of overwhelming ambiguity it is often those leaders that hold a tangible vision, the power to enact change and the determination to succeed that end up taking the reins, shaping the future as they imagine it (whether for good or ill). While changing tack under volatile market conditions may feel risky, for those with the courage to do so it can be the perfect time to reassess and realign one's business according to deeper principles. If, as global studies suggest, we are seeing consumer priorities shift at a profound and unprecedented level, then reflecting the values that are driving these changes is a powerful way for organizations to both attract and retain the best talent, as well as maintain relevance with consumers. From under the well-worn cloak of corporate social responsibility, businesses are already venturing out towards the richer, more nuanced concepts of brand identity and mission. From the well-established buy-a-pair, give-a-pair approaches of companies such as Toms Shoes and Warby Parker, to the work of activist brands such as Patagonia and Ben & Jerry's, there is a rising tide of businesses that are recognizing the value of profit with purpose.

The swelling ranks of certified B-Corp companies, for instance (businesses that have met the highest standards of verified social and environmental performance, legal accountability and public transparency to balance purpose and profit), reflect a deepening desire the world over to buy from, work for and invest in those businesses we believe in. Positioning their certification process as 'the most powerful way to build credibility, trust and value for your business', at the time of writing, the B-Corp group includes brands as diverse as Hootsuite, Allbirds and Eileen Fisher, and with over 3,821 businesses already qualified, their followership looks set to keep growing.[3] The members of this pioneering collective, however, are not the only ones heeding the moment. Given that a whopping 81 per cent of Millennials expect companies to make public declarations of their corporate citizenship,[4] and 73 per cent are willing to pay more for sustainable goods and services,[5] it is no wonder that ethics, social impact, genuine brand personality and treatment of employees have been reported as the most influential triggers for enhancing reputation.[6] Gone are the days in which a product merely had to do what it said on the tin to satisfy the customer. Now, as the Reputation Institute report notes, a business must be more than the sum of its parts if it is to succeed. Rather, its reputation must be built not only upon the quality of its products, but on positive societal influence, acts of fairness, and the behavioural ethics to which it adheres.[7]

On good behaviour

Once only a clarion call for those 'do-good' organizations and NGOs willing to sacrifice profit for purpose, the notion of ethical business practice (and its impact on trust and perceived brand value) has finally made it to the boardrooms of even the most profit-driven corporations, and for good reason. In a massive online survey looking at 40 global companies common across the United Kingdom, Germany and the United States, Edelman discovered a powerful dynamic playing out between ethics and competence in the cultivation of trust.[8] With competence referring to ability (being good at what you do), and ethics comprising purpose (trying to make a positive impact on society), integrity (being honest) and dependability (keeping your promises), the study found that no institution – whether NGOs, governments, industries or the media – was perceived as both competent *and* ethical. The data was damning – although the only institution seen as competent was business, the industry failed to meet respondents' expectations for ethics (only NGOs met this standard, but they in turn failed to meet expectations for competence).

These results may not seem particularly surprising, but given that **ethics** were found to be *three times* more important to building company trust than competence, if businesses are to appeal to consumers in the long term, ethical practice must be front and centre of their operations. Indeed, while utility, price and convenience may still be primary motivators for many consumers, depending on context and category of the purchase, the study revealed that a whopping 64 per cent of customers already identify as belief-driven buyers. Given that this majority will choose, switch, avoid or boycott a brand based on its position on societal issues, it seems clear that standing for something (and the cost of failing to do so) is an issue that brands can no longer afford to ignore.

So what does this mean in practical terms? When it comes to understanding customers, the study identified three key segments: leaders, joiners and spectators. As you might guess, people who classified as 'leaders' were those who held strong and passionate beliefs, which they expressed in part through the brands they bought from. The 'joiners' were more flexible, reporting that they would change their purchasing patterns depending on the issue and the brand, and the 'spectators' didn't make belief-driven purchases, nor punish brands that took a stand. While useful as a framework from which to understand and map out belief-driven personas (which we will explore when we look at values in Chapter 5), this approach doesn't address how to navigate the risks endemic in relating to consumers on such terms.

As customers move further into the leaders and joiners camp, brands and business leaders are struggling to keep up, with those at the sharp end falling prey to what some might describe as a spectacularly ruthless 'cancel culture'. Not only the fate of ill-advised companies (countless celebrities and individuals have also met this sticky end), this peculiarity of our time refers to a form of social and professional boycott, in which public support is withdrawn from the entity deemed to have violated social justice norms. Whether the transgression is large or small, recent or historic, the offending brand or person will typically be so thoroughly group-shamed across media and social channels, their reputation and social standing so irreparably damaged, that their ability to participate in public and economic life is essentially 'cancelled' by those scrutinizing their misdemeanours.

Whether for or against such admonishments, the resulting stigma and ostracization is a plight most would strive to avoid. In this light, then, what can businesses do to eschew such an outcome when mistakes are made? Well, where there is rupture, there is also room for repair – but only if we are able to understand the nature and extent of the damage. When trust is broken, it can undermine even the most established relationships, leading not only to customer disappointment (and in the extreme, rage), but also to a loss of sales and competitive advantage.[9] If businesses are to avoid such hits, then learning how to spot the early warning signs and make amends before things escalate is absolutely vital. Whether you use social listening tools, chatbots or live customer support, your first line of defence will almost always be **verbal**. Customers will find ways to tell you (or others) what they are unhappy with, but it is what you choose to do with that information that can make the difference between a loyal customer or a lost relationship. When it comes to complaints, there are various approaches you can take to deal with the issue, from apologies, denial and promises, to giving explanations, sharing information or advertising. Not all strategies, however, are created equal.

No stranger to public controversy, United Airlines have at various times been in the spotlight for their underwhelming performance in customer service and the poor treatment of their passengers – from the events that led to the now famous viral video, 'United Breaks Guitars',[10] to the barring of two teenage girls for wearing leggings while travelling under an employee travel pass (which included a dress code).[11] But in 2017, United surpassed even their own abysmal track record in a debacle that would cost them more than just their reputation. As reported in Inc.com, having overbooked a flight, United Airlines cabin staff requested that passengers volunteer to disembark so as to make space for standby crew. According to a witness, 'they randomly selected people to kick off', until they came to one man, Dr David Dao, who refused to leave the aircraft as he had hospital patients to attend to at the other end.[12] What should have finished there quickly escalated into a bloody scene, with concerned passengers shouting in protest as the doctor was forcibly dragged from his seat by three security guards. Undeterred by growing complaints, the officers violently removed him from the aircraft, leaving the man with a broken nose, lost teeth and a concussion, injuries so grave that he had to be admitted into hospital for treatment (the irony wasn't lost on him either).

The entire ordeal was caught on camera by other passengers and immediately went viral, the internet holding its breath in anticipation of how the airline would respond. Time passed, and United finally issued an apology – not for the horrific treatment of an innocent, paying customer, but for (and I quote) 'the overbook situation'.

Announcing that 'further details on the removed customer should be directed to the authorities', the statement caused such an outcry that people flooded Twitter with a torrent of memes denouncing the airline's extraordinary behaviour, with many businesses stating they would never fly with United again. From what could have been an entirely avoidable scandal, United Airlines ended up paying out a multi-million-dollar settlement to Dr Dao,[13] whose subsequent book, *Dragged Off*, went on to document 'the many small but significant acts of racial discrimination faced on the way to the American Dream'.[14] The moral of the story (aside from refraining from unwarranted violence), is that denial usually gets sniffed out for what it is, and apologies will not tend to recover consumer trust unless they are sincere,[15] explicit and unreserved.[16]

When trust has been violated, sharing information and making promises to resolve the issue can also contribute towards repair, but only if the declaration is honest and the promise is supported by evidence that demonstrates the progress being made.[17] Regardless of the strategy selected, for any approach of promise-making to truly rebuild trust, it must be based on a robust understanding of the nature of the damage caused, so that appropriate reparations can be made. When the beloved *Simpsons* show announced that they would end the use of white actors to voice people of colour,[18] for instance, it stood as a clear (albeit belated) example of the kind of promise and commitment required to move towards redressing racial injustice within their industry. Not all interventions, however, may be so direct or straightforward, and, in many cases, repairing lost trust will depend on a more complex and complete commitment to organizational restructuring, as we shall see in Chapter 5.

The real thing

Whether you are seeking to build connection or repair damage caused, the success or failure of a given strategy will depend on how authentic it is perceived to be. Despite being woefully oversold and underused, the concept of **authenticity** (from a psychological perspective) refers to the quality of being real, true and genuine, and in a brand context tends to relate to the congruence between the company's norms and values, and those of their customers.[19] From a philosophical, existentialist position, it is the extent to which your actions are aligned with your desires and beliefs, despite the force of external pressures. Most of us have an intuitive sense for what it means to be 'true' to ourselves, yet for various reasons, this state of genuineness can be elusive (and at times costly) to maintain. When Ralph Waldo Emerson opined that 'to be yourself in a world that is constantly trying to make you something else is the greatest accomplishment',[20] he was pointing not only towards one of the most difficult, invisible challenges we can face as individuals, but also the difficulties we encounter in the groups and structures we create. While the ability to inhibit or suppress certain aspects of ourselves can be useful at times (you wouldn't get very far if you shouted at your boss every time you felt angry), as we touched upon earlier, our ability to live according to a set of beliefs and values can have profound and positive effects, both in our personal lives and beyond.

Conducting oneself with authenticity, however, need not entail grand gestures or the recitation of lengthy mission statements. In the realm of the influencer, for example, even the simple act of portraying oneself without the perfect hair, make-up and filter can be subversive. Amidst all the meticulously lit, impeccably staged performances and selfies, it is no wonder that gems such as comedian Naomi Watanabe stand out from the crowd. Perhaps best known to western audiences for her celebrity appearance in *Queer Eye: We're in Japan!*,[21] not only is Naomi the most-followed person in her country (known as the 'Beyoncé of Japan' for a series of famous impressions), she is also a vocal champion for body positivity in a culture where the subject remains, as in many places, taboo.

What is refreshing is that along with the high-fashion, techni-coloured press shots that pepper her Instagram feed, she also posts fresh-faced, non-airbrushed photos and videos of herself to her 9 million-plus followers. I remember one post in particular that caught my eye when the lockdowns hit. A split-screen selfie, the left half showed Naomi's fresh-out-of-the-shower face, and the right, her striking alter ego complete with neon-pink hair and brightly coloured make-up. In the accompanying text, she wrote that she would be on YouTube Live at a specific time that evening, and, knowing that many people would be eating alone, she invited her fans and followers to 'Come eat a meal with me'.[22] This juxtaposition of the unfiltered and the picture-perfect, alongside a genuine expression of kindness, struck such a chord that the post itself received more than 280,000 likes. But it is not just influencers that stand to gain from bringing a more complete version of themselves to the table.

With remote working now a widely adopted norm, many of us have come to realize the extent to which our lives and identities (and those of our colleagues, no matter their seniority) exist beyond the personas we bring to work. In attempting to negotiate the blurring of our private and public spheres, we have inadvertently laid the groundwork for some deeper changes to take place in terms of how we relate with one another professionally. This new reality really hit home for me one afternoon late in August 2020, when I called the insurers Allianz about my policy. Rather than the usual, insistent jingle I was anticipating, I was instead greeted by a pre-recorded message acknowledging that callers might hear pets or family members in the background, as their staff were working remotely to ensure they could continue serving their customers. I was surprised (and dare I say it, even delighted) that the company had named and framed the situation so clearly – it felt refreshingly human, and actually made me feel more open and responsive when a representative finally did pick up my call.

While this vignette gives a nice snapshot as to how we might weave authenticity into a specific customer touchpoint, being 'authentic' across all aspects of one's business can be difficult to achieve and can even result in unintended consequences when we do. Given the risk and investment involved, it can be tempting to ask yourself, what's the point? Well, from a brand perspective, perceived authenticity can lead to a whole host of desirable outcomes. From improving the consumer–brand relationship and increasing people's receptivity to your message,[23] to boosting brand trust[24] and the perceived quality of your products or services,[25] businesses that conduct and express themselves authentically stand to gain a competitive advantage over those that don't. Given the benefits, then, it is no wonder that so many campaigns – from Coca-Cola's 'the real thing' to Nike's 'authentic athletic performance' – have aimed to hit this note.

Of course, a sharp eye might be quick to point out my inclusion of the word 'perceived' ahead of authenticity. You may be asking yourself, if it's just about perception, what is the point of all the hard work when you could just fake it? The answer has to do with mental stress and trust. In the 1950s, a psychologist named Leon Festinger put forward a theory of **cognitive dissonance**, which proposed that in order to function well in the real world, human beings strive for internal psychological consistency.[26] If our internal values and belief systems contradict one another, or our actions go against our ideals, the psychological stress we experience as a result is so uncomfortable that we will try to justify the stressful behaviour either by adapting what we're doing, changing what we think about our actions, or avoiding contradictory information and contexts that might augment our sense of dissonance. In everyday life, this can show up as the discomfort we feel when we want to stand up for someone on the principle of inclusivity, but somehow fail to do so; or when we commit to reducing our waste only to buy from a supermarket that wraps everything in plastic.

The problem is that for many of us this experience is painfully familiar. Despite a desire to orient ourselves around cherished values, the tensions and complexities of everyday life can make it challenging to live up to them in every context. At some point, whether as individuals or brands, all of us will fall into the *value-action gap* – situations in which our values fail to systematically materialize into action, whether through lifestyle choices, purchasing behaviours or business decisions. When this happens, we have to try to make amends with (and reduce the dissonance between) past and present behaviours, closing the gap between our actions and the values we aspire to live up to. Although this may be tricky, we can turn to others to lend a hand, which is where trust comes in.

If you are familiar with the field of psychology, you will know that entire libraries have been written about the biases that underpin human behaviour. Try as we might, with so much of what we do and think governed by unconscious machinations, it's a wonder that we are able to change our behaviours at all. Yet change we can, and with deliberate, concerted effort, we have the power to make choices that reflect the people we wish to become. Because it requires energy and commitment, when a consumer makes the decision to trust (and buy from) one brand over another on the basis of shared values, if the brand fulfils their promise and enables the consumer to better live their ideals, this can build towards longer-lasting trust, credibility and loyalty. Known as **consumer–brand identification**, this cultural fit – where a brand's norms and values are congruent with those of its consumers – is also a powerful driver of brand authenticity (as we saw earlier),[27] which in turn can enrich the consumer–brand relationship. If such promises are broken, however, the cost of dissonance for the consumer can be so great that they may never purchase from that brand again.

We have the power to make choices that reflect the people we wish to become.

So returning to the question of faking it: although you could indeed choose to signal authenticity without walking the talk, the majority of consumers are now so well equipped and invested in seeking out brands that support their values, that those unable to meet their needs authentically will end up being called out and left behind, and not without attracting a fair amount of social shaming in the process.

Cognitive dissonance, however, is not restricted to the realm of individuals and consumer behaviour. From claims about transparency and equal gender pay, to sustainability and inclusive hiring practices, it is not uncommon to hear stories of organizations making values-based appeals to attract stakeholders and employees, only to fall short when it comes to enacting them. Where once this kind of friction may have been tolerated or even expected, as the majority of the workforce skews towards the values-driven Millennials and Gen-Zs, failing to be coherent in word and deed can now spell disaster for organizations wishing to attract and retain talent. So what can businesses do to conduct themselves more authentically?

A word on authenticity

Well, there's a lot of research that reveals which characteristics a brand can express to signal its authenticity to others. From **indexical** authenticity (which relies on objective, evidence-based facts[28]), to **iconic** authenticity (which results from a consumer's feelings and imagination about how the brand 'ought to look'[29]), there are many things a brand can do to better convey that it is 'the real thing', distinct from its competitors. Take, for example, a craft beer brand from Barcelona that wants to convey a message of authenticity to its consumers. It could either talk about how the hops are locally sourced and processed in Catalonia (indexical, fact-based authenticity), or it could design packaging and marketing materials that reflect the culture and associations its consumers might expect in such a product (iconic, impression-based authenticity). Given that perceptions of authenticity are usually informed by subjective and objective facts, an approach that draws on both is likely to have the most impact.

What is more, the concept of brand authenticity can also be broken down into practical steps that you can readily apply. Broadly speaking, for a brand to embody authenticity business-wide, it must express its values and norms in three key ways. It must be *consistent* and be able to fulfil its brand promise at every touchpoint, showing stability and continuity through a mission statement that is supported by past behaviours. It must conduct itself with *honesty*, by demonstrating credibility, a commitment to quality, and having a reliable track record. Finally, it must show that it is *genuine* by conducting itself with integrity and sincerity, expressing its individuality without succumbing to external pressures or pandering to the latest trend. In a nutshell, if a brand can reflect its core values and norms in a consistent way, using facts and feelings to express itself with integrity, people will perceive that brand as being true to itself, and will respond more favourably towards it.

Given that our desire for authenticity can be especially strong during times of uncertainty and change,[30] it may come as no surprise that brand authenticity can also be influenced by a sense of continuity and **nostalgia**. When life is difficult, we look for reassurance that things will work out, and one of the ways in which we comfort ourselves is through seeking out experiences that feel familiar and reassuring. Psychologically, nostalgia is a curious phenomenon – not only do we process pleasant information more accurately and efficiently than things we don't like,[31] but when we tell nostalgic stories we also use more optimistic words and phrases than we do for everyday events.[32] Known as the Pollyanna principle,[33] this positive bias we have when thinking of the past is not just something that makes us feel good; it can actually boost our sense of meaning in life.[34]

This is why, when a brand has a legacy and a tradition behind it, reminding people of this story during hard times can be a powerful, emotionally resonant way of reconnecting with and uplifting them. Whether proactively communicating a brand's history, relaunching historical products and package designs, or reviving old brand claims, there are many ways to reignite a sense of nostalgia that connects consumers to a beloved brand. One of my favourite examples here is the story of a New York deli, Katz's, established in 1888 in the Lower East Side. Home to millions of newly immigrated families, this bustling and vibrant neighbourhood would see flocks of people congregate at Katz's every Friday to eat their famous franks and beans. A beloved focal point for the community, Katz's survived the pandemic of 1918 and the First World War, but when the Second World War arrived, conscription came knocking and all three of the owners' sons were deployed abroad. Concerned they wouldn't be eating well, Grandma Katz decided to send her grandsons some carefully wrapped salamis, the only food durable enough to make it through long postal delays and poor conditions. The idea caught on, and a new tradition was born as the trademarked company slogan invited New Yorkers to 'Send A Salami To Your Boy In The Army'.

Fast-forward through the Great Depression, the Great Recession and 9/11, and the famous deli found itself caught in another pandemic, COVID-19. Having weathered all manner of storms, Katz's hunkered down, reprinted their slogan, and through their partnership with Feed The Frontlines[35] they found new ways to 'Send A Salami' to those most in need – not troops in trenches, but the medics, nurses, teachers and key workers across New York experiencing food insecurity while working to protect the lives of others.[36] Although Katz's also received funding from the US government this time around, it is unlikely they would have made it through such extraordinary challenges without their integrity, authenticity and a longstanding reputation as a gathering place at the heart of their community.

This sense of history, of a narrative that inextricably weaves a brand's past with that of its patrons and employees, is another key factor that influences how authentic a brand is perceived to be. By maintaining their brand's style and behaviour (their signage has barely changed since it was first conceived), and communicating their **heritage** and **traditions**, Katz's was signalling that they were the real deal, a business that could be relied upon to weather the storms from one generation of customers to the next.

But brands needn't have been around as long as Katz's to benefit from this sense of heritage. In fact, studies show that even in the absence of objective facts, using a communication style that emphasizes a brand's tradition can be enough to influence its perceived authenticity.[37] For new businesses that don't yet have traditions to refer to, there are other strategies that can be used to convey authenticity. One of these pertains to **commercialization**, the degree to which a business is willing to subordinate (or compromise) its values and norms in the pursuit of profit. In fiercely competitive markets where it can be tempting to cut corners, it is vital to note that inconsistent behaviours can irreparably damage a brand's reputation, which is why communicating one's values with clarity and committing to go beyond profitability have an integrity-boosting effect.[38] Whatever your organization, to be perceived as authentic means abstaining from any short-term marketing actions that could undermine your values, such as fake testimonials, unsubstantiated claims and short-term pricing tactics. It also means steering clear of aggressive advertising campaigns, or working with tools and distributions channels that go against the brand's core principles.

Finally, a conversation around authenticity would not be complete without talking about brands' key representatives: employees. When it comes to how a brand is perceived, **employee passion** plays a vital role in customer satisfaction and the overall brand experience. If employees are intrinsically motivated, genuinely friendly and enthusiastic, the customers they interact with will attribute this passion to the brand,[39] creating a positive association and laying the groundwork for a richer, stronger, long-term relationship. Not only does this contribute towards a more resilient reputation, it can also create deeper emotional bonds with the consumer, enhancing their loyalty, purchase intention and willingness to pay a premium and, crucially, increasing their propensity to forgive bad brand experiences when things go wrong.

Key takeaways

- Trust is fundamental to happy, well-functioning relationships, and in a business context can increase brand attachment, commitment, customer loyalty and consumer resilience towards negative brand information.
- The most influential triggers for enhancing brand reputation are ethics, social impact, having a genuine brand personality and the fair treatment of employees.
- For apologies to work they must be sincere, explicit and unreserved. Promises must be supported by evidence demonstrating the progress being made.
- Authenticity is vital to business reputation and refers to the cultural fit between a company's norms and values, and those of their customers. Congruence results in consumer–brand identification, which can boost brand trust, enhance perceived quality of products and services, and increase people's receptivity to your message.
- When our values fail to materialize into action, we fall into the value-action gap and can experience cognitive dissonance, which we will strive to resolve.
- Brands can signal authenticity through facts and evidence (indexical) or impressions and feelings (iconic). For this to work, brands must be consistent, honest and genuine.

- In periods of uncertainty, the desire for authenticity and nostalgia increases, making messages around tradition, heritage and brand history more powerful. Compromising brand values and norms in the pursuit of profit (commercialization) should be avoided, and nurturing employee passion and enthusiasm prioritized.

CHAPTER THREE

Living the good life

Life is never made unbearable by circumstances, but only by lack of meaning and purpose. VIKTOR FRANKL[1]

From pleasure to purpose

As a species, most of us are hardwired to seek out pleasure and avoid pain. From streaming our favourite show with a glass of wine, to losing ourselves down interminable rabbit holes of social media distraction, this deeply ingrained dynamic is one of the strongest forces that propels human behaviour. This is why, for the better part of our history, we have bought and sold products and services specifically designed to alleviate suffering or enhance enjoyment. The problem is that there's often a catch. Even though buying that beautiful bike or luxury watch may bring us a rush of pleasure, we generally recognize that it's unlikely to offer long-term happiness. And while most of us would agree that comfort and financial freedom are important, when taken to the extreme, materialistic values are implicated in a whole host of unpleasant outcomes.

Defined as a value system that centres around one's possessions and projected social image, **materialism** offers a very particular way for people to signal their social status and try to meet social needs. The issue is that in our indefatigable drive to acquire ever more impressive belongings, we can end up making unintended sacrifices to meet needs that will never be fulfilled by the next big thing. Despite such aspirations, people who score highly on materialism not only tend to report lower levels of wellbeing, social functioning and psychological adjustment,[2] they are also more likely to experience greater levels of unhappiness and anxiety,[3] and may suffer from lower-quality social relationships than their lower-scoring peers.[4]

The problem is that merely being exposed to desirable goods (walking past a gorgeous shop window) or consumer cues (seeing a seductive product ad) can be enough to shift us into a more materialistic mindset, which in turn can arouse unpleasant feelings and even reduce our desire to be socially involved with others.[5] Easily triggered by simple situational factors (one of the reasons why advertising works so well), this mindset can be hard to avoid. Even the language we use in the media and more broadly – referring to the public as 'consumers' rather than citizens, for example – may influence the way in which we behave, biasing us towards values that reflect self-enhancement and potentially activating a mindset of consumption. (A brief note – I use the terms consumer and customer throughout this book not to devalue the individual, but because it is the language most familiar to the context of business.)

Yet despite these omnipresent cues, in recent years a curious shift has begun to emerge. Contrary to the prediction that economic growth might increase our focus on materialism and money, this pattern has not borne out in the data. Instead, figures suggest that countries that enjoy greater economic freedom tend to be *less* materialistic, not more. In a 2020 study that drew on data from the World Bank, the Economic Freedom of the World project and the World Values Surveys, researchers found a correlation between countries with a higher gross domestic product (GDP) per capita and less materialism (and vice-versa),[6] raising questions not only about the impact of wealth on our behaviours and values, but also around the future of business in general.

Given that economic freedom is associated with better education outcomes, increased job opportunities and more diverse, higher-quality products, it should come as no surprise that it also holds positive correlations with proxies of wellbeing, including higher life expectancy and literacy,[7] fewer human rights violations,[8] greater income equality (in some instances),[9] and greater levels of life satisfaction and happiness.[10] From a consumer perspective, as our level of wealth increases, we become free to contemplate and focus on non-material things. For businesses, then, resilience may no longer depend on setting the trend and making the next new shiny thing; rather, it may rest on their ability to use behavioural insights to create the kind of value people will pay for.

The tricky thing is that our perception of value is rather mutable. Whatever your age, chances are you will be familiar with the old proverb 'money can't buy you happiness' – and with studies suggesting that happiness tapers off after a certain income level,[11] we might be tempted to believe that the story ends there. But the relationships between wealth and wellbeing never did run smooth, and

Resilience may rest on one's ability to use behavioural insights to create the kind of value people will pay for.

more recent research hints that things may be more complicated than we once thought. In the United States alone, one massive study found that for people of higher socio-economic status age 30 and older, the happiness–income link has steadily strengthened over the decades, and despite hypotheses to the contrary, this trend shows no sign of slowing after the US $75,000 mark.[12]

Elsewhere, data suggests it is not the amount we spend, but rather *how* we spend it that contributes to our sense of wellbeing. Whether investing in experiences (as opposed to material goods), trading money for time (such as paying for a cleaner), or splashing out on others (rather than oneself), there are several ways in which we can spend to boost our happiness,[13] some of which may be influenced by one's generation. It's a topic I reach out to César Christoforidis, Senior Vice-President (SVP) of Global Partnerships & Strategy of Emplifi, and Julio Sosa Sr, Consultant at Emplifi, to shed some light on. Drawing on research from their Sustainability Brand Index, César explains that Centennials, Millennials and Gen-Z 'would much rather trade an experience for material gain', and that, 'If you want to keep any level of loyalty you now have to provide an exceptional experience in that journey to those clients.' With the number of communications on social media around sustainability 'on the increase across the board', their study's findings reflect what appears to be a growing, general trend – that the value we placed upon financial success only a decade ago, is finding new loci of attention.

It is not the amount we spend, but rather how we spend it that contributes to our sense of wellbeing.

Beyond this shift towards experience and sustainability, however, there is another, more individual factor that can influence how satisfied we will be in our purchasing decisions. Since we typically prefer people and places that reflect our personalities (living in a diverse, artsy neighbourhood might reinforce one's self-concept as a hip bohemian, for instance), it stands to reason that making purchases that align with our traits, preferences and needs would also result in a greater sense of satisfaction. But how might we measure this?

The value we placed upon financial success only a decade ago, is finding new loci of attention.

From a data perspective, the widespread use of banking apps has made it easier than ever to conduct natural research with real people to examine spending patterns out 'in the wild'. It is this approach that was used by a group of Cambridge University psychologists when they conducted a field study of UK bank transaction records to explore the impact of consumer behaviours on wellbeing.[14] Looking through a psychographic lens, their results showed that people who spent more on products that matched their personality reported greater satisfaction than those that didn't, to the extent that one could deliberately boost one's level of happiness by altering spending behaviours in this way. To give an example, when participants were offered a voucher for either a bookshop or a bar, those who scored highly for introversion reported greater happiness when receiving the former, whereas extro-

Research points towards a future consumer quite different to that of the past.

verts were fairly happy with either. In fact, finding the right *psychological fit* between personality and spending was so impactful that it even had a stronger effect on happiness than total spending or total income – meaning that if you are less wealthy but you spend in a way that matches your personality, you will actually get more bang for your buck. Who knew that keeping up with the Jones's could be so simple?

So what does this mean in terms of unfolding consumer behaviours? If we consider the broader trend of wellbeing alongside the generational, values-based shifts we explored earlier, the research points towards a future consumer quite different to that of the past. While we may historically have relied upon expensive or trendy items to signal our worth and ideals to those around us, we are increasingly prioritizing and paying for interactions with brands that not only share our values, but that help us to express and enrich our sense of meaning and wellbeing. Although it is improbable that our impulse to communicate status will disappear, this desire will likely find new expression through signals that reflect evolving consumer norms (the hashtags #blessed and #living-mybestlife spring to mind). It is a topic I reach out to Lewis Garrad, occupational psychologist and partner at Mercer, to discuss.

When I ask him if he is seeing a shift in terms of what we value and how we broadcast this to the world, he tells me that priorities vary according to our life stages, and that for younger adults seeking to boost their status and attractiveness in the eyes of others, 'perhaps that equation is changing, and what people consider to be high status is a very different lifestyle'. Rather than aspiring to spend all their time at work in pursuit of money, 'the people who are respected and who are revered are the ones who are quite the opposite. So they don't need to be wealthy, but, wow, look at all the fun stuff they're doing.' If, as Lewis suggests, 'Technology's almost facilitating that change by high-lighting aspirational lifestyles that are not so much about wealth, but far more about the quality of life that you're living', then for organizations to thrive, they must be positioned to respond accordingly. Whether on social media or IRL (in real life), as each generation subverts and reinvents the social norms of its predecessors, so burgeoning trends around fitness, veganism and conscious consumerism are likely to become adopted by status seekers as signals of value, possibly consigning cruder, more ostentatious displays of wealth to the past. So how can we meet these evolving expectations?

In pursuit of happiness

We're all searching for it. Whether through relationships, experiences or the things we buy, happiness is that elusive thing we just can't get enough of. Yet despite our collective obsession, a coherent definition for the subjective state of happiness has proven remarkably tricky to pin down. Although consensus around its exact meaning among academics and practitioners remains elusive, in recent years a more layered and nuanced conversation has started to take shape. By approaching happiness and wellbeing through the lens of pleasure and purpose, researchers have begun to explore the distinction between these states, leading to some fascinating implications for both brands and businesses alike.

Drawing from Aristotle's writings about what constitutes the 'good life',[15] many psychologists have come to differentiate the **eudaimonic** or meaning-oriented state of happiness, from the more **hedonic** or pleasure-focused kind. Viewed through this dual lens, hedonic happiness focuses on the presence of pleasant feelings (and the absence of bad), whereas the eudaimonic state gives primacy to qualities of psychological wellbeing and personal expressiveness. Curiously, these two types of happiness are not only philosophically distinct, they also appear to be neurologically different. In his seminal work, *Thinking, Fast and Slow*, Daniel Kahneman revealed that while hedonia was connected to the fast, heuristic mode of System 1, meaning-oriented eudamonia was linked to the more intentional, slower decision-making of System 2[16] (which may explain why it is easier for us to recall hedonic purchases than eudaimonic ones).[17]

But if hedonically pleasant experiences are more seductive, faster to process and easier to recall, what is the benefit of focusing on the labour-intensive eudaimonic stuff? Well, from a health perspective, evidence suggests that eudaimonic wellbeing is linked with all manner of benefits, from better immune function, lower cardiovascular risk and better neuroendocrine regulation, to better sleep and more adaptive neural circuitry.[18] From a consumer point of view, when you examine people's purchasing patterns, many decisions do not appear connected to pleasure at all. From marathons and tattoos, to assembling flat-pack furniture or getting waxed, we seem willing to pay for all manner of effortful, unpleasant experiences, and our determination to pursue such goals clearly shows we must be getting something back, or else we wouldn't choose them. Beyond pleasure or fun, then, there must be deeper dynamics at play, the likes of which could empower brands to provide something richer to their consumers. So what might these factors be, exactly?

First, the theory. In a research paper in 1989, psychologist Carol D Ryff proposed a framework for psychological wellbeing that would come to transform the way in which we view eudaimonic happiness. Her seminal work outlined, for the first time, six crucial factors that can determine our sense of wellbeing: autonomy, positive relationships with others, environmental mastery, personal growth, purpose, and self-acceptance.[19] Based on Aristotle's Nicomachean Ethics, Ryff's psychometric inventory offers not only a road map with which we might achieve a sense of contentment for ourselves, it also functions as a valuable tool with which to assess and optimize how well a brand performs across each dimension.

Let's take a closer look. The first factor, **autonomy**, refers to our level of self-determination and our ability to regulate our behaviour from within, independent of external pressures. Described by the famous psychologist Maslow as a 'resistance to acculturation',[20] people who are 'self-actualized' tend not to abide by all the social norms and diktats of their culture. Rather, they find a way to maintain their own internal compass even when this runs contrary to the prevailing ideologies or general consensus of the time. There are many cultural icons who, by virtue of their autonomy, have stood out and transformed the way we see the world, whether through the exuberant rejection of received gender norms by artists such as Prince or Frida Kahlo, or the visions of human equality embodied by Emmeline Pankhurst and Martin Luther King Jr.

Ryff's second factor explores our ability to establish meaningful, **positive relationships** with others, the kinds that are reciprocal, empathetic, affectionate and intimate. Whether viewed through the lens of philosophy, psychology or physiology, friendship and love have long been known to have profound effects on our wellbeing, and from a cultural perspective they are almost universally endorsed as a vital feature of how to live.[21]

From here, we move on to **environmental mastery**, the third factor on the scale. Generally speaking, we like to feel as though we have some control over our lives, and when it comes to mental health, the ability to create or choose an environment that suits our needs (whether a quiet, ordered space to relax in, or a vibrant, noisy social setting) can mean the difference between a sense of wellbeing or a perceived loss of control. We have all experienced the relief that comes from shutting a door to retreat into our own private space, so it should come as no surprise that the ability to 'extend the self'[22] by controlling complex environments is emphasized as vital by various theories of wellbeing.

The fourth factor, **personal growth**, is the aspect of wellbeing that comes closest to Aristotle's concept of eudaimonia. Rather than striving to attain a fixed, immutable state in which all our problems are resolved (which is impossible, anyway), this factor relates to a more continual process of development. It is about being open to experience, and exploring our potential in a way that is dynamic and fluid. Given that life will always throw new challenges our way, it is our ability to focus on the journey rather than the destination that will support our trajectory towards self-actualization.

Having a **purpose in life** (sometimes easier said than done) is the fifth factor, and it refers to our sense of direction and the conviction that life holds meaning. Particularly valuable during times of difficulty, it relates to our sense of intentionality and passion, and our desire to strive for goals that evolve and emerge at different stages of life. Whether pursuing youthful ambition or seeking out creativity and emotional integration as we mature, our capacity to reflect on what matters to us and to cultivate beliefs that offer a sense of meaning, are some of the most valuable skills we can develop in pursuit of a life well lived.

The sixth and final factor is about **self-acceptance**, and our ability to accurately perceive our emotions, actions and the motivations behind them. While the ancient Greeks might have implored humanity to 'know thyself', anyone who has experienced some version of therapy will recount just how uncomfortable and laborious such endeavours can be. Despite our capacity for contemplation, the pursuit of self-knowledge is fraught with biases and blindspots, and it is usually only through dedicated practice or process (such as meditation or counselling) that we gain the ability to dive beneath the surface of self-reflection, to a more complete sense of self (or selves). As psychologists from Maslow to Jung have emphasized, this process is not just about self-esteem, it is also about our need for positive self-regard and coming to terms with our 'shadow' so that we might self-actualize, mature and reach a deeper sense of self-acceptance, flaws and all.

Given the uncertainty we face around the climate crisis, economic disruption and the fragility of our interconnected systems, it is no surprise that so many of us are re-examining our values and choices in search of deeper meaning. As progressively unstable conditions contribute to feelings of fear and anxiety, those businesses that can deliver both pleasure *and* purpose are the ones most likely to outlive the competition. If a business is to offer real value during turbulent times, their offering (whether goods or services) must be able to fulfil a trifecta of needs. It must provide *utilitarian* value (something that is functional or necessary, such as water, rent or technical support); *hedonic* value (give pleasure or comfort, such as a round of beers shared with friends); and *eudaimonic* value (it must provide meaning or impact, such as a transformative experience might offer).[23] Providing something that is useful or fun is something most businesses are already good at, but finding a way to integrate deeper meaning or purpose can be challenging to even the most competent. Given that we now have a psychological framework for understanding eudaimonic value, let's unpack an example of a business that is

Businesses that can deliver pleasure and purpose are the ones likely to outlive the competition.

applying these qualities throughout their ecosystem, and in particular, the user journey offered to their consumers.

One of the most referenced, established and beloved activist-brands, not only is Patagonia renowned for its bold, values-driven mission, but it has earned its stripes through an impressive track record of practising what it preaches. Founded in 1973 by American environmentalist and climber Yvon Chouinard, the outdoor gear and clothing manufacturer has historically pioneered unusual actions (from the self-imposed 'Earth tax' and sourcing of sustainable materials, to community-based actions around sustainability) in order to protect the environment and promote conscious consumption. While it may finally be receiving the social recognition it deserves, it is when we view it through the lens of Ryff's framework that we really begin to see how well this brand meets the criteria for psychological wellbeing and, by extension, **eudaimonic consumption.**

When I visit their activism page I am greeted with the message 'We're in business to save our home planet' and the invitation to 'Join us'.[24] As I click through to the 'Answer with Action' page, I'm asked to confirm my location before viewing the categories of grants Patagonia supports. Alongside a button for 'All issues' are the options of biodiversity, climate, communities, land and water, and, once I make my selection, I am directed to a page that lists a variety of nearby environmental groups that I can now connect with and support. So how exactly does this function as a eudaimonic experience?

First, the user journey provides the *autonomy* to select my own path, by empowering me to direct the experience according to my own set of priorities. Second, by connecting me with local groups, it offers the possibility of developing new, *positive relationships* with others based on shared values. Third, it speaks directly to my need for *environmental mastery*, only on a much larger scale – in this instance, the invitation is not to act in a small way so as to control my immediate surroundings. Rather, I am offered the opportunity to engage with others so as to co-create an environment that could benefit a much wider circle (focusing on clean water, air and soil, richer biodiversity, and so on). Fourth, by enabling me to access local groups and change-makers, the website makes it much easier for me to pursue avenues for *personal growth*. For the fifth aspect, *purpose*, Patagonia's clear brand mission is closely aligned with the values I cherish. Finally, when it comes to *self-acceptance*, the careful balance between acknowledging the shadow aspect of human consumption (waste, landfill, pollution), and offering proactive ways to effect change (how we buy, and what we expect from brands and government), allows me to show up and engage without feeling ashamed for not being (or doing) good enough.

So, that is an example of how we might design for a eudaimonic consumer experience. The next step is to understand how we can apply these qualities within an organization itself.

Designing a eudaimonic culture

Given that so many of us are seeking more from the companies we work with, how might we begin to use some of these insights to design a culture that supports the pursuit of purpose and wellbeing? Well, if you are familiar with Maslow's famous hierarchy of needs, you will know that we are driven to meet a variety of fundamental necessities: **deficit needs**, those things we desire more, the more we are deprived of them (hunger becomes more intense the more we are deprived of food, for instance), and **being needs**, which result as a desire to grow as a person. When it comes to deficit needs, most workplaces go some way towards meeting our requirements for physiological survival and a secure environment, as well as our desire for love, belonging and self-esteem. The higher-level being need for **self-actualization**, on the other hand, is one that few companies are equipped to support – which is why those that do are so highly prized.

So what might a workplace that enables self-actualization look like? To understand this, we must first explore what the term means. According to Maslow, self-actualization is characterized by an acceptance of ourselves and others (as we saw earlier), and refers to a state in which we are able to live according to our values with a sense of spontaneity and creativity. It encompasses a deeper appreciation for life, a capacity to express our emotions freely and clearly, and living in a way that is guided by a strong set of ethics. In terms of its outcome, the effects of self-actualization are profound and appealing – from feelings of surrender, ecstasy and awe, to those of humility, self-unification and transcendence,[25] it is no wonder so many of us yearn to move in this direction. Yet there are many misconceptions around how self-actualization can be 'attained'. Rather than some singular experience or ultimate destination at which we might hope to arrive, Maslow considered self-actualization to be a slow, integrative process, akin to a series of steps we might take into the dark unknown.

It is a theme that has attracted renewed interest in recent years, due in no small part to the fascinating work of renowned humanistic psychologist, author and podcaster Scott Barry Kaufman. When we speak, he tells me that far from being a static, end state, 'The path towards self-actualization is a constant process, a North Star goal that we never achieve but we move towards whenever we make decisions that are conducive to growth.' When I ask how we might best direct our efforts, he tells me, 'One of the biggest ways of growing is to get outside your comfort zone, to lead with your values, to lead with a sense of mission or purpose, usually a pro-social purpose, a humanitarian purpose.' He explains that it's 'really wanting to realize a future image of yourself. When you move towards that future self, or a future vision of society that you see for yourself, I think you are moving in the direction of self-actualization.'

When it comes to translating this to the workplace, Maslow suggested adopting what he called **eupsychian management**, an enlightened theory aligned with the idea of humanity 'moving toward the ultimate of mysticism, a fusion with the world, or peak experience, cosmic consciousness… a yearning for truth, beauty, justice, perfection and so on'.[26] With his latter studies suggesting that 'self-actualizing people are, without one single exception, involved in a cause outside their own skin',[27] his writings help shed light upon why so many people are now flocking to organizations that purport to hold a higher mission. Of course, while Maslow's theories have been around for a while, until recently, interest in his work has largely been confined to the realms of psychology and self-help, and it is a topic I bring to John Featherby, founder of Shoremount (one of the UK's founding B-Corps), to discuss. While these themes may finally be enjoying a moment in the business world, he tells me, 'It's easy to forget that it was literally only two or three years ago that we were being laughed out of corporate meeting rooms, talking about things like purpose and meaningful work and that kind of stuff. Now everyone talks about it like it has always been there, and they were always interested, but it's total nonsense. This topic was woo-woo and out there, and it's not what serious businesspeople did. And then it becomes mainstream because enough people talk about it, and it creates a social permission, and then it becomes socially accepted, and then it becomes socially expected.'

It has become so expected, in fact, that a failure to offer employees a sense of purpose and meaning is fast becoming one of the biggest risks a business can take. When I speak to Amy C Edmondson, author and Novartis Professor of Leadership and Management at Harvard Business School, she tells me, 'In knowledge-intensive work, and that's just about everything, if people do not have a sense of purpose and meaning they simply will go through the motions – and that may be good enough, but you don't want good enough. You want great. You want people to really use their brains, really use their heart and soul, to work with each other to contribute to something that matters. So if you don't have a compelling value proposition to offer your employees – along the lines of, "If you work here you get to contribute to something that matters" – I think you're really losing a serious opportunity for better performance and better engagement and all of the things that come with that.'

But it is not just about the performance and engagement of one's workforce, as Rita Clifton CBE, a global brand expert and former Chair of Interbrand, points out. 'If you look at those organizations that seem to have a strong meaning or strong purpose, they seem to be outperforming the average of all others. If you look at an organization like Unilever, their purpose-led brands have been outperforming all of their other brands in that stable. Therefore, you have seen the business evidence and frankly, you've also seen the business risk.' In the wake of the COVID-19 pandemic, she tells me, 'We've also learned that things can happen very quickly when we want them to, and so when we come to big issues like climate change or addressing issues like biodiversity, there's been a sea-change. There's been a sea-change in business and investor sentiment about the importance of sustainability and long-term impact.' She explains that when we see 'people like Larry Fink, who is the global head of BlackRock, a global investment management firm, talking about how they are investing in and gearing their investments towards longer-term sustainable assets, and taking money from non-sustainable assets', and there are 'programmes like Oxford Saïd business school doing studies on enacting purpose for businesses of all kinds, and the people that you see around the table in those conversations aren't the usual suspects', it is an indication that deeper changes are afoot.

Although research points towards younger generations as the progenitors of these shifts, award-winning writer and CEO of PTHR, Perry Timms, tells me that this transformation may be broadening beyond these groups, 'There are a lot of career transitioners in their 40s and 50s that are also saying, "I've had enough of working for the soulless entity. And I want something that gives me a greater sense of fulfillment for those that follow me." So I think it's rippled out even beyond the age brackets you're talking about.' And no wonder, since meaningful work is known to provide feelings of worth and boost self-esteem and dignity, all of which can support us in actualizing our full potential.[28] Given the myriad benefits, then, how can businesses offer their employees a deeper sense of purpose and meaning?

Since self-actualizing individuals tend to be motivated by (and loyal to) the values they cherish, if an organization wishes to improve its culture and ability to attract talent, it must first identify its own set of values upon which to structure and guide its operations, from recruitment and HR strategies, to communication and the relationships it cultivates throughout its business ecosystem (more on this in Chapter 5). And if, as Maslow argues, self-actualization reflects our need for 'ongoing actualization of potentials, capacities and talents, as fulfillment of mission… as an increasing trend towards unity, integration and synergy within the person',[29] then an organization that actively supports its people to recognize, develop and apply their skills (especially in service to a goal that holds personal meaning), will not only be more attractive to high-calibre talent who wish to continually develop and grow, it will also enhance its ability to adapt and thrive in the face of accelerating change.

Key takeaways

- Materialism is a value system that centres around possessions and projected social image. People who score high on this report lower levels of wellbeing, social functioning and psychological adjustment, greater unhappiness and anxiety, and lower-quality social relationships.
- It is not what we spend but how we spend it: investing in experiences, splashing out on others and trading money for time can boost wellbeing.

- Centennials, Millennials and Gen-Z would rather trade experiences for material gain.
- We prefer people and places that reflect our personalities, and will spend more on products that offer a good psychological fit.
- Happiness falls into two categories: hedonic (seeking pleasure and avoiding pain) and eudaimonic (seeking meaning, wellbeing and self-expression).
- Eudaimonic consumption is on the rise, with consumers prioritizing brands that share their values and offer purpose and meaning.
- Carol D Ryff proposed six factors that determine our sense of wellbeing: autonomy, positive relationships with others, environmental mastery, personal growth, purpose and self-acceptance.
- If a business wants to deliver real value, they must provide utilitarian, hedonic and eudaimonic value.
- Maslow suggested we are driven to meet deficit and being needs. Our pursuit of self-actualization is about self-acceptance, self-development and living according to our values, and employees are increasingly looking to companies to support them in this.

CHAPTER FOUR

Up close and personal

Deepening the people–business relationship

Unexpected kindness is the most powerful, least costly, and most underrated agent of human change. BOB KERREY[1]

A little thought goes a long way

From the branded emails that flood our inboxes to the content on our social feeds, it is hard to escape the world of personalization we encounter every day. Designed to mirror our preferences and predict our desires, the business benefits of adopting a personalized (and often automated) approach are many – from driving customer engagement to increasing sales, few would turn down the chance to boost the bottom line. As countless studies evince the effectiveness of matching content to people's personalities, predilections and past behaviours, personalization has become so commonplace as to barely raise an eyebrow anymore. This may be precisely why, when a business decides to take a more nuanced, relational and consumer-led approach, people are quick to notice.

Back in spring 2019, with all the florists, chocolate shops and card vendors primed for Mother's Day, it looked set to be yet another year in which no one would escape the tidal wave of marketing hitting UK stores. One of the most profitable holidays of the season, not a thought would be spared for those who might not want to be reminded of the mothers in (or out of) their lives. None, that is, except from a small florist based in London which, having received a handful of messages from customers requesting to opt out of Mother's Day messages, decided to push an email to their entire database, asking if anyone else would like to opt out. This bold, sensitive move by the digital-first company, Bloom & Wild, elicited such an over-whelming response (almost 18,000 opted out, and over 1,500 got in touch about the campaign via phone, email, Instagram and Twitter) that it was quickly picked up by national and specialist media alike.[2]

From those who had lost a loved one to people who simply appreciated the thought behind the action, this small gesture was greeted with such an avalanche of positive sentiment that customer-brand interactions quadrupled in number on Twitter alone.[3] Recognizing that they had touched upon something important, Bloom & Wild went a step further, removing any mention of Mother's Day from their website for those who had opted out and making it possible for customers to select their preferences for other sensitive occasions, effectively handing them greater control from the get-go. This considerate and compassionate approach was so well received that Bloom & Wild went on to establish the 'Thoughtful Marketing Movement', an initiative aiming to bring together a cohort of thoughtful, like-minded brands, in an effort to change the face of marketing. To qualify, businesses must commit to offering customers the ability to opt out of sensitive content, and with more than 150 brands already subscribed (including *The Telegraph*, Paperchase and Treatwell), it is a project that is already making waves.[4]

What was it, then, that made their campaign so successful? Beyond the attention and respect paid to people's individual situations, the power of this simple intervention lay in granting people some agency, a quality that, at least online, is becoming increasingly hard to come by. Although personalization does have its problems (and profound ones, at that), this case study shows that when used appropriately and consensually it can be a powerful means through which to respect consumers' boundaries and better meet their needs. But why should this matter in a business book about values, uncertainty and resilience? Well, if we want to build more sustainable, mutually enriching relationships with our customers, employees and business partners, we must understand the dynamics that undermine them, so that we can better equip ourselves to thrive.

When problems around personalization arise, they generally do so for two main reasons. The first stems from our tendency to either be unaware of, or unable to effect, the extent to which our online environments are being manipulated. This shows up, for example, every time we scroll through 'news articles' in our social feeds, and assume that the content we are seeing is also being broadcast to our peers and wider society (when in reality it has been algorithmically selected to match, augment or reorient our existing perspectives and political views). In this instance, while personalization may serve to create what feels like a fluent, frictionless experience (in which none of our assumptions or values are challenged), the diminished array of perspectives we encounter actually thwarts our deep-seated need for growth, and curtails possibilities for expanding our horizons. By removing any narratives that may offer a different, more nuanced understanding of our complex world, when applied in this way, personalization can blinker us to the lives, experiences and viewpoints of others, truncating not only our capacity for empathy, but also our potential for growth and self-actualization – fundamental qualities that characterize what it means to be human.

The second, related issue arises when, alongside the proliferation of our individual filter-bubbles, any kind of public 'commons' of shared facts and understandings becomes so eroded that we no longer have a wider context within which to locate or relate our subjective experience. In the absence of a shared news channel, or the possibility of even glancing over the headlines from a selection of newspapers (as used to be the case when entering a newsagent only a decade ago), the breadth or consensus of facts we would otherwise encounter cannot reach us, and we are left to the confines of what we are served in our own individuated channels. Of course no system is perfect, and while it is true that news and prevailing social narratives are usually penned by the hands of the powerful (and therefore subject to their whims, biases and ambitions), the fact that a shared, public narrative exists at all, yields the possibility that it might be challenged and improved upon. Unescorted by such a narrative, the fracturing of society into smaller, increasingly polarized fragments becomes ever more probable, as does the likelihood of descending into tribalism and social unrest – which brings us back to the issue of relationships and control.

Considered two (out of three) of our fundamental psychological needs (as we shall see momentarily), the ability to form and maintain healthy relationships and retain some agency over our lives is vital to our health and wellbeing. Proposed by psychologists Ryan and Deci in their ground-breaking **self-determination theory**,[5] these needs are thought to be universal, innate and essential, and if met across our lifespans, can give us an ongoing sense of integrity and eudaimonia.[6] The benefits of meeting these needs extend beyond the personal to the professional: not only can they enhance our self-direction, motivation and performance (which business wouldn't want that?), they can also bolster our confidence and contribute to a deeper sense of purpose more broadly. The reverse, of course, is also true: spend too much time in social environments that undermine these needs, and we can end up feeling distressed, alienated and controlled, which in the extreme can lead to mental health crises. Whether you are interested in applying these insights to deepen your relationship with your customers, colleagues or even your friends and family, by understanding how these fundamental drives shape our behaviours you will be better placed to create conditions in which your relationships and business can flourish over the longer term. So what exactly are these needs, and how can we design contexts that will help satisfy them?

Well, the first need is that of **autonomy**, which is about living in a way that feels authentic and uncoerced, in which we experience full volition over our own behaviours. Although we may be tempted to mistake it for selfishness, individualism or independence, when seen through a psychological lens, autonomy actually relates to a feeling of agency (from a cultural perspective, it has even been related more positively with collectivism than with individualism[7]). In the case of Bloom & Wild and the 'Thoughtful Marketing Movement', simply giving customers control over the marketing messages they receive was a powerful way of respecting and meeting this need, an intervention that resulted not only in happier customers, but a boost in PR and the start of a wider conversation around the role of ethics and consent within marketing more generally.

The second need is **competence**, our desire to be effective and capable in achieving our goals. Whereas autonomy relates to the freedom to direct our own lives, competence is about feeling that we are taking useful actions that will help us achieve a desired outcome. Experiencing ourselves as competent not only boosts our self-confidence and makes us feel good, but if you couple it with autonomy (and track how these needs are being met over time), you can even start to predict daily fluctuations in mood, vitality and self-esteem.[8] In fact, satisfying both of these needs has even been found to boost our intrinsic motivation, a desirable state in which we feel engaged with something for the sheer joy and interest of it, rather than for any external incentive or reward.

Beyond the personal, psychological benefits of believing that you are making effective progress towards your goals,[9] designing environments that encourage competence also hold broader implications for society, democracy and even corporate culture, especially if we think back to the motivations driving younger people in the workforce today. These implications may be part of the reason why Bloom & Wild enjoyed such a positive, widespread response to their initiative – in a virtual world designed to strip us of our agency and the power to do anything about it, if you can give people back some sense of autonomy (I have the freedom to make a choice) *and* competence (I have the skill to enact it), chances are they will be grateful for the opportunity and will express greater motivation to engage with you in the long run. But if we really want to cultivate greater relational resilience between individuals and the businesses they interact with, we must fulfil a third and final criterion.

Known as **relatedness**, this need is about our desire to belong, to feel accepted and understood by our significant others. One of the strongest predictors of healthy relationships and wellbeing,[10] relatedness (and our need for intimacy and validation) is one of the most powerful drivers of human behaviour, and where we experience this alongside a sense of security, our intrinsic motivation is again much more likely to flourish.[11] Given that it is exactly this kind of motivation that meets our deeper needs, it will come as no surprise that emphasizing intrinsic aspirations (such as seeking community and personal growth) is positively associated with self-esteem and self-actualization, both indicators of wellbeing.[12]

So where can we find examples of brands that align with intrinsic aspirations and meet our three basic needs? Well, think back to the suite of purpose-driven B-Corps, and we will find a whole ecosystem of businesses designed to do just that. Given their mission to 'balance profit and purpose' by using growth to create a 'positive impact for... employees, communities and the environment',[13] it is clear that these companies (and their customers) value more than just external markers of success. From bakeries to plastics manufacturers, the differentiator for these brands is that they are offering more to their stakeholders than the garden variety triumvirate of wealth, influence and image. Instead, they are providing customers with a path to *autonomy* (living in a way that feels authentic to their values), *competence* (buying from ethical brands to effect real change) and *relatedness* (creating community with their customers, and giving back to local groups of people) – and it's an approach that appears to be working.

When it comes to building **resilience**, especially in times of uncertainty, it is often these needs – for autonomy, competence and relatedness – that are first to come under assault, leaving us feeling disconnected, anxious and fearful. When we feel as though our lives are no longer in our control, that we cannot effect change in our environment or be with the people we love, it is our ability to find the little wins and moments of human connection that can draw hope into an otherwise bleak landscape. It is for this reason that some businesses thrive where others flounder – those that intentionally create cultures, customer experiences, products and services that meet our fundamental needs are simply better placed to engage with people at a deeper, more meaningful level. And when things go wrong, it is often the store of goodwill and loyalty that has been built over time that will carry such businesses through the hardships.

Getting attached

The past decade or so has witnessed a groundswell of interest in the world of behavioural science, with businesses and individuals alike clamouring to understand the hidden dynamics behind persuasion and decision-making. If you are familiar with this field, you'll know that behaviour change rarely results from appeals to reason – instead, we must rely on evoking emotional responses to encourage the desired outcome. This underlying tendency is one of the reasons why, when we're looking to attribute consumer behaviours (such as an increase in sales) to a specific action (an ad campaign), one of the most useful tools we can employ is sentiment analysis. Whether through biometrics, text analysis or natural language processing, it is our ability to identify, extract and analyse how people *feel* about something that will help us to better meet their needs and reach our goals. It is also why unimaginable sums have been invested by some of the world's wealthiest companies in researching and developing such techniques.

There are a whole host of reasons why measuring sentiment can be valuable, but when it comes to brand resilience there is one in particular that stands out. Whether as individuals, societies or organizations, our ability to cope with adversity and bounce back depends largely on the quality of our relationships, and our capacity to form healthy attachments to the people we care about. The idea that emotional bonds might be fundamental to our wellbeing was first proposed in the 1960s, when British psychiatrist John Bowlby developed the **attachment theory** to explain how our early experiences with our primary caregiver(s) influence our social and emotional development.[14] According to the theory, we are driven to create strong emotional bonds to meet our basic human needs, starting from our earliest experience with our mother (or primary caregiver), and evolving through friendships and romantic relationships as we grow older. As the attachments to our friends, family and lovers vary in strength, so too do the rewards they offer us: typically, the stronger the attachment, the greater the sense of connection, love, affection and passion we experience.[15]

What is interesting from a brand perspective, is that when we form a strong attachment to someone, we are much more likely to invest in and commit to them, and we are also more likely to make sacrifices for that person.[16] Given that many organizations intentionally craft public-facing identities or 'personalities', it stands to reason that we might also expect similar dynamics to play out between consumers and their favourite brands. Whether we're interested in a customer's loyalty or willingness to make financial sacrifices (such as pay a premium) in order to obtain specific goods or services, gauging a person's strength of attachment can be a powerful way of unpacking how best to meet their emotional needs.

What's more, attachment doesn't just show up in our relationships; it can also apply to objects. If you think for a moment of your most cherished, irreplaceable possessions, chances are they are few in number, and hold significant and profound meaning for you.[17] Because our attachments to such items are woven, in part, through emotional memories that connect them to us,[18] if brands are able to create emotionally resonant narratives that similarly connect them to their customers, they stand a better chance of building a deeper form of attachment for specific items (and, by extension, to the brand as a whole). It may sound fairly straightforward, but attachments, as with all human behaviours and drives, rarely come in one shape and size. To give you some context, while Bowlby's theory revolutionized how we conceive of relationships, it wasn't until developmental psychologist Mary Ainsworth expanded upon this that we came to understand some of the key attachment styles – secure, avoidant and anxious – familiar to us today.[19] While I will not dive into details here, suffice it to say that our style of attachment can profoundly influence how we relate to others of all kinds. So, what has this got to do with business?

Well, emotional bonds don't just develop between people – as I alluded to earlier, they can also be nurtured between brands and their customers to enhance the success and long-term prosperity of the organization,[20] making brand attachment one of the most valuable assets you can cultivate, particularly during periods of uncertainty. Outside of unsettling times, there are also significant benefits to be had in terms of profits – not only is the revenue generated through strong attachment generally less at risk of disruption,[21] but if your customer base is fiercely loyal, they are also more likely to repurchase with you 'against all odds and at all costs', even when tempted by incentives to switch.[22]

Brand attachment also comes in useful when you want to make behavioural predictions. When markets are volatile and income streams erratic, the ability to form a clear, evidence-based assessment of how to adjust your approach can make the difference between survival and a rather sticky demise. The problem is that when attempting to make such predictions, many businesses focus on the wrong thing. Rather than gain a complete picture of their customers, they limit their scope to **brand attitude**, inadvertently missing out on some of the most valuable data they could be using. So what exactly is brand attitude? Essentially it measures a person's judgement of how good or bad they perceive your brand to be. The problem is that because we can form these evaluations at a distance, it is possible for us to hold attitudes (positive or negative) about any number of brands or products, without them being important or central to our lives. And while it may be useful to know what people think about you, since attitudes are based on thoughtful processing that can be formed quickly[23] without any direct brand contact, it will not tell you what your customers really *feel* about you.

Instead, for a richer, more complete picture of the consumer–brand relationship, we need to look at a different type of dynamic. Similar to Bowlby's theory above, the theory of **brand attachment** describes the emotional bond that develops between the brand and the self over time. Unlike the remote evaluations that form our attitudes, when brands nurture an emotional attachment with their customers it can cultivate a cognitive bond in which the consumer believes the brand to be relevant to who they are.[24] While brand attachment is not the only factor that drives loyalty or a customer's willingness to pay more, over time, it can evoke the kind of connection, affection and passion[25] that transforms a walk-in customer into a life-long evangelist, building a client longevity many companies can only dream of.

Since brand attachment reflects a deeper relationship and commitment on the part of the consumer, it should come as no surprise that it is also a stronger predictor of consumers' intentions to invest time, money and even their reputation in a brand. It is also more accurate in predicting actual purchasing behaviours and the likelihood that a customer will choose your brand over another, which is especially useful if you want to shore up your position against the competition.[26] This is all to say that brand attachment is not merely a nice-to-have – as the global marketplace becomes more complex, understanding how to assess and cultivate meaningful brand attachment will enable you to build deeper emotional bonds that boost customer loyalty,[27] helping to shield your business against the vicissitudes of an uncertain future.

The ties that bind

So how exactly do we build stronger brand attachment? It comes down to four key drivers. The first is **brand responsiveness**, which connects back to the three basic psychological needs we explored earlier. Responsiveness and familiarity are considered as the foundations of healthy attachments with others,[28] which means that if you can respond appropriately to a consumer's needs for autonomy, competence and relatedness, they will be more likely to form an emotional attachment to you. Why? Because when a relationship meets these needs, not only do we experience a greater sense of wellbeing, self-esteem and vitality, we also gain a feeling of security, satisfaction and commitment to the relationship. What's more, when conflicts and disagreements unavoidably arise, we are more likely to be understanding and respond with less defensiveness.[29] From the perspective of a brand, if you can enhance a consumer's sense of relatedness and autonomy without inhibiting their sense of competence, you will create the right conditions for strong brand attachments to flourish.[30]

The second crucial driver of brand attachment is **self-congruence**, a concept that sits at the heart of many of the world's most persuasive and successful ad campaigns. In this context, self-congruence refers to the extent to which a brand's image or identity is congruent with our 'actual' or 'ideal' self-concept,[31] and it is a powerful way for brands to grab our attention and move us to action. The curious thing here is that the pursuit of self-congruence can actually lead us down two distinct paths.

Although brands have historically relied on aspirational visions of our future to get us to buy (purchase this product and you will land the big promotion, gorgeous partner or the perfect body), there is evidence to suggest that sometimes keeping it real (reflecting the 'actual' self) is more likely to hit the mark, especially when it comes to boosting people's perceptions of your brand's authenticity.[32] Why? It comes back to cognitive dissonance. As we explored in Chapter 2, this experience of psychological stress shows up when we hold conflicting values, ideas or beliefs,[33] or when we engage in actions that go against our ideals – a state that is so uncomfortable that we will go to great lengths to resolve the contradiction. It is for this reason that we often prefer brands that promote an image or identity that reflects our real (as opposed to ideal) self-concept,[34] and it also explains why inclusive, body-positive campaigns, such as Rihanna's Savage X Fenty lingerie ads, can have such a profound impact when executed well.

Then, of course, there is the tried and tested path of the aspirational brand, which seeks to present customers with a vision of what their 'ideal' life could be. This approach is persuasive for another reason – its ability to tap into our desire for greater self-esteem. Our human desire for self-enhancement is so strong, in fact, that it can lead us to buy from those brands we think will help us to project and achieve our ideal selves.[35] Countless studies now confirm what advertisers have long understood: that our preferences for certain brands (and our attitudes towards them) are influenced by our level of *ideal self-congruence*. This means that the better the fit between a brand's image and who we aspire to be, the more likely we are to buy from them. The problem is, of course, that we are complex beings who are also susceptible to social comparison – so if a brand is selling us a vision that offers an ideal self that seems out of reach, it can actually end up evoking negative feelings and the whole thing can backfire.[36]

The trick is in discerning which approach is the better fit for your target audience, and knowing how to craft a campaign that will elicit the desired effect. Take the Scottish brewery and pub BrewDog, for example. As concerns about our impact on the planet intensify, growing numbers of companies have been responding by making commitments to become carbon neutral. Unconvinced of the impact of such actions, in August 2020 BrewDog officially announced that it had become carbon negative, making it the first international business of its kind to achieve this remarkable status.[37] For those of us who share these concerns, companies such as BrewDog offer a desirable way in which to literally put our money where our mouth is, and move one step closer to the aspirational, ideal version of ourselves (and the planet) that we wish to inhabit. By creating the potential for self-congruence (where the company's climate values align with those of their customers), BrewDog has created the perfect opportunity for consumers new and old to deepen their attachment with their brand, thus boosting their resilience for the longer term.

While it may sound obvious that we tend to prefer and maintain longer-lasting relationships with brands whose identities reflect our own,[38] creating such attachments can also lead to unintended consequences. When a brand achieves this kind of fit (when their identity matches with our own), we can get so attached that we become dependent, even to the point of becoming anxious when we are unable to access that product or service.[39] In turn, the separation we experience can actually increase our love of that brand,[40] with the joy of being reunited sparking a kind of virtuous circle. Perhaps one of the most notorious examples of this is the now classic story of the 'New Coke' that was launched over 35 years ago, in April 1985.

Originally created in 1886 by American biochemist John Stith Pemberton, Coca-Cola had more or less retained its original formula (minus the actual coke) for 99 years or so. Long established as a much-loved brand, when their rival Pepsi started inching in on their market share they had to do something about it, and so a massive rebrand was attempted. Unfortunately for them, it was an epic failure. Coca-Cola's loyal followers were so crestfallen by the change in taste of their favourite beverage that, within 79 days of the new product hitting the shelves, the company backpedalled and resumed supplying their fans with the Coca-Cola Classic they so sorely missed. The New Coke received its own rebrand (Coke II) and continued being made until 2002, but despite enjoying a very limited appearance in 2019 (in partnership with *Stranger Things*, the Netflix series set in 1980s America) it never replaced the original.[41] Whatever your line of work, this case study serves as a brief illustration of just how powerful brand attachment can be, and the lengths to which a business may go to repair any rifts when the emotional bond (and bottom line) is threatened.

The third factor in driving brand attachment is **sensory brand experience**, which explores how emotional bonds can be fostered through rich, multi-sensory customer experiences – a principle that Austrian energy drinks brand Red Bull knows well. Rather than stick within the more traditional parameters of product marketing, Red Bull was one of the first companies to really conceive of and realize what has since become a coveted ecosystem of multi-sensory experiences for people to participate in. From its lowly beginnings, the brand's expansion into extreme sports, sponsorship of cultural events and the attempting (and marketing) of audacious stunts not only opened up new revenue streams extending beyond canned energy drinks, it also enabled a fundamental identity shift, crystallizing the Red Bull brand as avant-garde and exciting in the minds of would-be consumers. From the Red Bull Cliff Diving World Series to more extravagant stunts, such as the Stratos space diving project (which involved skydiver Felix Baumgartner freefalling from a high-altitude helium balloon), Red Bull have succeeded in carving out a very particular and visceral space, creating a 'brand myth'[42] that people can directly experience and aspire to.

But creating a compelling sensory brand experience need not be complex and expensive – even the addition of a subtle, distinctive scent (the likes of which you will find in Anthropologie stores) can be enough to yield desirable effects. By adding such an olfactory layer to the mix, a shopping experience that might otherwise remain in the realm of the visual and tactile suddenly expands to include a more visceral dimension. If this experience is positive and repeated over time, not only can it lead to greater emotional attachment to the brand,[43] but when memorable it can also lead customers to identify more with the brand itself.[44]

The fourth and final factor that drives brand attachment is **corporate social responsibility** (CSR). Known to influence how customers evaluate products,[45] a good CSR strategy can also help brands to establish and strengthen emotional bonds with consumers, especially for those who are less avoidant (remember our attachment styles?) and value warm relationships with others.[46] While research suggests that good CSR (or indeed, ESG) strategies can help foster greater brand attachment or 'consumer–retailer love',[47] if you want to take it one step further, a data-driven approach that segments customers along personality and values-based traits can provide additional depth to your insights. In this instance, a good old-fashioned loyalty card (for consensually collecting consumer data) could be combined with incentive programmes so as to help brands better understand the consumption patterns associated with customers' personality traits and value systems (the latter of which we will be exploring in the following chapter).

While it is true that firms with sustainability policies typically outperform those that don't over the long term (both in terms of accounting and stock market performance),[48] if you are looking to increase your positive impact it may be reassuring to know that you needn't be all things to all people. In a seminal study conducted by Harvard Business School, researchers found that rather than focus on a wide range of ESG issues, firms with good ratings only for 'material' ESG concerns (issues likely to affect the company's operating performance or financial conditions) typically outperformed competitors that took a broader, financially immaterial approach.[49] Of course, with younger generations, activists and NGOs increasingly well equipped to apply targeted pressure at an ever-expanding scale, it is becoming harder for businesses to get away with inadequate policies and behaviour. Concerns that may arguably have been financially immaterial yesterday (such as workplace harassment or lack of inclusive hiring practices) can quickly become material, creating all kinds of legal, reputational and financial difficulties for businesses that don't measure up. As many of the world's cultures, in the workplace and beyond, become less permissive of bad behaviour, the issues we fail to address in our companies today may well become the #MeToo's of tomorrow. It is for this reason that organizations and their leaders must be better prepared to anticipate and respond to evolving ESG concerns as they unfold – their very survival depends on it.

A new kind of leadership

New challenges require that we shift how we work. As we move away from traditional, hierarchical supply chains towards ecosystems built around digital platforms and dynamic partnerships, the success of any given organization is becoming increasingly contingent on the state of its larger network. When reciprocal, vibrant and healthy, a strong network of relationships can keep its members buoyant during times of hardship, in a form of interdependent resilience that extends beyond one's immediate sphere. How, then, can we increase the relational wellbeing of a business and its ecosystem? It starts with leadership.

If I asked you to explain how businesses are typically structured and led, chances are you would describe some version of a traditional hierarchy, in which a founder or CEO is charged with envisioning, communicating and directing the future of the enterprise. Sometimes described as **heroic leadership**, this industrial-era model still exists today, with many organizations drawing a clear boundary between those in positions of power and the people who report to them. Although one particular leader may be more charismatic, transactional or transformational than the next, scratch beneath the surface and you will often find the same well-trodden, unidirectional flow of power, with the person at the top establishing policies and practices designed to minimize any friction that might impede the desired progress of their vision.

While this leadership style serves a function, its fault lines and limitations are becoming increasingly difficult to ignore. As the pace of change accelerates, more people are noticing that when agency and autonomy are concentrated in the hands of the few, it is done so at the expense of the many. Yet despite its potential costs, for many leaders this particular approach may be the only mental model they know – and since resistance to change can be great, the old ways maintain their hold. This stubborn inflexibility is something that Cindy Gallop, founder and CEO of MakeLoveNotPorn, knows only too well. When I ask her if she thinks we are starting to see a shift in terms of the leadership qualities we are coming to value now, she states that one should 'never, ever ask that question in the passive tense'. She explains, 'We only see a shift when you and I, and everyone else, makes that shift happen. Shifts do not happen as a naturally occurring phenomenon. Shifts happen when human beings, extremely motivated, determined and utterly committed human beings, make those shifts happen.'

And so the old model persists. Rather than inviting employees to actively participate in the economic and cultural development of an organization (likely disrupting the status quo), they are instead expected to fulfil the roles assigned to them, ideally with as little dissent as possible. Whether achieved through punitive measures meted out by authoritarian leaders, or the positive reinforcement of a charismatic boss, the resulting structures look fairly similar. By wielding power over others to make unilateral decisions, the heroic leader takes decisions autocratically, and in so doing, robs the organization of its chance to generate more diverse, creative and innovative solutions to difficult problems. Eventually, as the gap between dependency and empowerment yawns ever wider, this form of leadership can become self-defeating, leading to a self-reinforcing culture in which micromanaging and bullying become the norm. Play this out for long enough, and employees end up feeling stifled and disengaged, resulting in lower productivity and heightened absenteeism, a spiral that can descend into a rapid race to the bottom. So what is the alternative?

Here we must turn to the lessons learned from the chaos of the COVID-19 pandemic. Of the many revelations to emerge from the crisis, one of the most fascinating was the relationship between the success of a country's coping strategy and the leadership that conceived it. Among the nations that were initially able to keep their death rates low while others were spiking, the majority shared one particular commonality: they were led by female heads of state. From New Zealand's Jacinda Ardern, to Tsai Ing-wen, the president of Taiwan, data suggests that the most successful strategies for containing and coping with the virus came from women-led nations. But why?

Despite narratives to the contrary, large-scale quantitative studies suggest that when it comes to leadership, gender differences in talent are either non-existent or, where they do exist, tend to favour women.[50] Yet while it may be tempting to assert that success for the above countries simply fell along gendered lines, if we look more closely, we will see a more nuanced picture emerge, a picture that – even prior to the pandemic – has long captivated the imagination of Professor Tomas Chamorro-Premuzic, whose illuminating book *Why Do So Many Incompetent Men Become Leaders? (and how to fix it)* explores this complex territory. When we speak, he opines, 'In a logical or normal world, we shouldn't have needed a pandemic to realize that people, groups and societies are generally better off if their leaders are smart, kind and honest.' The problem is that, 'In essence, we prefer male incompetence to female competence. When we select, nominate or appoint leaders, we're focused too much on style. We select them based on confidence, narcissism and charisma.' Yet despite the evidence and shifting social pressures, Tomas explains, 'When you have the things that you need to have to lead effectively, things like competence, humility and integrity, we almost overlook you or ignore you for leadership roles… Basically, the gender gap can be explained in not really so much gender, but by the fact that we focus on the wrong traits.' So what traits should we be focusing on, exactly?

Let's look to the Nordic block for an example. While neighbouring countries were struggling to keep their mortality rates low, Finland stood out as a beacon, with fewer than 10 per cent of the deaths of nearby Sweden. Led by Millennial prime minister Sanna Marin, it was not simply her gender that shaped the outcome of their approach, it was her leadership style. At the time of the crisis, she wasn't governing alone – unusually perhaps, she was working with a coalition of four female-led parties to establish responsive strategies that would help minimize the fallout. Rather than opt for a simpler, top-down approach, this collaborative process required careful negotiation in order to co-create a more comprehensive, strategic perspective – qualities that characterize the lesser-practised (but highly effective) style of **post-heroic leadership**.

Summarized beautifully all the way back in 1924, in her book *Creative Experience*, Mary Parker Follett wrote that 'Leadership is not defined by the exercise of power but by the capacity to increase the sense of power among those led. The most essential work of the leader is to create more leaders.'[51] A management thinker ahead of her time, Follet (like Hannah Arendt after her) understood that if business leaders could instil a sense of *power with*[52] versus *power over* their employees, they would be able to tap into and cultivate leadership capacities that might otherwise lay dormant throughout an organization's networks. Much as the skilful orchestra conductor seeks to identify and nurture each individual's unique strengths, so the post-heroic leader invests in their employees, instilling in each individual the power to fulfil their potential, thereby enhancing the performance of the whole.

Although leaders of all stripes are vested with the authority to make decisions for the collective, the post-heroic leader seeks to be more participative than their autocratic counterpart, acting instead as a skilful facilitator to get the best from their employees. Rather than promoting only their own solutions and relying on contingent reinforcement to drive results (a bonus for good outcomes, versus a penalty for bad, for example), this leader develops the skills to ask open questions, creating not only a sense of shared ownership among the people they manage, but also an intrinsic motivation to succeed. Given that freedom from extrinsic concerns can actually help us to produce more original ideas,[53] adopting a leadership style that focuses less on monetary rewards and more on divergent, innovative thinking not only makes greater eudaimonic sense (we feel more purpose-driven and empowered to actively participate), but in the long run it also works out better economically.

It is this kind of enlightened leadership that Scott Barry Kaufman touches upon in his fascinating book *Transcend: The new science of self-actualization.*[54] When I ask him about how we might foster environments that support a greater sense of fulfilment, he points towards the importance of job crafting, and explains, 'We leave so much potential at the table because we have such a misguided view, or limited view, of what sides of ourselves we're supposed to bring to any given situation.' If we really want to maximize potential, he suggests, we must invite workers to bring 'more of their unique personality characteristics and talents to the table', and create conditions that support, rather than stifle, self-actualization.

It is a theme I hear again when I speak with Stephanie M H Moore, a lecturer in business law and ethics at Indiana University. When we discuss the future of business, and how we might create more resilient, flexible organizations that empower people to thrive, she suggests, 'We need to stop thinking about work in the more traditional ways that we've been thinking about it. We need to be more creative in our thought processes as leaders, and understand that everyone has a different way of working, a different way of being creative, a different way of processing information.' From an HR perspective, she points out that, 'Connections and support are so important to people, especially younger employees, younger workers. They are really wanting that support and connection, and that meaningful purpose out of their work. It is becoming more and more important.' If we are serious, then, about eliciting the best from those we employ and work alongside, it is clear that we must first

Leaders must use their authority to model the values they wish to pass on.

relinquish the old, outdated models of admonishment and instruction to make way for the new. Rather than issue orders and expect compliance, leaders must use their authority to model the values they wish to pass on, so as to create organizational cultures within which creativity and collaboration can flourish, and performance excel.

To explore how we might do this, I reach out to Barbara Kellerman, faculty member at the Harvard Kennedy School for over 20 years, and the author and editor of many books on leadership and followership. When I ask her how she conceives of leadership, she explains that we must look at it 'not through the lens of a single person, but as an equilateral triangle, with three parts that are equally important. One is the leader, two are the followers, and third... is the context', which includes 'not just the nature of the organization or the community or the country, but also the moment in time.' Barbara explains that 'followers are getting much more demanding than they used to be', and that 'weaker leaders and stronger followers are in many ways evident in the corporate sector'. Now, 'CEOs have, in general, much shorter tenures than they used to, they find it harder to lead... two generations ago, a CEO could simply say "Do this" or "Do that", and now it is not nearly so simple. They have, in general, more attentive boards of advisers that are not simply in their hip pocket. They have multiple constituencies that are screaming and yelling at them all the time, whether it is the press, or the public, or their customers, or their clients, or their supply chain sources. So it is a far more complex environment, obviously, than it used to be, giving less leeway to leaders, even the top leaders, to do what they want, when they want.' And when it comes to leading through the largest, most intractable issues of all, she tells me that, 'To change the world as it needs to be changed, in order to address the climate emergency, will require a level of collaboration among nations, between nations, and among sectors, between sectors, that is unprecedented.'

As daunting as this may sound, there is cause for optimism as the green shoots of change begin to burst through. With more organizations designing inclusive cultures that support greater agency and self-development, it is clear that some businesses are already meeting our deeper needs for relatedness, autonomy and competence. Instead of relying on blind obedience to get the job done, this more sophisticated, human-centred approach is fast paving the way for a whole host of positive outcomes. Known to be linked with higher levels of team performance, productivity and engagement,[55] transformational leadership such as this will be vital if we are to skilfully respond to increasingly dynamic, ambiguous and complex environments, and it is this approach to which businesses such as Mercado Libre, a popular e-commerce company headquartered in Argentina, owe their success.

In alignment with their sustainability initiatives around education and entrepreneurship, social development and the environment, Mercado Libre covers all kinds of benefits for its staff, from flexible work hours (without pay reduction) and childcare programmes, to nursery rooms and parental leave.[56] Beyond the obvious appeal of such perks, there is another reason why the company is such an attractive place to work. They encourage their staff to become 'knowledge nomads', support-ing employees to actively enhance their autonomy by forming communities through which they can collaborate and engage in self-directed learning. By intentionally structuring an environ-ment in which this kind of agency is rewarded, and family life supported, the company not only meets the deeper psychological needs of its staff and their dependants, but also sends a strong message of care to customers, demonstrating that their ethos is one that is lived from the inside out.

For the greater good

Of course, these are not the only qualities leaders must develop to create healthier cultures and relationships. There is also the question of how they approach difficult situations when they arise. Back in 2015, when Dan Price went out for a crisp hike along the beautiful Cascade Mountains with his long-time friend, Valerie, he could not have known that he would come back from this walk a changed man. As they trekked along the ridges overlooking Seattle, their conversation turned towards deeper questions of life, and Valerie shared some of the struggles she had been facing. Despite serving 11 years in the military and working two jobs that clocked up an eye-watering 50 hours a week, she was barely making ends meet. Her rental had just shot up by US $200 a month, and despite a strong work ethic and an annual salary of $40,000, the rise in economic inequality meant that she could not afford a decent home. Dan's story, in comparison, was worlds away. Having founded Gravity Payments (a credit-card-processing company) in his teens, the business now served around 2,000 customers, and at the tender age of 31 Dan was already a millionaire CEO. As he listened to his friend, it dawned upon him that Valerie's experience might be more commonplace than he had thought.

Determined to shift the scales, at least for the people he employed, Dan set about making some fundamental changes to his business. He calculated that if he wanted to raise his company's minimum salary to a comparable figure of $70,000, he would have to take a whopping $1 million pay cut (90 per cent of his salary), give up his stocks and savings, and mortgage his two houses. Most people might balk at the idea, but Dan? The story goes that when he announced these plans to his staff, he was met with such stunned silence (and, one might imagine, disbelief) that he had to repeat himself just so the news could sink in. For one-third of Dan's employees, the jump in minimum wage was so large that it doubled their salaries in one fell swoop, enabling many of them to buy their first homes (from 1 per cent pre-initiative, to over 10 per cent in the next five years).[57] Of course, news travelled fast, and it wasn't long before Dan's unorthodox approach was attracting the scorn of critics. Derided as 'pure, unadulterated socialism' by right-wing radio host Rush Limbaugh, Dan's move incurred the wrath of those who saw his sacrifice as a sign of weakness. But when Rush stated, 'I hope this company is a case study in MBA programmes on how socialism does not work, because it is going to fail',[58] he couldn't have predicted that while it would go on to be studied, by Harvard

Business School, no less, it would not be for its socialism nor its failure, but for its unbridled success.[59]

There was fallout, of course. Not only did Dan make personal sacrifices to stand up for his values, he also took hits at the workplace, with two senior employees resigning in protest, lamenting that the move would make staff uncompetitive and lazy. But here's the rub – with the raise in salaries, Dan's employees were able to pay off debts, move closer into the city and take holidays without fear of losing money. By creating an environment in which people were valued and supported, they actually pulled more weight and performance increased. Instead of training their focus on the extrinsic motivation of making enough money to scrape by, when employees knew they would make enough money to look after themselves and their loved ones, the focus shifted towards intrinsic rewards.

While it may be tempting to stop here and bask in the glow of these psychological and performative payoffs, this was not the end of the story. When COVID-19 crashed onto the scene in early 2020, Gravity Payments, like so many other businesses, was dealt a massive blow. Their revenue slashed to 50 per cent and they were losing around US $30,000 per day. If things didn't change, and fast, they would be out of cash within five brief months. All the fanfare of having achieved a higher minimum wage for their workers would come to nothing if the company went out of business, so they cut expenses where they could, but it still wasn't enough. Raising their prices and laying off staff was an option, but their clients were primarily small and independent businesses that were already suffering, and they wanted to avoid making any redundancies wherever possible. In the end, after exhausting all other options, the majority of Gravity's employees volunteered to take a temporary cut in salary in order to protect the company. Dan's willingness to sacrifice his personal gains was now paying dividends, and within 24 hours the majority of his staff had pledged $400,000 (roughly 20 per cent of their total payroll), and offered to give up between 10 per cent and 100 per cent of their wages over the following month to help keep the business afloat.[60]

What is remarkable is not that the pay cut succeeded, but that the solution came from the employees themselves. By collaborating to solve the problem, the staff took shared ownership over the process, giving them not only a greater sense of autonomy and control, but also greater motivation to make it work. At the time of writing, Dan's company is still going strong and he has become a vocal advocate for the reformation of how we build business. From taking responsibility and making personal sacrifices, to transforming workplace culture and engendering reciprocal commitments from his staff, Dan's story highlights some of the most important qualities we need in our leaders today.

Integrity and the four Cs

From fledging start-ups to global multinationals, if we are serious about contributing to the wider good we must ask ourselves some fundamental questions. What resources or expertise do we have, both as organizations and as individuals, that we can use to serve society? And how might we alter our processes and goals so as to effect longer-term change? In the realm of incentives there are several approaches that can be successful in curtailing corporate myopia. One such intervention made the headlines in 2018, when the American Accounting Association released a peer-reviewed study containing some rather compelling figures. Having analysed data during periods in which the United States changed reporting-frequency mandates, they found that the frequent publishing of earnings reports actively led to a decline in investments, operating efficiency and sales growth. In contrast, companies that issued reports just once a year enjoyed not only an annual sales growth almost 3.5 per cent greater than their quarterly-reporting competitors, but also an average of 10 per cent greater annual sales as a percentage of their assets.[61]

While the study garnered a lot of attention, the findings themselves were not new. Rather, they provided further vindication for an approach that had already been trialled some years before. When Unilever's CEO, Paul Polman, announced back in 2009 that the company would cease issuing quarterly earnings reports, their share price dropped by 8 per cent, with many concerned that this move would be a bad one. Explaining that the company needed to 'remove the temptation to work only towards the next set of numbers' if they were to accomplish the goals of their Sustainable Living Plan, Unilever held its ground and, as a result, Polman has since reported that 'Better decisions are being made.'[62]

But businesses need not confine themselves to one approach alone – incentives can also be shaped by changing the way in which bonuses are structured. The United Kingdom, for instance, has already made strides to shake off the chattels of short-termism, by extending the minimum period that a CEO must hold onto their shares from three years to five,[63] effectively providing the individual with a longer time horizon within which to make their decisions. Not only does this kind of intervention curtail the appeal of quick wins, it also creates a context in which leaders and shareholders are freer to make decisions based on a deeper set of values. For Unilever, this meant meeting and developing its sustainability goals. For Dan Price, it was creating a business that could support both the financial and emotional wellbeing of his employees.

Whatever the deeper principles that move you, there is one final element that modern leadership and those with the power to make change demand now, and that is **integrity**. Despite its prevalence in modern conversations (or perhaps because of it), integrity has fast been reduced to a buzzword, its meaning stripped away as swiftly as its adoption – yet it remains essential to building trust and long-lasting relationships, both in business and beyond.[64] Whether you view integrity as an unwavering commitment to certain moral principles, such as justice, fairness and honesty,[65] or an adherence to your own set of values and ethics, at its core, integrity rests on the ability to abide by what I conceive of as the four Cs, even (or perhaps especially) when doing so incurs a personal cost or sacrifice:

1 *Making a commitment to your values.* In the business realm, this can mean committing to principles such as fairness, respect, justice, responsibility, empathy, openness and honesty,[66] to name a few.

2 *Being congruent in word and deed.* This is about aligning what you say with what you do,[67] and adhering to the values you have committed to. In practical terms, it is about walking the talk and being truthful in your communication, ensuring that you fulfil the promises you make. Given that this kind of congruence affects employee performance and influences their level of commitment towards the organization,[68] this 'C' can yield valuable benefits when built into the DNA of your business.

3 *Being consistent over time.* Like trust, integrity is built over time and requires more than lip service to a social justice issue or a throwaway campaign to establish properly. Real integrity requires the patience to establish a track record across different situations and moments, so that your reputation becomes synonymous with the values you espouse.

4 *Being coherent in your intention and behaviour.* While this fourth and final 'C' may sound lofty, in an ideal world businesses would not commit to certain standards of behaviour simply to comply with laws or trends – rather, they would do the right thing for the right reasons. Rather than take a utilitarian path in which the ends justify the means, businesses that really care about integrity engage in certain actions not because they look good on paper, but because they reflect a deeper set of principles and beliefs. While the two outcomes

may appear the same on the surface, if you only engage in 'responsible' practices because there is a payoff, it undermines the very integrity you're chasing after.

While the values we cherish may vary from one nation to the next (a topic I explore in my book *Webs of Influence*[69]), the basic tenet of walking the talk remains the same, no matter the local culture. Wherever a business may be, if we wish to lead with greater compassion and integrity we must endeavour to treat our customers, employees and partners with respect, transparency and fairness, taking responsibility for our actions and making every effort to ensure we conduct our business ethically. Ultimately, since the world we inhabit is so interlinked, it is no longer tenable to expect old, outdated models of business to successfully address the issues we now face. The rate at which we now see crises unravel, and interwoven economies collapse, should give us a clue as to the scale and depth of change in approach we need to take, in order to charter a path forward. Integrity and collaboration need not put paid to healthy competition, nor marketing advantage, but if we wish to stand a chance of creating the conditions within which organizations and their people can thrive, now is the time to lay new foundations, starting from the ways in which we lead.

Integrity remains essential to building trust and long-lasting relationships, both in business and beyond.

Key takeaways

- To engage consumers we must respect the three fundamental psychological needs for autonomy, competence and relatedness.
- Self-determination theory states these needs are universal, innate and essential, and can bring a greater sense of integrity, eudaimonia, purpose, self-direction, motivation, confidence and performance.

- According to Bowlby's attachment theory, we are driven to create strong emotional bonds. The stronger the attachment, the greater the feeling of connection, love and affection. Strong attachments elicit greater investment and commitment, and emotional bonds towards brands can boost business prosperity and success.
- When predicting consumer behaviours, sentiment analysis and brand attachment are more useful measures than brand attitude alone.
- Brand attachment can be cultivated by boosting brand responsiveness, enhancing self-congruence, creating sensory brand experiences and establishing good CSR or ESG strategies.
- Leadership can be viewed as an equilateral triangle comprising the leader, followers and context.
- Complex, ambiguous contexts call for leadership styles that elicit diverse, innovative and creative solutions from their followers. Heroic leadership is fast ceding ground to the more participative, collaborative style of post-heroic leadership, which can boost team performance, productivity and engagement.
- Integrity is essential to building trust and long-lasting relationships, and must fulfil the criteria of the four Cs: commitment, congruence, consistency and coherence.

CHAPTER FIVE

The lure of woke-washing

Values and virtue signalling

When you adopt the standards and the values of someone else... you surrender your own integrity. You become, to the extent of your surrender, less of a human being.
ELEANOR ROOSEVELT[1]

Walking the talk

It was 25 May 2020 when the news of George Floyd's brutal killing blazed across screens around the world. Another needless, merciless death to add to a heartbreakingly long list, the footage fuelled an already powerful movement to condemn systemic racism and police brutality, under the now famous rallying cry, #BlackLivesMatter. Barely a week later, and two music executives, Brianna Agyemang and Jamila Thomas, would call upon workers in the music industry to go silent in solidarity, and 'take a beat for an honest, reflective and productive conversation about what actions we need to collectively take to support the Black community'.[2]

Originally under the hashtag #TheShowMustBePaused, what started out as an industry-specific action quickly spiralled out into the public sphere, with people of all stripes clamouring to show their support under the larger, rolling banner of #BlackoutTuesday. As celebrities, brands and social media users caught drift of the rapidly trending topic, millions were quick to post black squares to their timelines, under the hashtags #BlackLivesMatter and the abbreviated #BLM. Despite good intentions, the hashtags became so flooded with these squares that many grew concerned the action was now silencing the very voices it purported to champion – those activists who relied upon #BlackLivesMatter and #BLM to share vital news, information and resources with one another. What started out as a way of publicly expressing solidarity quickly drew accusations of optical allyship, as social channels and newsfeeds filled with empty words and campaigns. Of those ensnared in the maelstrom, there was one company in particular that caught my eye.

Since much of the work I do centres around the psychology of online behaviour, I am always watchful for interactions and campaigns that might demonstrate the principles I teach. As company after company rolled out messages of support for #BlackoutTuesday, it was through this lens that I approached Reebok's US website. Their usual homepage had been replaced by a large black space that spanned the width of the screen, with a message that read, 'Without the Black community, Reebok would not exist. America would not exist. We are not asking you to buy our shoes. We are asking you to walk in somebody else's. To stand in solidarity. To find our common ground of HUMANITY.' Directly beneath this message ran a bright-red banner, sporting an all-caps invitation to submit an email address and 'Pair up with us and get 15 per cent off'. This contrast between such an overtly moral statement and the explicit nudge to buy something felt so jarring that I decided to explore what other people were making of it.

I didn't have to look far. From Nike and Spotify, to Apple and Adidas, I found plenty of examples of brands touting their solidarity while their messages of inclusivity failed to materialize at the highest levels of governance (made painfully apparent by the predominance of all-white, typically male executive boards). From articles denouncing brands' messages of support as hypocritical, to others naming the dissonance between companies' stated values and those informing their internal operations, the reactions on social media and publishing platforms alike pointed towards a disconnect that would likely backfire unless addressed head-on, and swiftly.[3] Despite the stakes, I have to say my expectations were not high. But as the weeks drew on and a more nuanced conversation began to emerge, I noticed that some appeared to be taking the complexity of the situation onboard. I returned to Reebok's US site just over a month later to see if anything had changed. This time, I was greeted by a split screen – on the left, a black space imprinted with white words that read, 'We won't continue to accept the status quo. Here's what we are doing about it'. On the right, a white space emblazoned with the hand-written statement, 'BLACK LIVES MATTER', followed by slides outlining Reebok's longer-term plan to 'Invest in the Black community', 'Invest in our people' and 'Hold ourselves accountable'. Under each heading were bullet points explaining the specific ways in which the company intended to honour each public commitment. From supporting organizations that work to end systemic injustice, and providing university scholarships for students, to reforming their hiring policies and being held accountable by a third-party investigator, the list went on.

As I read, the qualitative difference between these structured, longer-term commitments, and the platitudes issued only weeks before, really struck me. Something had caused this company to reconsider their initial response and reflect on how they might transform their words into meaningful, longer-term actions. But as much as this heartened me, I remain keenly aware that such pledges can amount to nothing unless accompanied by transparency around timelines, and making publicly available the evidence (and results) of any actions taken. After all, for a business to truly take responsibility, they are the ones who must furnish the evidence of their actions, rather than leave it to concerned customers and stakeholders to seek out.

So what can we learn from this snapshot of what is undoubtedly a much longer, more complex journey? First and foremost, this story expounds the perils of making public commitments to values you do not intend to uphold. Whether as a brand, business or individual, engaging in such conspicuous (but vacuous) expressions of moral values has come to be known as **virtue signalling**. A pejorative neologism widely credited to the British journalist James Bartholomew,[4] the term describes what has since become an exceedingly common phenomenon, in which a party broadcasts their socially accepted alignment on a given issue.

Facilitated by the design and pervasiveness of social media, our collective obsession with signalling has become so strong that it is common to see brands jump on the bandwagon, in many cases 'supporting' a just cause and appropriating the language of social activism in a bid to resonate with specific target groups. This trend has become so widespread as to make it practically indistinguishable from the modern marketing practice known colloquially as **woke-washing**. A political term originally derived from the African American expression to 'stay woke', the word itself refers to an awareness of social and racial justice issues, with roots tracing back to the abolitionists of the Wide Awake group – young, uniformed men who marched in support of Abraham Lincoln's run for presidency in 1860.[5] These days, with its growing association to left-wing politics and culture, the word 'woke' has not escaped the claws of criticism, with companies and people vying either to signal their wokeness, or to lambast it. Although decried by many for its insincerity and appropriation of real values-driven movements, in reality the practice of woke-washing can have some effectiveness – at least in the short term.

In a bid to reach out and sell to the virtue-signalling masses, brands across the spectrum are creating campaigns and products intentionally designed to help consumers broadcast their position on any given issue – and in many instances this approach is working. In a study investigating the conspicuous consumption of particular products and brands on Facebook, researchers found that such virtue signalling not only enabled consumers to project their ideal self to friends and peers, it also enhanced their self-esteem in the process.[6] But they also found two other important dynamics at play.

The first is **social comparison**. Whether we're looking to evaluate ourselves more accurately, find inspiration, connect with others or regulate our emotions and wellbeing, the desire to compare ourselves to other people in our social group is a natural one. The problem arises when we start to spend time in environments in which upward comparison is at best, unavoidable, and at worst, actively reinforced through the quantitative validation of likes, views and other engagement metrics. With countless studies expounding the threat of upward comparisons to our self-esteem and wellbeing[7] (comparing myself to yet another yoga influencer is enough to bring on a cookie binge), it is fair to say that social media creates spaces within which the darker side of our behaviours can run rife. From heightened preoccupations with our appearance, to symptoms of depression and social anxiety,[8] the apps that serve as idealized windows into the lives of others can, if unchecked, exert profound and deleterious effects on our sense of self and wellbeing.

Apps that serve as idealized windows into the lives of others can exert profound and deleterious effects on our sense of self and wellbeing.

Beyond social comparison, the second dynamic, our **need for uniqueness**, can also cause problems. Although social platforms offer a valuable means through which to stay in touch with loved ones, the vast expansion of our hitherto small social circles has exacerbated our need to differentiate ourselves from the next person (particularly if we are higher in extraversion or narcissism). While this need for uniqueness is not bad per se, if we're not mindful it can lead to unintended consequences – which is where we circle back to the Facebook study I mentioned earlier. Through their investigations, the researchers found that those most likely to engage in conspicuous consumption and virtue signalling were people with a higher need for uniqueness, and those who were more attentive to social comparison content (folks who zone in on the post of a friend's coveted new sneakers, for instance).

While this may seem like a very modern problem (and in some ways, it is), the use of branded merchandise to send specific signals about who we are, or would like to be, is nothing new. You need only glance back at the mountains of portraits commissioned through the ages by those wealthy enough to afford them to understand how deep-seated our need for uniqueness and a positive self-image (both private and public) has always been. Whether it is power, wealth or status, or something that reflects the values of a life well lived, humans have long adorned themselves with symbols that communicate our various ideas of 'success'. The issue we face today is that the growth and revenue of the biggest social platforms are largely predicated on stimulating an ever-growing hunger for self-validation and status-seeking.

In the past only the rich could have afforded the impression-management services of a flattering painter, whose work would hang in a grand hallway or room to impose itself upon the occupants below. Now, with the swipe of a filter, or the flash of a luxury bag, anyone with enough money to buy (or borrow) the right props can avail themselves of this artistry. Nowhere was this more poignantly illustrated than by the swathe of influencers who were recently caught faking it on social media. With some celebs making upwards of US $1 million per post, there is a lot of pressure to make it big, so it is no wonder that many are opting for easier routes to the jackpot. When the Twitter user known as 'maison-melissa' published a series of posts comparing different celebrity images taken on what looked like the exact same private plane, she made the headlines exposing these highflyers for what they were – literally, jet-set. Through her investigations, she revealed that these influencers had simply paid a photographer to take snaps of them in a professional LA studio with a fake backdrop.[9] The desire to signal a lavish lifestyle (however deceptive) has become so popular among some circles that it has even given rise to a whole new industry – 'the influencer backdrop economy'.[10]

Whatever your thoughts on the ethics or effectiveness of such practices, they do reveal something of the dynamics that shape consumer behaviours today. Whether people are buying from brands in order to feel good, look good or do good, it makes sense that businesses would want to adapt their strategies to harness these motivations. Many, of course, will be tempted to cut corners and fake it, exploiting the language of current trends in order to garner attention in the short term. Of course, in the age of citizen journalism and social media, misrepresenting one's business endeavours and capitalizing on cultural moments is a sure-fire way to imperil one's reputation, undermining as it does the four Cs of the previous chapter (*committing* to your values, being *congruent* in word and deed, being *consistent* over time, and remaining *coherent* in your intention and behaviour). Far better, then, to take a more robust approach – one that understands the deeper values that drive consumer behaviours – so that we can design business strategies that work towards a longer-term vision, the kind that resonates far beyond the scope of empty signals.

The personality problem

From the famous Marlborough Man of the 1950s, to Dove's body-positive skincare ads, the branding and advertising worlds have long drawn upon the power of personality to influence consumer behaviours. Whether you want to build trust and attachment, or boost purchase intention, commitment and loyalty, there are a lot of perks to be had if you can create a brand or product image whose 'personality' resonates with its intended audience. This is why, when something comes along that promises to render the whole process more effective, it is bound to become popular.

These days, when organizations gather their brightest minds to better segment and drive engagement with their customers, rarely a conversation goes by without **psychometrics** cropping up. Concerned with the scientific study of psychological measurements, such as personality traits, intelligence and attitudes, in an online context, psychometrics have come to be synonymous with the large-scale qualitative and quantitative analysis of personality data. Made infamous by the Cambridge Analytica scandal of 2018, the personalization of content to mirror specific audience traits has become so commonplace as to make it hard to imagine any alternative – yet this approach is not the silver bullet many claim it to be. While psychometric profiling is now widely practised within the personalized ad industry (with varying results and despite legitimate concerns around informed consent and data privacy), when it comes to informing consumer choice and decision-making, the role of personality is less clear-cut than many would have us believe.

If you are familiar with the field of psychographics, you will already know that many of the preferences we express online can be used to predict aspects of our personality,[11] and that certain traits are known to influence consumer behaviours (risk-takers, for instance, tend to make more impulsive purchase decisions[12]). Yet despite their popularity and widespread implementation, predictive models tend to interpret broad traits, and therefore yield rather limited insights as to *why* people choose to buy from one brand versus another. And when it comes to the relationship between brand personality and human personality, although the research spans several decades, as a field of study it has not escaped criticism over issues of measurement, conceptualization and generalizability.

For one, the measures we employ to map out a brand's personality typically fall along different dimensions than those we would use for a living, breathing human.[13] Take the Big Five, for example, which measures the traits of extraversion, conscientiousness, agreeableness, emotional stability and openness. Although widely accepted as the standard framework for human personality,[14] boasting a robust track record for validity, reliability and stability over time,[15] research suggests that the five dimensions cannot be mapped onto brands,[16] despite our tendency to 'recognize' attributes and traits as comparable to our own.[17] Whereas our personalities arise through an interplay of biological predispositions and the environment in which we are raised,[18] the same cannot be said for brands – rather, their 'personality' must be deliberately crafted and conceived either by their founder, or by the team employed to develop it.

What's more, perception of a brand's personality can vary wildly depending on the personality of the consumer being polled. For instance, while a car brand might be perceived as more exciting in the eyes of an extravert (as compared to an introvert), a customer that is high in conscientiousness or agreeableness will likely report a different impression altogether.[19] Given that differences in personality can significantly alter how a brand is viewed from one person to the next, if we want a more robust understanding of the forces that shape consumer behaviour we have to dig deeper.

Where personality research can give us insights into our general preferences and behaviours, **values** reveal the deeper drives that motivate our actions. Defined by psychologists as a set of guiding principles that reflect desirable goals (such as wanting a life of excitement, or personal freedom), human values influence the ways in which we judge events and situations, shaping how we live and, by extension, what we buy. From the way we feel about our employers,[20] and the degree to which we identify with brands,[21] to our propensity to engage in socially responsible consumption,[22] values have a strong hand in shaping a whole variety of life outcomes. Although it is true that values and personality traits are interlinked and can influence one another (since both are aspects of the self), values actually form a distinct psychological construct from personality,[23] and it is through this lens that we can begin to understand why two people might buy the same product, but for entirely different reasons. Where personality traits can tell us about our dispositions and typical styles of behaviour (an extravert will be more outgoing and gregarious, for example), our values speak to the underlying motivations that drive our behaviours and shape our aspirations.[24] And unlike the weak predictive power of personality,[25] values are good predictors of consumer choice[26] – so if you're looking to develop a more rigorous approach to mapping out and predicting consumer behaviours, exploring values-based positioning is a powerful place to start.

Taking a stand

In the face of mounting social, environmental and political pressures, consumers are becoming more deliberate and active in their purchasing decisions, both in terms of what they buy, and from whom. If businesses are to survive in this new environment, then, Professor Tomas Chamorro-Premuzic suggests, 'It's really important that brands have a clear and distinct reputation… the worst thing that can happen to a brand is if it's meaningless and people don't know what it delivers, what it's meant to do and what it stands for.' He explains, 'Because of the rise of ethical demands, and altruistic or pro social acts within or by brands, we're seeing, I think, bigger demand from people for brands to express where they stand and what they think about complex and heated, often controversial, political issues.'

In fact, as values become increasingly relevant to consumer choices,[27] evidence suggests that those companies that can successfully articulate (as well as enact) the values they espouse, also stand to gain an increase in financial returns.[28] One of the many factors contributing to the swelling interest in purpose-driven marketing, it is no surprise that brands are flocking to align themselves with values deemed most attractive to their intended consumers. But there is another reason why businesses might wish to consider taking a more meaningful approach. When Accenture conducted a massive study of 30,000 people back in 2018, results revealed, even then, that 62 per cent wanted to buy from brands whose beliefs and values matched their own – and with 47 per cent reporting they would walk away from a company that failed to step up on a social issue (where the brand's words and actions appeared incongruent with their own values),[29] it is clear that failing to adopt a values-driven strategy may be more risky than it is worth.

Yet given the extensive benefits of actively communicating one's principles (and indeed the risk of failing to do so), many organizations still struggle to express their values clearly to a wider public. It is a theme that comes up in conversation with César Christoforidis, when he explains that communicating a company's values is 'now also becoming the job of the brands, because at the end of the day, they have the power to reach – whereas if you go on a corporate page of a company, they only have a small followership'. He continues, 'The most successful messages around sustainability or corporate responsibility have been the ones that have been driven from the CEOs', however if an organization is to really land their message, César suggests they must 'recruit the real brands, the ones that the consumers engage with on a day to day', to act as ambassadors of the work they are doing with corporate governance and beyond. From an experiential perspective, it is the difference between communicating your message around ESG practices via the brand of Ben & Jerry's, for instance, versus its parent company, Unilever. When a customer can scoop, taste and munch their way through a direct, sensory experience of a brand whose products are sustainably and ethically sourced, the quality of interaction will be far more evocative than any response an advert from the parent company might elicit. It's primarily for this reason why the resilience of a business, or any organization for that matter, depends largely upon the success and integrity of its public-facing part.

The resilience of a business depends largely upon the success and integrity of its public-facing part.

So how do values connect with and shape consumer decisions? Whether we are aware of it or not, whenever we buy something our values act as a standard against which to evaluate brands and their products, with different types of products eliciting different kinds of judgement. For example, utilitarian objects (such as scissors) tend to invite more rational evaluations related to their function (do they cut effectively?). On the other hand, an item such as a guitar that is bought for pleasure, or to express an aspect of one's identity, invites a different kind of evaluation altogether (does it sound good, feel good to hold, and express who I am?). In this instance, the product can take on a more 'symbolic' and intimate meaning, eliciting a more holistic judgement as to whether or not to buy it.

Beyond shaping how we evaluate products (which, in turn, influences what we purchase), values can also predict consumer behaviours in other interesting ways. Research shows, for example, that we are more likely to endorse products that reflect our own values,[30] which, considering the proliferation of conspicuous consumption, underscores again the importance of expressing what you stand for as a brand. Whether to manage how we view ourselves, or the impressions we make on others, what we buy also helps us to communicate who we are. Thinking back to self-congruence (our desire to maintain consistency between our ideal and actual self), our choices as consumers can also support or undermine our efforts to live according to our values, which is why we tend to buy products that help us create, maintain and reinforce our sense of self[31] (for instance, buying organic might support your self-concept of being an ecologically responsible citizen). Given that we prefer to remain internally consistent (and experience distress when we can't), if we are able to buy from a brand whose ethos aligns with our own we are likely to feel much happier about our decision and, by extension, our relationship with that brand. But the power of values does not stop there. From a business perspective they can enable us to better predict and adapt to consumer behaviours, and they can even help us understand and change consumer opinions of a product.[32] So how can we utilize them?

Our values act as a standard against which to evaluate brands and their products.

It's all about values

In light of the shift we are seeing away from purely hedonistic consumption towards that which is more conscious and eudaimonic, it is important that we understand the fundamental relationship that exists between values and our sense of health and wellbeing. If you are in the fortunate position to be able to actualize (or live according to) your values, you will probably be familiar with the wonderful sense of enhanced wellbeing that this can bring. On the flipside, you might also recognize that when our efforts are thwarted and our values blocked, wellbeing can take a significant hit.[33] But what does this have to do with business? Well, given that (1) we are facing multiple crises that pose a significant risk to our health and wellbeing, (2) younger generations in particular are seeking greater meaning and eudaimonic satisfaction in their lives, and (3) we generally prefer to buy products that express our values and identity – those businesses that are able to embody a core set of values that reflect those of their consumers (and the wider public in general) are more likely to meet their eudaimonic and values-based needs, thereby enhancing their wellbeing, and contributing to the foundations necessary for more resilient customer relationships to develop. And that's just from the consumer-facing side.

As Professor Tomas Chamorro-Premuzic is quick to point out, we are living at a point in time in which 'there is now some moral pressure, or outside pressure, to really play your cards and show what you stand for'. While taking a stand certainly carries the risk of upsetting certain people (as we will see in Chapter 6), he explains that it is 'also going to make other people proud and more loyal to your brand'. In fact, 'The problem really comes from the inside, because often brands... haven't taken even a course in ethics. They don't have philosophical or moral issues at the top of the agenda.' But the issue is not just about succumbing to external pressure, or increasing consumer loyalty – it's also about ensuring there is resilience from an organizational perspective. Whatever your industry or offering, Tomas asserts that, 'If you want to attract the smartest and brightest and most hardworking and valuable employees, certainly young people, they will be more wary, and there will be more scrutiny as to what it really means to work in your place.' Here again, values play a pivotal role, since an employee's ideals essentially serve as 'their inner mental compass or their map of where they are going to be happy, thriving'. When it comes to intrinsic motivation the research is clear, 'We've known for so long that the best way to motivate people is to not motivate them at all. Just assign them to a role or task they love and then they will be self-motivated. They will be more creative and in a state of flow, and you'll probably have to try to stop them from working because they're going to want to work so much.'

If this sounds like an appealing proposition, then let's take a deeper dive into the world of values so that we can learn how to

work with them. First conceived by social scientists to understand and explain people's responses to conflict (be it moral,
social or political), value models were originally developed to
understand the higher-order principles upon which we appear to
make our decisions. While various academic frameworks exist,
there is one in particular that is considered the most robust and
influential. First proposed by social psychologist Shalom H
Schwartz, back in 1994, the **Theory of Basic Human Values** has
come to be the most widely accepted. Refined over decades to
accurately measure values that are recognizable across cultures
and time,[34] Schwartz's theory proposes that there are 10 basic
universal values, which fall under four higher-order groups.

FIGURE 5.1   Schwartz's circular continuum

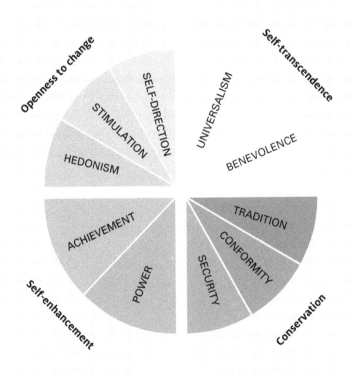

Depending on who you are, these values will differ in terms of their importance in your life, and you can see how they map out on Schwartz's circular continuum in Figure 5.1.

As you will see from this continuum, the first higher-order value is **openness to change**, which comprises the following basic values: *self-direction* (being independent in thought and action, with the freedom to create, explore and choose), *stimulation* (seeking novelty, excitement and challenge in life) and *hedonism* (valuing pleasure and your own sensuous gratification). In behavioural terms, a consumer who prioritizes this set of values would be more attracted to experiences, careers and brands that give them a greater sense of autonomy, novelty and delight. A good example of a matching brand identity would be Apple, whose famous slogan to 'Think Different' is the very embodiment of self-direction. Another example of a compatible brand would be Red Bull, whose popular high-octane, multi-sensory events provide a very visceral experience of stimulation and hedonism (as we saw earlier).

Schwartz's second higher-order value is **self-enhancement**, which incorporates *achievement* (pursuing personal success by demonstrating competence according to social standards) and *power* (seeking social status and control or dominance over people and resources). Consumers driven by these values would be more attracted to brands that convey success, status and prestige – characteristics beautifully exemplified by the car brand BMW. Globally recognized as a high-performing luxury car, its use as a symbol of status and wealth is widely recognized across cultures, which makes it a popular brand among consumers seeking something both exceptional and hard to attain.

The third higher-order value is **conservation**, which includes the basic values of *security* (seeking harmony, safety, and the stability of society, relationships and oneself), *conformity* (complying with rules and laws, and restraining from actions that will upset others and violate social expectations) and *tradition* (respecting, accepting and committing to cultural and religious customs). Consumers who prefer the reliability and status quo of tradition would be attracted to messages that promise a sense of continuity, with classic and legacy brands being particularly appealing. A great example here would be the luxury watch brand, Patek Philippe, whose advertising slogan, 'You never actually own a Patek Philippe. You merely look after it for the next generation', perfectly captures the timeless quality of heritage, longevity and conservation exemplified by this value.

The fourth and final higher-order value is that of **self-transcendence**, which speaks to the values of *benevolence* (the desire to preserve and enhance the welfare of people you are in frequent contact with) and *universalism* (understanding, appreciating, tolerating and protecting the welfare of all people and the wider web of life). As climate and biodiversity crises worsen, these two values are increasingly drawing the focus of purpose-driven marketing. From the now-familiar activist brands such as Patagonia and Ben & Jerry's, to companies that are launching sustainable sub-branded products (such as 'Space Hippie', Nike's low-carbon footwear that uses recycled plastics), businesses from all sectors are beginning to harness the attraction of self-transcendent values. While this speaks of course to the earlier trends we explored in terms of generational differences, as consumers become increasingly sensitive to the damage being wrought by food and fuel industries and beyond, this set of values will become ever more attractive and indeed impossible for businesses to side-step.

Of course, the values we prioritize vary greatly from one person to the next, and they can also be mediated and influenced by our cultural context. This means that from a business perspective, when it comes to standardizing your strategy, a one-size-fits-all approach is unlikely to cut it. Let's say, for example, that you represent a British brand with a *self-enhancement* identity, and you want to appeal to very individualistic consumers in the UK (in this case, targeting people who consider the self as fully autonomous). If you want to expand your reach overseas, you will have little difficulty resonating with other individualist consumers from culturally similar markets such as the United States. But try to penetrate more collectivist markets such as China (where the self is viewed as part of a collective, in which hierarchy is more widely accepted) and you will have to change tack.

To successfully target a second market that is so culturally distinct from the first, your brand concept must resonate with the value profiles of both audiences, without losing the heart of what the parent brand represents. In practical terms, this means identifying where each market sits on the values diagram, and then localizing your approach by crafting sub-branding strategies that hold different (but coherent) meanings to that of the parent brand.[35] Returning to the example above, if your business sells luxury electric cars, and its brand identity is built on the value of *self-enhancement* (helping people demonstrate dominance and success), your UK advert might depict someone in a lavishly upholstered car driving through the streets of London, displaying all the symbols of a carbon-free lifestyle, exuding power, prestige and status. For a Chinese market, however, your sub-branding strategy might focus on the neighbouring value of *conservation* (which sits beside *self-enhancement* on the values scale), resulting in an ad that shows a successful businessperson driving the same coveted car as his or her peers, valued principally for its safety and conformity.

Informed by cultural and genetic underpinnings, the values we hold dear are also shaped by our upbringing, with the degree of influence varying from one value to the next.[36] Yet despite their relative stability, under certain circumstances values can change, especially when they come into conflict with one another, or someone we care about brings to light inconsistencies in our values and behaviours[37] (for instance, when your drive for *self-direction* clashes with the desire to *conform* to your friends). To better understand the conflict and compatibility between values, take a look again at the values diagram. Values that sit opposite one another in the circle will tend to have conflicting motivations (leading to conflicting behaviours), whereas values that are adjacent to one another will hold motivations and behaviours in common. So while *self-direction* is not the antonym of *conformity*, the contradicting motivations that underpin each will give rise to behaviours that appear opposite (carving your own way versus following the crowd, for example). In contrast, neighbouring values such as *universalism* and *benevolence* actually share motivations, resulting in similar outcomes (in this case, treating other people and the natural world with care and respect). In even simpler terms, if we divide the circle into the four higher-order factors, we can split them into opposing pairs, in which *self-enhancement* conflicts with *self-transcendence*, and *openness to change* rubs up against *conservation*. Since holding opposite values as important can cause inner conflict and inconsistent behaviours (which can cause social problems and damage our wellbeing), most of us will tend to value one side of the circle over the other.[38]

Generally speaking, where changes to our values and personality do happen, the most significant shifts typically occur amidst the turbulence of early adulthood, as we run up against a whole gamut of life changes[39] (such as leaving home, starting our careers, taking on new roles and responsibilities – the list goes on). What's interesting is that when our values shift, it doesn't happen randomly – rather, they change in a coherent way. This means that if one value (such as *universalism*) grows in importance, so too will its neighbouring values (such as *benevolence*), while conflicting values (such as *power*) will tend to weaken.[40] Beyond the significant effect of life events, values can also change with time. As we grow older and become more set in our habits, more embedded in our social networks and less preoccupied with our own concerns, our priorities for *self-transcendence* and *conservation* can strengthen, and the relative importance of *openness* and *self-enhancement* diminish.[41] Given the breadth of consumers that are out there, this point is an important one if you are thinking about segmenting according to generation or age.

Where values themselves remain stable, the way in which we express them can vary depending on the context. If your friends and family are tolerant, for example, you may find it easier to express values of *universalism*. If you are wealthy, it may be easier to express *power*. But it is not just our social and economic situations that shape our values. Considering the unrelenting flood of social content that permeates our lives, it may be sobering to read that the media we are exposed to can also have an impact,[42] a point that raises significant questions about responsibility, ethics and the spread of disinformation (a topic for another day). What is concerning (or adaptive, depending on the context) is that we appear to adjust our values according to the circumstances of our lives. Rather than serve as immovable anchors, our values can become more or less important depending on how easy or difficult they are to obtain.[43] For instance, if you are in a job that offers greater agency and freedom of choice, over time you will come to prioritize the values of *self-direction* over those of *conformity*,[44] a shift that can have knock-on effects in other areas of your life. But while this kind of acclimation (where ease enhances importance) occurs for some values, it doesn't happen for all of them.

When it comes to values that connect to our sense of security and material wellbeing, if we are unable to attain them (often for reasons beyond our control), a compensation mechanism kicks in. Based on Maslow's deficit needs for safety, belonging, self-esteem and physiological requirements (for food, water, shelter and warmth), when these material values are curtailed, the deprivation we experience actually boosts our feeling of need, and with it our desire to obtain the valued goal (as we saw in Chapter 3).[45] This is one of the reasons why power and security are often valued most by those who haven't had either,[46] and why social stability and the attainment of wealth are typically valued by those who have endured social upheaval and economic hardship.[47] So, given the complexity of values and their increasing importance to our professional lives, how can we apply these insights in the service of brand resilience? Before I outline a specific tool you can use to achieve this, let's first map out how values show up within the wider business ecosystem.

Putting it into practice

From the cultural and organizational structure of a business, to its public-facing brand identity, values form an integral part of a company's DNA. Whether to inform internal management practices or the newest advertising strategy, if an organization is to thrive, it must be able to articulate and abide by a clear set of values that inform how it relates with its employees, partners, customers and wider society. When I ask HR expert Perry Timms about how values can be enacted within a company, he suggests that while 'values in themselves are great', they are actually underpinned by principles, and that 'sometimes we just need a set of principles to start with'. It is all too easy to attach a values statement to a single word, such as 'We value *honesty*', without it ever resulting in tangible changes in behaviour. Yet if we ground our values in a principle, such as that suggested by Perry, 'We'll talk truth to power and we will want candid feedback at any given time', people are much more likely to turn around and say 'those principles, I totally get'. He explains that since one's 'principles can very strongly exemplify and mandate the ethics that you want to be part of', the declarations that arise from these can then be 'ethically tested in where you go, what you do, who you rely on'. In this way, one's values and attendant principles can be held accountable through their expression in tangible, measurable outcomes.

Of course, not all values will necessarily help organizations build resilience in the face of uncertainty, so when I ask Perry what quality he believes to be vital for the long-term success of a business, his response of 'virtuousness' intrigues me. He explains, 'The more virtuous an organization is, the more likely it will last the term. So by that I mean ethical, good... it has to show its virtuousness in everything it does.'

From a talent and recruitment perspective, this can mean focusing on 'how you present your company to the world, how you then go about people applying to come and work for you, how you make sure that you're removed from bias'. In this context, Perry suggests that human resources act 'almost like a steward or a voice of conscience to the organization. So if they are having high attrition because their toxic leadership is creating mental ill health with people, they don't just keep recruiting people, they actually go back and say, "Hang on, what's the ethical breach here in how people are either deployed, supported, or enabled in their work?" And if they find it, then they stand in the space and say, "That's not humane, that's not good enough, that's got to change." And then they have evidence to back it up.'

Beyond recruitment practices, Perry suggests, it's also about 'pricing, it's distribution of profits, it's looking after employees, it's giving back to the community, it's about planetary regeneration'. It's about a company's 'choice of supply partners and material acquisition, as in where they get their parts from or their raw materials or whatever it might be'. Ultimately, while accountability for our actions may be said to stop at the limits of what we directly control, it is perhaps precisely when we go 'beyond what we are contracted to do, and we show a degree of connection, and empathy, and help' that our true colours – both as individuals and the organizations we represent – most clearly shine through.

Of course, not everyone considers pro-social and pro-business values to be quite so distinct or separable from one another, as I discover in conversation with Stephanie M H Moore. When I ask her what she believes to be the biggest risks and opportunities facing business right now, she explains that, 'Business issues are social issues, social issues are business issues. So for me, I think the biggest opportunities and the biggest risks are the same. Businesses have to decide where they are placed in society. Are you part of the solution? Are you part of the problem? Are you trying to be part of a global positive change, a global positive net impact?' From diversity and inclusion, to equity and justice, she tells me that it is 'frustrating that we don't all come to the table, every single person, understanding that these kinds of things are meaningful and important to everyone'. In the grand scheme of things, and especially as businesses face increasingly complex challenges, she believes that 'Every single piece of what you do as an organization has to be aligned with the things that you say you care about. Those are the most successful organizations, and those will continue to be the most successful... because employees know that you mean what you say.'

And therein lies the crux. As business values become increasingly important to stakeholders of all kinds, one of the major challenges organizations will face is in demonstrating that they are in fact enacting the principles they claim to uphold. When I raise this with Perry, he suggests that we may start to see more services offering a 'score card for businesses, not just what their market value is, but almost like an ethics index'. Something similar, perhaps, to the approach taken by JUST Capital, an independent non-profit that, according to their website, 'tracks, analyses and engages with large corporations and their investors on how they perform on the public's priorities'.[48] In an ideal world (and if trends and human psychology are anything to go by), as more organizations seek official channels through which to demonstrate their standing, we may yet witness the birth of a living, breathing leaderboard, one that shines a light upon those that are guiding the way.

The Values Map

Despite the fact that most organizations naturally prioritize certain values over others, as constructs, they can be tricky and expensive to measure. Where businesses wish to realign their strategy according to a new set of values, a robust road map can be complicated to plot out, with traditional methods often proving expensive and time-consuming to implement. Take the method of means–end chain analysis, for example. While the process of interviewing consumers about their product preferences (and the underlying reasons for them) can yield detailed information, the nature of extensive interviews means that this approach can be expensive and lengthy to run. What's more, finding and incentivizing enough customers who are willing to fill in self-report questionnaires and be profiled, raises not only ethical considerations (especially in the EU with existing GDPR regulations), but also questions around budget and scalability.

Given the technological advances we have seen in the collection, storage and analysis of data, methods that rely on remote profiling (such as inferring meaning through free text analysis) can provide alternative, if ethically questionable, routes to understanding one's consumers at a more intimate level. But for those of us who don't wish to profile individual consumers by mining their online behavioural data, there is another, more 'virtuous' and inexpensive way.

In the study of human relationships, there is a dynamic known as **similarity-attraction theory**, which proposes that we generally prefer people we believe to be similar to ourselves. Whether in terms of demographic characteristics,[49] values, beliefs, lifestyle or shared experiences,[50] or indeed any element we might share in common, when it comes to being drawn to one person over another, similarity plays a big role. The same is true for the brands we choose to buy from. As we saw in Chapter 4, we tend to develop stronger attachments to brands we perceive as congruent with our actual or ideal self, and while this applies on the level of personality traits (if you are high in extroversion you will be attracted to extraverted brands and messages), research shows that values-based congruence actually leads to stronger consumer–brand relationships than when focusing on personality congruence alone.[51] So where does that leave us?

Well, if you want to map out the existing values of your business, design more resonant messages, or locate a coherent direction in which to develop your brand identity, there is an approach you can take that is swift, straightforward and robust. In collaboration with Dr Kiki Leutner at Goldsmiths University, I have developed *The Values Map*, a values-based online tool designed to help you analyse and understand your values archetype, and what this means in terms of the characteristics and goals that drive your business, brand or team. Based on Schwartz's values questionnaire, this process is the one that I use in my consultancy practice to help clients identify, develop and communicate the psychological values they stand for. From feedback detailing how your values are expressed through company culture, to recommendations on how to enhance your marketing and communications, this tool provides scientifically rigorous insights that can help shape and inform your business and branding strategies moving forward. If you want to try it out, you can find it at the following link: thevaluesmap.com.

Key takeaways

- The conspicuous, vacuous expressions of moral values is known as virtue signalling.
- Woke-washing is the marketing practice of claiming to support a just cause, appropriating the language of social activism so as to engage specific groups.
- Although psychometrics are commonly used to drive engagement, values are better at predicting and explaining consumer choice.

- Consumers prefer brands and products that reflect their values, and that help them create, maintain and reinforce their sense of self.
- Schwartz's Theory of Basic Human Values provides a framework through which to accurately measure higher-order (and basic) values. These are: openness to change (self-direction, stimulation and hedonism); self-enhancement (achievement and power); conservation (security, conformity and tradition); and self-transcendence (benevolence and universalism).
- In an organizational context, when underpinned by principles, values can be held accountable through their expression in tangible, measurable outcomes.
- According to similarity-attraction theory, we prefer people we believe to be similar to ourselves. In a business context, values-based congruence can lead to stronger consumer–brand relationships.

CHAPTER SIX

Emotionally intelligent communication

What not to do

When dealing with people, let us remember we are not dealing with creatures of logic. We are dealing with creatures of emotion. DALE CARNEGIE[1]

Holding up a mirror

It was the year 1964, and Joseph Weizenbaum was sitting at his desk working on a prototype computer program that he hoped would one day simulate human conversation. A professor at what were then MIT's Artificial Intelligence Lab, his efforts to build a natural language processor were making progress, and looked set to demonstrate first-hand the superficiality of communication between people and machines. Step by step, using methodologies of pattern matching and substitution, the program began to take shape, until one day, it was ready. If all went well, his creation would be able to convincingly craft the illusion of a real conversation with a human. Naming his progeny ELIZA, he set about developing various scripts upon which the program could run, chief among which was a particular curiosity called DOCTOR[2] (presumably named after the language patterns of Rogerian psychotherapy upon which it was modelled). Designed to echo back elements of speech typed in by a human user, this script would offer 'therapeutic' non-directional questions in response.

If, for instance, the computer opened the conversation with, 'Please tell me your problem', and you answered 'I'm feeling anxious', a follow-up question might be 'How long have you been *feeling anxious?*' If you then responded 'Since I quit my job', ELIZA would invite you to 'Please go on', and reflect whatever you typed in next ('I don't want to end up broke') in the follow-up question ('What would it mean to you if you *end up broke?*') and so on. In this way, the program would simulate some version of a therapeutic framework and, in the process, emulate the sense of empathy and rapport one might find from a warm-blooded person. In the event, ELIZA turned out to be a resounding success, yet despite his many careful calculations the professor had failed to predict one crucial thing – quite how convincing his creation would be.

Having worked alongside him throughout the development of the machine, Weizenbaum's secretary was keen to try ELIZA herself, and try she did – but the dalliance didn't last long. The story goes that after only a few sessions, despite understanding how the machine had been built, the secretary requested that she be left alone with ELIZA so as to have 'a real conversation'. Dismayed that his endeavours had the opposite effect to what he had intended to prove (the superficiality of communication between people and machines), Weizenbaum reportedly lamented, 'No one understands, no one is there.'[3] Despite his best efforts to demonstrate that the program was incapable of conversational and computational depth, Weizenbaum had inadvertently birthed an entity to which users were attributing complex human characteristics. Of course, ELIZA couldn't really understand or empathize with the text being typed into her system – the computer was running on a script far more rudimentary than its many chatbot descendants we encounter today. So if ELIZA was only faking it, what exactly was happening to make her so convincing?

Well, it comes down to the quality of verbal interaction between the two parties. In ELIZA's case, where the conversation consisted of green lines of text blinking across an old-school computer monitor, the user's subjective experience of empathy and understanding depended on the words on the screen. In everyday life, the quality of our conversations can vary greatly from one experience to the next. Whether with our colleagues or friends, we all know what it is like to be trapped in a one-way torrent of verbiage, or to clunk our way through a dialogue that just doesn't seem to connect. So when we do come across a conversation that flows, we tend to pay attention. Of course, the difference between a good conversation and a bad one comes down to a few key things. In ELIZA's case, the brilliance of the interaction was its simplicity. Despite being programmed to operate within very limited parameters, the act of reflecting back and **mirroring** the user's experience in their own words was enough to elicit a sense of compassion and rapport, creating an impression that ELIZA both cared and understood. But why was this so powerful?

The language we use is loaded with nuance and meaning and can convey subtle differences that are important to the speaker. So if you told me 'I went to the most *exhilarating* show the other night', and I answered, 'What made it so *exciting*?', you wouldn't feel as understood as if I had asked, 'What made it so *exhilarating*?' While the two words might be closely related, they would mean different things to you. By listening carefully and paying attention to the details, I would be demonstrating that I cared about understanding your subjective experience. This is why, when we encounter someone who literally speaks our language, we can experience a powerful sense of kinship, understanding and trust.

Though the idea is simple in theory, for this technique to work well it must be approached with a certain level of **emotional intelligence**, or EQ. Made famous in 1995 by Daniel Goleman's book *Emotional Intelligence*,[4] the term itself originates from a large body of psychological literature, and refers to our capacity to reason about emotions and use them to enhance our thinking.[5] Far from being simple expressions of mood, our emotions contain valuable information and meaning, and can give away clues as to possible actions we might take in a given situation. For example, if you are shouting to express your anger (emotion), the reason may be because you have been treated unfairly (meaning). In this instance, you might decide to respond with retribution, peace-making or withdrawal (action), depending on the context and what you hope to achieve. Being emotionally intelligent is not just about being able to identify specific feelings – it is also about understanding and reasoning with what they signify.

According to the seminal work of psychologists Peter Salovey and John D Mayer, emotional intelligence comprises four key abilities.[6] The first is the degree to which we can accurately *perceive*, identify and discriminate between different emotions, both our own and other people's. This means being able to detect and decipher non-verbal expressions of emotion in everything from faces, gestures and voices, to pictures and cultural artefacts. The second is about our ability to *use* our emotions to facilitate different kinds of cognitive processes, such as thinking and problem-solving. In a practical sense, this can mean understanding how to harness the changes in your mood to best fit the task at hand. If, for example, you had to go through the tedious, meticulous task of completing your tax return, you would be best served doing it in a slightly sad mood (as if the very thought of completing a tax return were not enough to elicit this feeling anyway). Not only does this subdued state appear to aid careful processing, it also benefits all kinds of methodical work that require attention to detail or deductive reasoning.[7] Happier states, on the other hand, tend to stimulate more innovative, creative thinking.[8] So whatever your goal or mood, being able to identify and then leverage the natural changes in your emotions can be a powerful tool for boosting your performance, competence and sense of wellbeing.

The third aspect of emotional intelligence relates to how we *understand* emotions, both in terms of the complex relationships between them, and the nuance and variety between closely-related feelings. For instance, while there is clearly a connection between feeling happy and feeling ecstatic (both are joyful, energizing states), there is also a difference in quality and intensity between the two. Understanding emotions also means being able to recognize and describe how they might change over time (for example, how shock can give way to grief and sadness).

The fourth and final element of emotional intelligence is our ability to *manage* and regulate emotions, both within ourselves and in other people. This does not, however, mean trying to be happy all the time, or shunning away uncomfortable feelings. While some of us may prefer to keep a lid on things in order to avoid 'embarrassing' displays of emotion (the definition of which depends on cultural context), being able to manage your emotions can also mean knowing when to amplify a specific state in order to elicit a desired reaction from others. This is something the world of politics knows well – you need only watch presidential debates during an election cycle to witness candidates amping up their righteous anger in order to provoke that same feeling in their viewers. In a nutshell, emotionally intelligent people are those who have developed the skill to identify, regulate and harness emotions in order to achieve their desired goals.

Let's return to ELIZA for a moment. While Joseph Weizenbaum did not endow his machine with real emotional intelligence, by designing a script that mirrored language use and emulated Rogerian patterns of speech, his program was able to elicit the powerful sense of feeling heard and understood. However inadvertently, the good professor had succeeded in creating a subjective, conversational experience resembling what we now describe as **active listening**. An intentional process designed to foster trust and rapport, active listening is about being attentive to the person speaking, and deliberately reflecting back or paraphrasing what they have said, without pushing forward your own opinions, judgement or 'advice'. The idea is that by listening deeply and holding up a mirror to the speaker's experience, they will feel more valued and understood, and therefore more willing to open up and speak candidly.

What's surprising (as ELIZA showed us) is that being a good active listener doesn't necessarily depend on your ability to read and regulate non-verbal communication (which is curious, given that body language plays a powerful role in transmitting our emotions, as we shall see later). Rather, studies suggest that active listening is primarily associated with good *verbal* social skills.[9] This means that if you can identify and practise the techniques for initiating and maintaining a conversation, you will be able to create a dynamic in which your partner – whether a friend, colleague or customer – feels more understood, and their emotional needs better met. So what are these techniques, exactly?

There are many factors that come into play in active listening,[10] but one of the most important is the attitude with which you approach the dialogue. Since the language we use tends to reveal how we feel about things (whether we are delighted or disappointed by what we are hearing), one of the most skilful aspects of active listening is intentionally using language that is neutral and non-judgemental. For instance, if your partner is describing what sounds (to you) like a tantalizing opportunity, rather than ask them a leading, yes-or-no question, 'Doesn't that intrigue you?' you could instead say, 'How do you feel about that?' Not only does this allow your partner to respond with more detail and accuracy (they may feel intrigued, but maybe apprehensive too), it can also create a safer space within which to answer more honestly. By asking open questions like 'What does that mean for you?' or 'What would be the ideal outcome?' not only will you invite a richer, more in-depth response, you will also gain a clearer understanding of the person you are speaking with. If there is something you haven't understood, it is important to ask for clarification and reflect back what is said to check you have grasped the intended meaning.

Beyond the questions you ask, it is also vital that you give the conversation room to breathe – if your partner needs a moment to pause and think, don't rush in to fill their silence. Yes, it may feel a bit awkward or uncomfortable, but by hitting your internal breaks, you will give them the opportunity to express themselves more clearly. It can also be tempting to offer advice or interject; however, in many cases what the other person wants is simply to be heard and understood, so if you want to show your support you can offer silent, non-verbal feedback by maintaining good eye contact, leaning in and nodding or smiling where appropriate. When the conversation feels that it is coming to an end, or the issue in question has been addressed, offering a summary of the key points can be a useful way of checking in with the other person, and closing the dialogue.

Although the techniques outlined above may seem simple enough, they can be deceptively tricky to put into practice. Of the things that should be fastidiously avoided, the usual suspects of interrupting, being distracted and faking your attention are fairly obvious (it can be tempting to zone out when touching uncomfortable subjects or emotions), but there are other, more subtle habits that can also derail a dialogue. Sometimes mistaken by the perpetrator as a display of empathy, in my experience, even (or perhaps, especially) folks who consider themselves emotionally intelligent will engage in a behaviour known as 'topping' the story. Imagine, for example, that you are sharing a personal, emotional experience with a friend, perhaps something that takes some courage to express. In an ideal world, you would find a sympathetic ear and the space to speak freely without feeling shamed or shut down. But in this instance, something else happens.

Rather than invite you to share more, or ask questions to better understand what you are saying, your friend replies, 'Oh yes, that reminds me of the time when…', and it's game over. Far from building trust and connection, by cutting in and immediately switching the focus back onto themselves your friend has steam-rolled the conversation and shut down the dialogue in the process. It's a dynamic most of us will be familiar with, and if you have experienced it you will know how frustrating and unpleasant it can feel to be on the receiving end. That's not to say that good conversation is just about listening – of course it isn't. When you are really in flow with someone, your voices and experiences will weave together into a dynamic dance that is more than the sum of its parts. But if you are looking to enhance the emotional intelligence of your communication, whether to build trust, resolve conflicts or deepen bonds, then active listening is one of the most powerful skills you can develop.

Mind the empathy gap

As we know, no discussion on emotionally intelligent communication would be complete without touching upon empathy. A well-worn word, **empathy** refers to our capacity to put ourselves in someone else's shoes, to understand or feel what they are experiencing from their unique vantage point. While the concept itself has a long history, it was Carl Rogers (the renowned humanistic psychologist whose work inspired ELIZA's code) who proposed that empathy is central to our personal growth and wellbeing, and more recent research now reveals its profound impact on the world of brands and customer experience. Far from being a fluffy concept or a nice-to-have, in service settings empathy has been found to reduce discrimination, revenge, anti-social and unethical behaviours,[11] and even to improve design thinking for innovations.[12] In the business realm, since empathetic employees are better able to understand and adapt to their customers' needs and desires,[13] they are invaluable in providing richer, more personalized service, which in turn boosts customer satisfaction[14] and the overall brand experience.

Thought to be the most powerful way in which we make sense of, and predict, our social environment,[15] empathy is not only vital for our survival and flourishing, it is also the social cognitive ability most complex and difficult for artificial intelligence (AI) to replicate.[16] Given that chatbots and robots are becoming increasingly commonplace (and their threat to people's jobs increasingly real), the value of empathy as a 'high-touch' skill that humanizes care[17] will become ever more important as we seek to build resilience in our workplaces and careers. Despite their ubiquity and utility in dealing with vast numbers of customer service interactions, when it comes to handling rare, complex or extraordinary issues, our current chatbots simply are not equipped to provide the empathy so often required to reach adequate solutions.[18] While empathy plays a role in the *instrumental* support we might receive (for instance, when you obtain practical help in the form of information, advice or suggestions), it is often the *emotional* support (such as the assurance or encouragement given by a human representative) that can make the difference between an underwhelming customer experience and a satisfying one.

Although our ability to recognize basic emotions is thought to be innate, evidence suggests that empathy can also be developed through specific training and exercises,[19] which is great news if this is something you want to augment in yourself or in others. In terms of how empathy works, it can be broken down into three different components. The first is affective or **emotional empathy**, our capacity to identify and respond to someone else's state with the appropriate emotion. If you noticed a glum-looking colleague, for instance, their eyebrows furrowed, hunched over a desk, you might pick up on their anxiety and offer some words of support or a gentle touch. This kind of compassionate, sympathetic response to another's suffering is called *empathic concern*, and it comes from an altruistic motivation to help others.

But our empathetic repertoire does not end there. Imagine for a moment that you are in the kitchen watching a friend cut a lemon and you see the knife slip, slicing through the top of their finger. In this scenario, not only would you respond to their emotional distress, you would probably also wince in sympathetic pain or **somatic empathy**, a physical response arising from mirror neurons in your somatic nervous system.

Beyond the emotional and physical, empathy also involves understanding other people's mental state or perspective. Known as **cognitive empathy**, this capacity involves *perspective taking* (being able to adopt other people's psychological point of view) and *fantasy* (identifying with fictional characters or imaginatively transposing yourself into fictional situations).[20] What is curious is that while empathy enables us to better understand the subjective experiences of others, emotional and cognitive empathy are actually two distinct constructs. Just because someone can empathize strongly on an emotional level does not mean they will be good at mentally adopting another person's perspective. In fact, in highly emotional situations, strong empathic concern can actually inhibit this ability.[21]

Given that empathy carries benefits for all aspects of the business ecosystem, from the workplace to the customer, it is also fundamental to building resilient organizations and good reputations. Yet empathy can also pose some tricky challenges, especially when it comes to communicating in the virtual world. With many of us now accustomed to interacting remotely (whether with colleagues or customers), it can be easier than ever to fall into the **hot–cold empathy gap.** One of the myriad cognitive biases that influence our lives, this gap describes our tendency to underestimate the influence of emotional situations and visceral drives on our own preferences, attitudes and behaviours.[22]

From physical states such as pain, thirst, hunger and sexual arousal, to any drug cravings or strong emotions we might be experiencing, these drives can have a disproportionate effect on our perception and decision-making processes. If it were a blisteringly hot day, for example, and you were feeling parched, you would respond more empathetically towards an advert showing a person in a hot place, also experiencing thirst. Watch the advert on a cold day with a nice cup of tea, however, and due to the difference in states between you and the protagonist, the empathy gap would be much wider. Whether it is thirst, pain or the all-consuming feeling of being in love, when we are in one of these 'hot' states we can become so focused on placating that sensation that we become blinkered to other goals, even to the point of impulsively acting out and losing control.[23]

The key thing here is that our ability to understand and empathize with other people is actually state-dependent, a fact that has important implications for the way in which we relate to one another. If we want to be emotionally intelligent in our communication, whether in exchanges with colleagues and partners, or in customer-service interactions, we must first map out where we are on the hot–cold spectrum, relative to the person we are speaking with. If, for instance, you are in a calm mood (a 'cold' state) and a client calls in, furiously screaming down the phone at you (a 'hot' state), it is going to be harder to empathize with one another, making resolution near impossible. If, however, you know the dynamics at play, and can swiftly recognize the difference in states, you will be better equipped to adapt your approach and address the situation, which is where active listening becomes invaluable.

By asking open questions and identifying the emotive language being used, not only will you create the space for customers to express themselves, you will also be able to reflect back their experience in their own words, bridging the empathy gap and stepping closer towards resolution. While this is useful in all manner of interactions, it is especially important when customers are feeling angry, not least because our primary response can be to freeze, fight or flee – outcomes that can lead to aggressive or avoidant behaviours, neither of which (in a modern context) tend to result in productive outcomes.

In social settings, yet another response opens up – the possibility to 'tend and befriend'. Underpinned by a suite of neurochemicals (including oxytocin, opioids and the dopaminergic pathways in the brain), our desire to affiliate with other people can provide a powerful means through which to reduce our stress, if they can provide the comfort and support we need.[24] This may be why, when it comes to helping angry customers, the most effective approach can often be to let them vent and express their grievances before offering words of emotional support alongside any practical solutions. The problem is that when it comes to reading, identifying and influencing other people's emotions, there can sometimes be other veiled, malevolent influences at play.

The power of contagion

Beyond the boundaries of conversant awareness lies a curious behaviour that most of us engage in every day, without even realizing it. Often unintentional and automatic, this process serves as a building block for our social interactions, helping us to empathize with and understand the experiences, thoughts and feelings of others. This strange phenomenon is known as **emotional contagion**, and it describes our tendency to synchronize and mimic the postures, movements, facial expressions and vocalizations of other people,[25] enabling us to experience an echo of what they are feeling. If, for instance, I asked you to mimic expressions for love, joy, sadness, fear and disgust, through this simple act you would actually feel some version of that specific emotion.

Considered a type of social influence,[26] emotional contagion is the means through which we 'catch' other people's emotions, and it can happen either with or without our knowledge. Most of us will have experienced meetings from which, for some seemingly inexplicable reason, we come away feeling buoyant or beleaguered, and it is often the hidden hand of emotional contagion that lies behind this effect. From a person's status and charisma,[27] to their level of facial expressiveness (higher levels of which can all increase transmission), there are a variety of factors that influence how contagious another person's state will be, and the degree to which they affect those around them.

From impacting our own wellbeing,[28] to the wellbeing of those with whom we are connected,[29] how we share our personal emotions online can have all manner of implications for the way we feel and behave – and not just in our private lives, either. This decade alone we have witnessed first-hand, and in real time, the power of emotional contagion to drive the spread of emotions that have galvanized some of the largest social movements in modern history.[30] Yet despite the wealth of experiments dedicated to examining this effect in the real world, in the early 2000s there hadn't yet been much research exploring how emotions propagate online. So when Facebook arrived on the scene it looked like an opportunity too good to be missed. Academically speaking, this was an exciting time, with researchers and institutes keen to avail themselves of the nascent technology (and hitherto inconceivable sample sizes) suddenly made possible through the widespread adoption of social media networks. People dabbled here and there, but it wasn't until 2014, when a massive, covert experiment was conducted across Facebook, that the far-reaching effects of emotional contagion were finally witnessed at scale.

Siezing their moment, a trio of researchers took to the platform to investigate whether emotional states could be transferred from one user to the next, through the medium of online posts. Within the bounds of what was legal at the time, the team 'recruited' 689,003 unwitting users, and set about manipulating their news feeds without their knowledge (or informed consent) by reducing the number of emotional posts they were exposed to.[31] The results were revelatory – just as anticipated, users who received a reduced number of positive posts went on to create fewer of these themselves, instead producing more negative posts (and vice-versa). Nicknamed the 'withdrawal effect', this behaviour demonstrated that it was indeed possible to transmit an emotional state without direct interaction between friends, thus proving that emotional contagion could occur without awareness, even in the absence of non-verbal cues (such as the mimicry we talked about earlier).

In one fell swoop, the researchers had successfully illustrated that mere exposure to another person's emotional expression (in this case, in the form of an online post) was enough to change a user's emotional state, with those receiving less emotional content (whether positive or negative) producing less in turn. Despite the small (but statistically significant) effect sizes, this controversial study provided – in the words of the researchers – 'experimental evidence for massive-scale contagion via social networks', the effects of which could have 'large aggregated consequences' when played out across social networks of such gargantuan scale.[32]

Of course, when the news broke and Facebook users finally realized that they might have been unwittingly manipulated, the ensuing outrage this provoked both intensified and elicited further outcry as it spread across social channels, ironically illustrating the very effect the researchers had identified in the first place.[33] In fact, people were so unhappy about the experiment that the data scientist who authored the paper eventually made a public apology via a Facebook post, conceding that 'the research benefits of the paper may not have justified all of this anxiety'.[34] Whatever we may think of the dubious ethics of such an experiment, it did serve to highlight what we already know: that the emotional quality of our communication has a real and tangible impact on the receiver.

But if the aim of social media platforms is to upregulate users' emotions so as to amplify the effects of emotional contagion (to engage more people, for longer), then increasing the intensity and frequency of the emotional content people are exposed to is not enough. Rather, to boost the transmission of emotion online, people must also be encouraged to share their own feelings – a behaviour that digital platforms have become all too adept at incentivizing. From likes and shares, to reposts and follower counts, the digital levers of positive reinforcement that characterize social platforms have become so ubiquitous as to render them almost unnoticeable. Yet if we examine how they influence social media use at a personal level, we will see just how powerful the effects of such conditioning can be.

Take Instagram, for example. I know from personal experience that if I've been inactive for a while, and I return to the app, seeing a bunch of activity (likes, comments, etc) 'batched' (as opposed to drip-fed as and when they occur) creates a greater sense of reward and excitement, providing a stronger incentive for me to re-engage, post more content and cue up the next dopamine hit. But we can take it one step further. On Twitter, it is possible to predict how many likes and retweets a tweet will attract, based on the emotional intensity of the content alone – the more intense the emotion, the greater the activity, with positive emotions enjoying a stronger effect than negative ones.[35] Ultimately, whatever the platform, any boost in engagement essentially rewards (and positively reinforces) our behaviour, encouraging us to express more emotion, thus perpetuating the effects of emotional contagion even further.[36]

A word to the wise

So what has this got to do with communication more generally? Well, in much the same way that cognitive intelligence doesn't imply wisdom, neither does emotional intelligence imply compassion. Despite the potency and virality of content designed to inflame and outrage, engaging people in such an explosive way is neither the most ethical nor the most effective means of driving generative outcomes. While such misanthropic approaches may indeed demonstrate one's skill in leveraging psychological dynamics, manipulating people's emotions to drive up some nominal metric of engagement (regardless of its impact on the viewer) is worlds apart from applying one's knowledge in a meaningful, humane way. When it comes to wielding power, especially across such a vast territory as the internet, it is our willingness to use this skill responsibly that sets us apart from the competition.

This is especially poignant given that the choices we make rarely stem from rational, deliberative reasoning processes. Contrary to what we may like to believe, countless studies demonstrate that when it comes to decision-making, we are far from objective agents. Rather, as renowned science writer and author Rita Carter puts it, 'where thought conflicts with emotion, the latter is designed by the neural circuitry in our brains to win'.[37] Online, as we engage across social and media channels awash with emotionally charged content, our ability to thoughtfully gather, analyse and process information can become further compromised, and our capacity to live according

How might businesses and brands engage in emotionally intelligent communication that is both resonant and ethical?

to our values, frustrated. Given that we are all subject to these hidden forces, how might businesses and brands engage in emotionally intelligent communication that is both resonant and ethical?

Whether investing in ads we hope will 'go viral', or crafting campaigns that will boost engagement and reach, most of us want to find better ways in which to connect with and convert the next possible customer. Yet typically, when we talk about viral content we tend to think of those videos, headlines and memes that evoke joy or anger or fear – those intense emotions that, once triggered, kick us into irrevocable action. What may escape our notice are the other, less visible dynamics that determine the content's emotional impact and whether or not we share. When it comes to transmitting our emotions to other people, there are other elements that can influence how (and to what extent) the process of contagion works. Emotions are not simple things, and in the virtual domain, where content can be shared across innumerable channels in all manner of formats, if we wish to transmit emotions successfully we must understand the three fundamental factors that characterize them.

The first factor is the **valence** of the emotion, which describes how positive or negative the feeling is – joy, for example, has a positive valence, whereas fear has a negative one. The second factor is **arousal**, the energy or excitement level with which the emotion is expressed. Where anger is high energy (and therefore high arousal), sadness is more subdued and therefore low arousal (see Figure 6.1). But emotions also vary in terms of their **dominance**, the degree to which we feel submissive or in control when experiencing them. If you watched something that made you feel fearful, for instance, you would feel less in control (low dominance) than if you consumed content that elicited a feeling of admiration or inspiration (high dominance).

In an online context, it is this triad of characteristics (the valence, arousal and dominance levels of the elicited emotion) that will determine the virality of any given piece of content.[39] The problem is that not all content and distribution channels are created equal. If we look at articles, for instance, those that attract the highest number of comments tend to evoke a combination of emotions that are high in arousal (such as happiness

FIGURE 6.1 VAD model

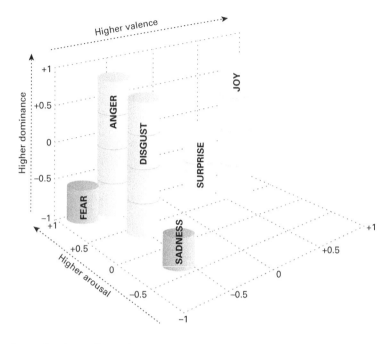

Source: Based upon diagram from Buechel and Hahn (2018) – emotion representation mapping for automatic lexicon construction (mostly) performs on human level.[38] Permission to use granted.

and anger), and low in dominance (such as fear, where people feel less in control), which goes some way to explaining why the most shared pieces are often the most charged and divisive.

When it comes to social channels, however, the VAD model tells another story. Unlike the high-arousal, low-dominance combination that drives commenting behaviours for articles, the factor that connects most with the social content we share is high dominance. Posts and updates that evoke feelings of admiration or inspiration, for instance, not only lift our mood, they also help us to feel more in control, which may explain why so many newsfeeds are replete with friends posting feelgood stories and updates of happy moments. Sure, you may say, but that still doesn't explain why so much of the content shared on social is negative. To answer this, we must look at some of the forces that shape what we pay attention to.

Unfortunate as it may be (and most likely for evolutionary reasons), when it comes to human reactions, our cognitive, emotional and behavioural responses tend to be much stronger and faster when we are faced with negative stimuli than when we encounter something that is positive or neutral.[40] Combined with our tendency to place more weight and attention on negative information, it is no surprise that unpleasant emotions are often more contagious than their pleasant counterparts. Of course, many of these effects become more visible when mediated by technology, so it can be tempting to assume that emotional contagion effects are more frequent, extensive and intense when expressed online. But while it is true that technology facilitates the reach and speed with which charged content can spread, the heightened frequency at which we are exposed to emotions (of any valence) can actually result in unintended effects, including emotional fatigue and habituation. If we're not careful, the very fact of being overexposed to a whole gamut of emotions can desensitize us and begin to mute our very ability to empathize.

But there is another phenomenon that can also steer the spread and impact of emotional content online. Since the revelations of the Cambridge Analytica scandal and concerns around the use of targeted ads such as those rolled out by the UK's Vote Leave Brexit campaign,[41] journalists, academics and business leaders alike have warned of the potential for politicized content to shape and subvert the democratic process. From the Arab Spring to the US elections,[42] social platforms have played a pivotal role in the dissemination of political and moral ideas and, as such, have had a hand in writing human history. With so much at stake, academics researching the science of emotion, morality and social networks have started to investigate these dynamics, yielding unsettling results in the process. Just as emotions can transmit from one person to the next, evidence suggests that so too can moral ideas.

With striking similarities to its emotional relative, **moral contagion** describes how the expression of moral emotions (via the content we share and create) can help diffuse moral and political ideas throughout social networks. In a watershed study in 2017, researchers from New York University investigated the content of 563,312 tweets from US users, in a bid to explore how people communicated about the divisive issues of climate change, same-sex marriage and gun control.[43] Unsurprisingly, results revealed that the mere 'presence of moral-emotional words in messages increased their transmission by approximately 20 per cent per word', and that this increase in diffusion happened within (rather than between) groups that shared the same ideological boundaries (liberals shared with liberals, and conservatives with conservatives). With results revealing a stronger contagion effect for moral-emotional words (such as 'hate', 'fighting' and 'shameful') than for moral or emotional words alone, the study raised important questions about the responsibility we take for the language we use, especially when it comes to discussing polarizing topics online.

Given the implications of such research, it is no wonder that social networks have started to engage with these issues, with Twitter and Facebook deciding to slap the equivalent of 'parental advisory' warnings on posts deemed politically inflammatory or misleading during the 2020 US presidential elections.[44] Yet when it comes to everyday media and our ability to shape it, the emotional valence of the content (how 'good' or 'bad' it makes us feel) is actually *less* connected to its virality than the emotion's dominance or arousal levels.[45] This means that if we want to boost the shareability of a video, for example, we need not resort to invoking the ire, sadness, fear or disgust of others. Rather, we can choose to create social content that is emotionally complex, surprising and joyful (where appropriate), thereby leveraging the dynamics of emotional contagion to lift the emotional states of those around us (even when trudging over political ground).

Perhaps an unlikely candidate, one of my favourite examples of an organization that is doing this well is the *Washington Post*. Where online news outlets have historically resorted to pushing out clickbait articles and provocative headlines in a bid to attract eyeballs and revenue, this particular newspaper has had astounding success in reaching new (largely younger) demographics on TikTok, by blending paid ads in amongst a stream of original, organic videos. A far cry from the provocative content one might find elsewhere, this otherwise traditional publisher posts satirical, timely videos on current affairs (often featuring their home-spun character, 'Dave'), bringing a more uplifting voice to the news, in a strategy that has earned them millions of impressions, comments and shares.[46] From lighthearted topics to hard-hitting reports, they have found a way to convey the facts to an audience that appreciates a more playful approach – and it appears to be working.

Whether you want to firm up positive associations with your brand, or simply to spread some cheer, choosing to propagate feel-good emotions both online and offline, can result in a whole host of desirable effects – and not just for your intended audience. From boosting the customer-helping behaviours of salespeople,[47] to increasing cooperation[48] and concession-making[49] in negotiation contexts, not only do positive moods make us feel good, they can also have a significant impact on the operation of our organizations. When it comes to cognitive performance and effort, for example, positive emotional states are associated with an increased ability to engage in more complex problem-solving and logical reasoning,[50] and, in the customer services sector, with better performance ratings.[51] Where the presence of negative emotions is associated with conflict (which in turn can be jacked up by bad moods, and our rejection of others), positive moods are actually connected with a greater acceptance of others.[52] In a very real sense, then, by choosing to do good, we can actually make it easier to be good.

Clear communication

When it comes to communication, articles and social content are not the only means through which emotions can travel online. Given the ubiquity of livestreams and conferencing platforms, it is important that we also understand how emotional contagion plays out across video. Whether pre-recorded, or via a live, virtual event, there are various factors that influence how emotion is transferred through the screen, many of which stem from our interactions in the physical world. When face to face, for instance, the energy with which we communicate our emotions will influence the extent of their transmission to others. From the facial patterns and gestures we engage in, to the tempo, loudness, pitch range and pitch level of our speech, the intensity with which we express ourselves can determine how contagious our emotions will be. This is why the same emotion, with the same degree of pleasantness, will be experienced and transmitted so much more powerfully when communicated with greater energy.

Take the unpleasant but low-energy emotion of depressed sluggishness, for example – we would expect this feeling to be less contagious than its high-energy counterpart, hostile irritability,[53] which makes sense when you think of the way in which we pay attention to the moods of those around us. If we circle back to charisma, for instance, chances are we all know someone who is the life and soul of the party, whose very presence lights up any room they enter. Here, the research confirms what we intuitively know – that people who are more expressive and forceful in their emotions are also more likely to attract attention, thus gaining greater exposure and a wider platform from which to transmit their emotions to others.[54]

What's curious is that this effect can be observed even when no one is speaking at all, as illustrated by an unusual study in which researchers asked trios of participants to sit and quietly face each other in a room for two minutes.[55] Intentionally designing the triads to include one highly expressive person and two who were inexpressive, the scientists invited each individual to report their mood before and after the experience. As you might predict, results revealed that while the inexpressive participants were more likely to have had their feelings influenced by the expressive person, the reverse was much less likely to occur. By demonstrating the effects of emotional contagion in such a brief, static setting, this experiment serves as a testament to our power to influence others, even in the absence of a single word. So what does that mean for us, in practical terms?

With so many of our daily interactions now happening online, if we can understand how best to create the conditions for resonant communication, we will be better placed to relate with others on a more satisfying, emotionally meaningful level. Since effective communication hinges in great part upon our ability to transmit and decode emotions with accuracy, when we are choosing people to represent our brand in the public domain it is important to consider their expressive capabilities. Take for instance the personality trait of extraversion (which shares similar qualities to emotions that are positive and highly energetic). When it comes to understanding the type of emotion someone is conveying, people who are high in extraversion are typically better understood.[56] On the flip side, when we encounter low-energy displays of emotions, such as depression, it can be much harder for us to correctly identify the emotion being experienced and expressed by the other person.[57]

This is not to say that we should prioritize certain personality traits, emotions or states over others, however. Rather, if we wish to communicate clearly, we must consider the context and goals we wish to achieve, and be mindful that high-energy displays will typically be more accurately received and understood than their low-energy counterparts. Given that we are more likely to respond to and share strong emotions, and that heightened energy can actually intensify our emotional experiences,[58] when it comes to developing marketing strategies (or indeed any form of communication) it is important to consider

135

whether our goals are best accomplished by drawing upon the charismatic, expressive and extroverted, or the quieter and more reflective. Successful communication is, after all, about so much more than a loud, one-way broadcast.

Key takeaways

- Mirroring words and phrases is a powerful means of establishing rapport and creating a sense of common understanding.
- To communicate persuasively we must cultivate emotional intelligence, which means perceiving emotions accurately, using emotions to think and problem-solve, understanding the nuance of emotions, and managing emotions within ourselves and others.
- Active listening can help us better understand and communicate with others by being attentive to the speaker, asking open questions, using non-judgemental language and reflecting back what is said.
- Empathy means putting ourselves in another's shoes, and comprises three elements: emotional empathy, somatic empathy and cognitive empathy. Central to our growth and wellbeing, it is the ability most difficult for AI to replicate.
- Our ability to empathize with other people is state-dependent, and in the absence of deliberate effort we can fall into the hot–cold empathy gap.
- Emotional contagion is a type of social influence through which we catch other people's emotions. It is transmitted through postures, movements, facial expressions and vocalizations and can occur without our awareness.
- Emotions are characterized by their valence, arousal and dominance levels, which, in an online context, can determine the virality of content.

CHAPTER SEVEN

How to recover when it hits the fan

To overcome difficulties is to experience the full delight of existence. ARTHUR SCHOPENHAUER[1]

Dealing with the inevitable

A couple of years ago, I moved into a beautiful little flat in the heart of a charming barrio in Barcelona. Freshly renovated, with dark herringbone wood floors and tall windows, it was practically perfect – except for one thing. We had moved in during a scorcher of a summer and, with the adjacent flat vacant, during those first few months nothing seemed amiss. But as autumn drew in, bringing new tenants with it (a family of six, not counting the dog), we noticed an enormous spike in our electricity bills. Our flat was the smaller portion of what had previously been a long, single apartment, and it appeared that in the midst of the renovations our electricity meter had been inverted with that of our neighbours. What should have been bills of around €50 per month were coming in at over €500, with the amount being direct-debited from my account without warning. In theory, the fix should have been simple – the energy company responsible for monitoring consumption would send out an engineer to check, report on and replace the meters, issuing a notice to our energy provider so they could correct our records and give us a refund.

In practice, the task turned into an 18-month ordeal, which at the time of writing still remains unresolved. Between endless phone calls to both companies (each refusing to communicate with the other), several failed attempts by engineers to arrange inspections (misdiagnosing the fault when they did) and an automated warning that our electricity would be cut if we did not pay our neighbour's bills, we were absolutely exasperated. By now on first-name terms with the nice-but-utterly-useless representatives of both firms, and despite continued reassurances from each, we were wasting precious time and money attempting to resolve what was essentially their mess. With no physical offices to complain to (how convenient), nor any effective email support, we were forced to spend hours on hold to ear-splitting jingles, just waiting for a representative to pick up, pull their finger out and actually do their job.

While service failures such as these are unavoidable, their negative impact on any given brand is not. Mistakes are bound to happen, and when they do, it is the way in which a company deals with them that will determine how much damage is incurred to both business and customer alike. Of course, in the aftermath of the annus horribilis that was 2020, many companies are now even more afraid to make mistakes, lest they incur the wrath of the masses. Making amends can be a delicate process at the best of times, but doing it online when public sentiment is divided, and identity politics at the fore, requires a very specific kind of resilience. If businesses are to deal with mistakes in a generative way, they must first identify and avoid the many traps that might entangle them – which include the impact technology can have on our behaviours.

On social platforms, for instance, the potential to present oneself anonymously (or at least under a pseudonym) can lead not only to a sense of temporary identity loss, but also to the unleashing of impulses[2] that might otherwise remain in check in the physical world. Known as the **online disinhibition effect**, this tendency to act out or self-disclose more frequently and intensely online than in person[3] can lead to exchanges escalating out of control, and it is something we must guard against if we are to manage our mistakes with integrity. Given the social pressures to respond in real time, it can be tempting to fire off a hasty tweet or lend one's voice and content to the argument, movement or cause of the moment. Yet if we want to act according to our values, we must grant ourselves the time to reflect upon the potential consequences of our actions before engaging in them, especially when the stakes are high.

Mistakes can happen in any part of the business ecosystem – between partner companies, within the organization itself, or between brand representatives and their customers. Whatever the issue, if mishandled, situations that might otherwise find a solution can quickly spiral out of control, damaging relationships, employee performance, organizational culture and customer loyalty in the process. But if we can find a way to side-step reactive response strategies, and instead draw upon scientific insights to guide our actions, we will be much better placed to engage in apology and recovery strategies that yield the results we want.

Revenge and reconciliation

So what can you do when it hits the fan? Typically, the first step is to diffuse the situation before it worsens. Here, we can begin by using the active listening principles outlined in the previous chapter to gain a better understanding of the situation, and identify what practical and emotional support the aggrieved party requires. Of course, if we are aiming to reconcile and reduce the possibility for revenge-seeking behaviours (a furious tweet or post can go viral at a moment's notice), then apologizing and demonstrating some empathy is a good place to start. When service failures happen, studies show that customers who receive empathy and a genuine apology not only tend to experience a greater sense of control (back to autonomy again), but also a renewed sense of self-esteem, both of which can boost the chance for meaningful reconciliation.[4]

But when it comes to apologies, some are more persuasive than others. As I mentioned earlier, those that are explicit and unreserved tend to be the most successful, but there are four additional factors that, when present, can have an additive effect on how appropriate an apology is perceived to be.[5] The first of these factors is **remorse**, which means expressing sadness about what you have done (for instance, 'I'm sorry I didn't call you back at the time we agreed'). The second is about taking **responsibility**, by acknowledging that your actions (or lack thereof) violated a social norm or rule of conduct (such as 'I know what I did was wrong'). Third, is a **promise of forbearance**, a commitment to be true to your word in the future ('I promise this won't happen again'), and the final factor is an **offer of repair**, in which reparation or recompense is offered to make amends for one's actions ('Please let me know how I can make this up to you'). While making an apology is rarely pleasant (mostly because it requires that we admit our own wrongdoing and face the consequences), it needn't be an arduous or painful process.

In fact, one of my favourite ad campaigns of recent years was created precisely as an offering of public apology. It was a cold English day in late February 2018, and the folks at KFC had woken up to realize that due to an unexpected shortage they wouldn't be serving Kentucky Fried Chicken anytime soon. With hundreds of UK stores forced to shut down, and the threat of a PR disaster looming, they needed to take action, and fast. But how? As a brand, KFC was known for not taking itself too seriously, and so it was that within 24 hours the marketing team (which belonged to the agency Mother London) set about plotting a response that would be apologetic but playful, irreverent but sincere.

Taking out a single, full-page ad in only two national UK newspapers (*The Sun* and *Metro*), they posted a photo of an empty KFC bucket set against a red background, its famous logo reordered to read FCK. With an all-caps headline that said 'We're sorry', the text that followed admitted, 'A chicken restaurant without any chicken. It's not ideal.' Acknowledging that it had been 'a hell of a week', KFC promised they were 'making progress, and every day more and more fresh chicken is being delivered to our restaurants'. With a sign-off thanking customers for 'bearing with us', the campaign exploded, amassing more than 1 billion impressions and an avalanche of precious airtime across news channels around the world. Hailed as 'a masterclass in PR crisis management',[6] the stunt even went on to win the coveted Print Gold award at Cannes. By crafting a message of *remorse, responsibility*, and a commitment to progress (if not *forbearance*) in their own inimitable style, not only were they able to strike the right note in terms of apology, they did so without compromising their brand identity.

Although KFC didn't provide any offer of *repair* to affected customers (a discount on your next meal, or a free side of chips, perhaps), their tongue-in-cheek campaign worked because it was accompanied by a competent resolution of the issue (ironing out the operational issues with their delivery provider). The problem is that in the absence of reparations not all apologies will be received with such widespread acclaim. Indeed, if issues escalate sufficiently, customers can end up engaging in coping strategies that look a lot like revenge and retaliation, especially if the service failure strikes a blow to our fundamental needs for competence, autonomy and relatedness (when we don't have the skill, ability or relational power to change the situation).

Even when businesses do manage to patch things up, the effects of critical service mistakes on the customer–brand relationship can be deleterious and long-lasting.[7] Unsurprisingly, the more severe and intense the failure, the bigger the impact on customer satisfaction, commitment and trust, and the more likely that person will engage in negative word-of-mouth.[8] Given that it is generally more costly for companies to acquire new customers than retain existing ones, if we are to mitigate these risks and reduce the likelihood of retaliation we must understand the dynamics from which such behaviours arise. First demonstrated by behavioural scientists Kahneman and Tversky back in 1979, their observation that 'losses loom larger than gains'[9] not only revealed that we typically prefer avoiding losses to acquiring gains – a phenomenon known as **loss aversion** – it also paved the way for further studies demonstrating that the perception of loss can be twice as powerful, psychologically speaking, than that of the equivalent gains (which is why losing £100 feels so much more acute than gaining £100).[10]

In a service setting, our tendency to give more weight to the losses of service failure, than the gains of reparation,[11] means that businesses must be particularly mindful of how they proceed if they wish to retain the loyalty and positive regard of the customer. Given that the performance of a business hinges in large part on how its employees handle such failures and recoveries, it is worth noting that when handled effectively the resolution of complaints can actually lead to better customer retention and loyalty.[12] Of course, for a recovery to work well, it must be seen by the customer as fair, both in terms of the exchange of value (such as a refund or discount) and the process itself (being treated with respect and courtesy, through a procedure that is fair and prompt).[13] If these elements are missing, consumers can feel that they have been wronged, and respond with one of three coping strategies in order to deal with the stress. To come to terms with the issue, they will either engage in an *active*, problem-focused approach;

they will take a more *expressive* route by venting or seeking out comfort to help manage unpleasant emotions; or they will try to *avoid* or *deny* the situation, dismissing the problem in a more passive way.[14]

Where reconciliation is not possible, customers may resort to retaliating against the firm, causing inconvenience in a bid to dole out punishment for the suffering it has caused.[15] With social media only a swipe away, such attempts to 'get even' can often happen very publicly, with exasperated customers taking to Twitter (or whatever their preferred platform) to give the offending party a good dressing-down. While this kind of approach can cause massive headaches for the organization in question, it can usually be avoided by engaging in social listening (for which many tools exist), and the provision of proactive, timely support to customers where failures arise. While most escalations can usually be avoided or nipped in the bud, occasionally service breakdowns can result in more of a cloak-and-dagger response, which can be disastrous to the firm. In these instances, rather than complain directly to the company, a customer may seek out more subversive routes to retaliation, from warning off friends and family, to creating a loss for the company involved, and, in the extreme, resorting to acts of theft and vandalism.[16]

Given that revenge and retaliation are typically paths of greatest effort and therefore last resort, most of us prefer reconciliation where this is possible. Here again, empathy plays a vital role. When expressed by employees during customer complaints, empathy is not only linked with customer gratitude, it is also connected with increased loyalty,[17] and through conveying an effort to understand the customer can improve the chances of reaching a more satisfying resolution. So how can we build upon these dynamics to find more successful paths to reconciliation when things go wrong?

Most of us prefer reconciliation where this is possible.

The hidden power of compassion

As you will know by now, our ability to build resilient relationships (and by extension, organizations) hinges in no small part on our capacity for skilful communication. Nowhere is this more important than when dealing with rupture, and when confronting 'socio-emotionally demanding situations' (the kind that involve relational conflict and emotional discomfort) there is one approach, NVC, that is known to be particularly effective, as we shall see momentarily.[18] Given that stressed employees are more likely to suffer from burnout, absenteeism, mental health issues and churn,[19] finding a robust, practical way to support one's staff not only makes sense from the perspective of performance and employee wellbeing, but also for the resilience of the business ecosystem as a whole.

Whether dealing with emotionally difficult interactions at home or at work, if we are ill-equipped to cope it can result in what is called **empathic distress**. Defined as the inability to tolerate the perceived suffering of another, empathic distress can arise in all kinds of contexts, resulting in the individual shutting down. If we are unable to regulate our own emotions well enough, or we have a lessened sense of distinction between self and other (between yourself and the person who is suffering),[20] the resulting feelings of tension and discomfort we experience can lead us to withdraw in an attempt to protect ourselves from the unpleasant emotions.[21] Unlike empathic concern (feeling compassion and sympathy for the other person), empathic distress is a self-focused experience, which when experienced over prolonged periods can foster a lack of compassion towards those around us. In some instances it can also lead to depression, anxiety and other mental and physical ailments, outcomes that not only result in losses for the individual, but also for the wider group as a whole. While conflict and workplace stress are unavoidable, there are some tried and tested methods that have been found to help reduce empathetic distress.

Well-loved for its myriad benefits, the popular practice of meditation (of various kinds) is known to improve emotion regulation,[22] enhance the quality of relationships and boost psychological wellbeing more broadly.[23] In terms of our context, it can also help people cope better with the suffering of others. In a study exploring the effects of meditation across five different contemplative traditions, where the practitioner's goal was to benefit others, meditation was linked not only to lower levels of empathic distress, depression and neuroticism, but also to higher levels of resilience, altruism and cognitive empathy.[24] Although it is tricky to generalize, evidence does suggest that mindfulness practices can support us in becoming more compassionate and better able to process our emotions over time.

But there is another technique we can also use to reduce empathic distress, one that works by enhancing our emotional and interpersonal skills. Known as **nonviolent communication** (NVC), this framework was initially developed by Marshall Rosenberg in the 1960s through his work with the US civil rights movement.[25] Based on the premise that we all share the capacity for empathy and compassion, Rosenberg proposed that we only fall back on harmful or violent behaviours when we are unable to find more appropriate or effective ways of meeting our needs. Rather than resort to retribution and domination (through the use of coercion, guilt, blame, humiliation, shame and threats), the NVC approach aims to help clarify communication so that all parties can attain what really matters to them. By enabling change within the individual, between people and within wider social systems and groups, the goal is to foster more open, restorative and trusting relationships based on mutual respect, within which one's needs can more easily be fulfilled.

Also referred to as compassionate communication, this technique is based upon four key philosophical assumptions, each of which connects with how we relate to others. The first assumption is that humans share the same universal needs (such as feeling loved and accepted), which, when met, result in satisfying states of being (feeling joyful, content and at peace). The second is that every action we take is an attempt to meet these needs. The third assumption is that our feelings reflect whether or not these needs are being met (when they are not, emotions such as anger, frustration and fear can show up). The fourth and final assumption is that we get our needs met through interdependent relationships with other people.

Now, in order to meet our needs in a more compassionate and productive way, the NVC approach suggests that we focus our attention on the following four elements. The first is *observation*, which means paying attention to the facts of the situation, without expressing subjective evaluations. By separating personal value judgements from what we observe, not only do we reduce the likelihood of triggering the other person's defences, we also create the conditions within which a more open exchange and greater understanding becomes possible. For instance, rather than saying, 'You rarely pay attention when I'm speaking', you could instead say, 'At the meeting this afternoon, I noticed that you were looking at your phone.'

The next step is to take responsibility for our *feelings*, by stating the sensations and emotions we are experiencing in relation to what we are observing, without adding in thoughts and narratives. While this may sound simple, it can require that we relinquish our assumptions about how emotions work. Where we might normally assume that our emotional states arise as a direct result of the words and actions of others, NVC suggests that people's behaviours are merely the stimulus for our feelings, rather than the cause. When viewed through this framework, the feelings we experience emerge as a result of how we choose to respond to the stimuli, meaning that we actually have a greater freedom in terms of how we relate.[26] For instance, if someone were to criticize you and say 'You're so stubborn', you could respond in one of several ways. You might react automatically, either by taking it personally, 'I really am stubborn', or fighting back, 'I'm not the stubborn one, you are!' Or you might take a moment and consciously name your own needs and feelings, 'When I hear you say that I'm stubborn, I feel saddened because I need some recognition of the effort I make to accommodate your requirements.' Rather than react impulsively, by explicitly connecting your feelings with your needs, this creates a space in which it is easier for the other person to respond with greater compassion. You could even take it one step further and include the other person's needs and feelings, by saying something like, 'Are you feeling (emotion X) because you require (need Y)?'[27] In this instance, by asking directly about the other person's under-lying needs, you invite them to share what they really hope to obtain from the interaction.

The third stage of NVC is to turn our attention inwards so as to identify the underlying *need*s that are giving rise to our feel-ings (or to guess what need may be causing the feeling in the other person). Here, the goal is to state one's need, without moral judgement, so as to clearly communicate what is happen-ing in that moment. For instance, 'I'm feeling uncomfortable (emotion) because I'm needing to be alone right now (need). Can we meet tomorrow instead?'

The fourth aspect of NVC is about making specific *requests* for action that can help us meet the need we just articulated. Rather than making hints and inferences, or stating what we don't want, a real request should be clear and positive, allowing for the other person to freely acquiesce, to say no, or offer an alternative (otherwise we are back in the territory of demands and domination). The central tenet here is that whatever our feelings may be, it is our own responsibility to get our needs met, and the responsibility of others to take care of theirs. For exam-ple, if you are with a friend or colleague at a busy social event, and you are concerned they have fallen silent, you might say, 'I notice that you haven't said anything in the last 15 minutes (observation). Are you feeling anxious (emotion)?' If they answer yes, you could share your own state and offer a course of action: 'I'm also feeling anxious, why don't we leave this group and head to the bar?' Or perhaps you might say, 'I'm really enjoying the conversation right now. How about we meet in half an hour when I've finished here?'

While the basics of NVC can be followed by practising the steps above, for the process to work well we must also possess a certain level of self-awareness so that we may accurately identify and name our own emotional states and underlying needs, as well as those of other people. Given that this kind of emotional literacy is fundamental to all manner of things, from emotional regulation and problem-solving to the quality of our relationships and social interactions,[28] our ability to develop a keen and subtle understanding of our internal landscape, both within and beyond the workplace, cannot be overstated.

Whether you are looking to communicate more effectively with your customers, colleagues, family or friends, not only will these skills support you when face-to-face, they can also be invaluable during virtual exchanges. When it comes to online communication, for instance, issues that might otherwise hinder relationship development (such as unexpected silences, and the limited sensory environment afforded by our screens) can actually be diminished by employing NVC, through the simple act of focusing on needs and feelings.[29] While our current technology cannot yet compensate for the loss of the many non-verbal cues that imbue our physical interactions with nuance and meaning, with some conscious attention we can make the most of the technology available to us to ensure that we are communicating with the care and consideration we each deserve.

A question of identity

As much as empathy and compassionate communication are important, there are times when it may serve a brand to strike out and take a stand at the risk of estranging others. While most brands will typically try to play it safe, there are those that intentionally court disruption by engaging in acts and campaigns deliberately designed to provoke debate. Intentionally or not, when a party chooses to mark a very public line in the sand between one value and another, it's likely to attract praise and ire in equal measure. This is exactly what happened when, back in 2018, Nike made the infamous decision to feature the former NFL quarterback Colin Kaepernick as one of the faces of their 30th anniversary campaign. Widely recognized for starting the *Bend the Knee* protests in the NFL in 2016, Kaepernick's decision to kneel during the American National Anthem to demonstrate against police brutality and racial injustice[30] was heralded by many as a powerful display of hope and solidarity, but denounced by others, and perhaps most famously by Trump, as 'a terrible message… that shouldn't be sent'.[31]

The backlash was swift and severe. Social channels were flooded by furious fans posting videos and images of burnt Nike apparel under the hashtag #justburnit, and it wasn't long before celebrities started weighing in on both sides. As the hashtag #NikeBoycott trended on Twitter, the resulting fallout saw Nike's stock price tumble by 3.2 per cent by the close of day,[32] a shock that left many questioning the wisdom of the brand's decision to run the campaign. Despite their track record for provocative marketing, this particular advert even aroused consternation at Nike HQ where, the summer before, it was reported that a debate had raged about whether to cut or keep the controversial quarterback.[33] Having become a free agent after his season of protest (and remaining unsigned, some argued, due to political reasons),[34] Kaepernick's public refusal to denounce his values had already attracted both the adoration and outrage of many.

Crucially, however, it appeared to have captured the hearts and minds of a particular segment of the population – those whose ideals and aspirations saw themselves reflected in the unflinching gesture of this football all-star. As commentators (and the public) speculated about Nike's whys and wherefores, some fascinating trends began quietly to emerge in various polls across the country. Commenting upon a 2018 YouGov poll that surveyed the support and opposition for anthem protests by age, political scientist and Newhouse Professor of Civic Studies at Tufts University, Brian Schaffner, tweeted that younger generations were indeed more likely to support anthem protests than their older counterparts (a fact, he suggests, that may have already been on Nike's radar).[35] Fast-forward a couple of years, and more recent polls by the *Washington Post*[36] and NBC–*Wall Street Journal*[37] suggest that most Americans now consider anthem protests to be appropriate and support the right of athletes to speak out. Circling back to Nike's anniversary campaign, whatever their original reasons, their provocation to 'Believe in something, even if it means sacrificing everything', not only acted as an implicit endorsement of the values Kaepernick knelt for, it also served as a rallying cry, one that both emboldened and estranged vast swathes of consumers.

While the campaign itself was not immune to criticisms of virtue signalling (taking any public position on heated issues is likely to draw this kind of fire), it did highlight the power of explicitly taking a stand and sticking with it, even in the face of great potential cost. So what was it that made this campaign so combustible? If we look beneath the values themselves, to the underlying mechanics that guide our social structures, we will find that there is a particular phenomenon that influences the ways in which we value and interpret the relationships we engage in.

Conceived by social psychologists Henri Tajfel and John Turner back in the 1970s, **social identity theory** was initially designed to explain how our self-concept (our idea of who we are) is influenced by the social groups to which we belong.[38] Whether it is a favourite sports team, religion, occupation or nationality, or one's gender, ethnicity or sexual orientation, our membership of a given group can influence our attitudes, our behaviours, and even our sense of self-esteem. Used to help expound intergroup conflicts and relationships (whether a pub brawl or the clashing of political adversaries), the original theory proposed that we exaggerate both the positive qualities of our own group and the negative traits of the 'out-group', so as to bolster and protect our sense of identity. From the conferring of gender-based privileges (the *in-group favouritism* of sexism), to the limits placed against people of a different skin colour (the *out-group discrimination* of racism), our social identities and the groups to which we belong can exert real and profound forces in our lives.

When we identify strongly enough with a group such that it defines who we are, it has the power to shape the ways in which we perceive both ourselves and those around us. From how we behave within a group (how susceptible we are to social influence), to our perception of others (including our propensity to stereotype), our membership of a given collective can strongly influence how we define and interpret our position within different social contexts. So how does it work exactly? Well, Tajfel and Turner suggested that there are three psychological stages that shape how we classify others as 'us' (part of our in-group) or 'them' (part of the out-group).[39]

The first of these stages is **social categorization**, our tendency to perceive people as belonging to specific groups, so as to understand our social environment with greater ease. By using categories such as our social class, gender identity and occupation, we create a shorthand that can inform us how to behave appropriately in reference to the norms of that group. If, for instance (as has happened on occasion), I am interviewing a guest of similar age for *The Hive Podcast*, and I discover we share a love of *Star Trek*, our 'membership' to this group will colour how we relate to one another. We may communicate in ways specific both to our Trekkiness (live long and prosper) and to our generation (through cultural references) that other groups and non-members might be deem irrelevant or even irritating. In identifying the groups to which we and others belong (an individual can belong to many), we gain vital information as to what behaviour is welcome and acceptable within a given social context.

The second stage is that of **social identification,** which is when we adopt the identity or characteristics of the group(s) to which we belong. If, for instance, you decided to go off and study painting in Florence, and you embraced the new category of 'art student', chances are you would adopt this identity and begin behaving according to the norms of that group (engaging in discussions about painting techniques over beers after school, for example). While identifying with a group undoubtedly brings riches and a shared social language, it can also carry issues, which leads us to the third and final stage.

Known as **social comparison,** this part of the process refers to the assignment of value or merit to a group and its members. Once our sense of identity is tethered to a particular collective, to maintain a positive sense of self-esteem our group must be deemed as performing favourably against potential rivals, which is where things can get messy. When your group gets compared to a competing cohort (one whose political views conflict with your own, for example), not only can the experience be emotionally laden, but any threats to your group can also feel highly personal.[40] In such situations, our desire to maintain positive self-regard can result in prejudice, and the mistaken belief that diminishing out-group members will protect our social standing. What is fascinating is that while we may fight with one another over various tribal alliances, many of the comparisons we engage in are arbitrary, and can change when the context permits. During the COVID-19 pandemic, for instance, key workers including nurses, refuse collectors and store clerks – people who might otherwise be afforded lower social standing than groups such as doctors and lawyers – were considered for the real value of their contributions to society, thus flipping assumed, everyday social comparisons on their head (the conditions under which such inversions might last is a matter for another day).

Whether such comparisons are made by people, the press or by brands, the resulting fallout can be catastrophic for members of the 'losing' group, whose distress may manifest not only in feelings of anger, but of increased vigilance and an appetite for risk-taking. On the flip side, experiencing discrimination from within one's own group can result not only in feelings of threat and shame, but also an increase in cortisol levels, vascular resistance and short-term memory impairments, which if left unchecked can lead to even more serious disorders over the long term.[41] In extreme cases, the 'othering' of people can lead to retaliatory acts of public defiance, such as the burning of Nike merchandise we saw earlier. Of course, given that we can each belong to a whole smorgasbord of groups (you could be a father, a Londoner, a lawyer and a feminist), the degree to which we identify with a group at any given time will depend on the context in which we find ourselves. So in the case of Nike, when fans' social identities as brand afficionados came into conflict with their identity as patriots (the kind whose values would not tolerate acts of protest during a National Anthem), each individual's most salient identity won out, resulting in a great deal of fracture and retribution.

As a brand, when it comes to choosing the right path to tread, it can be difficult to weigh up which social identity to stand behind, and which to let go of. Identities that value inclusion, for instance, may attract other liberal minds but repel the more conservative – but what if you want to appeal to both? While there will always be people at the edges of any group that you may never please, there is a way in which to bring differing identities and perspectives into dialogue. Where most brands stay on the tried and tested path of trotting out predictable, comfortable messages (the kind that maintain the status quo), some have found alternative routes to bridging distinct audiences.

Given our preference for similarity, and the fact that homophilous sources (those similar to ourselves) tend to be perceived as more credible, and therefore more influential in shaping our behaviours,[42] it stands to reason that so many brands would prefer to play it safe. Yet if we are to appeal to the changing needs of growing demographics, we must learn to get comfortable breaking out of the mould and taking informed risks. Those storytellers that can find the universal threads of experience that connect even the most disparate of lives, will not only ignite the curiosity and imagination of their audience, but also a deeper recognition that we all share common hopes and dreams.

This is exactly what the Indian tea company Brooke Bond Red Label accomplished with their video campaign, 'Taste of Togetherness – That Kind of a Woman'.[43] Opening against a black backdrop, the following words appear across the screen, 'We've all grown up believing some people are "bad people".' The text fades to be replaced by the question, 'What happens when we meet one of them?' Cut to a bustling scene of a busy train station in Mumbai, and we see a small crew of people assembling a Brooke Bond 'share a free chai' stall, the kind you might find at a summer festival. Its interior walls are adorned with homely prints and images concealing four hidden cameras, and we watch as an elegant woman in a fuchsia sari enters and sits, the camera cutting to a scene where she recounts her story.

Coming home from work, the 'free tea' sign had caught her eye, and so she had entered the booth. Once seated, another lady had walked in and sat across the table from her. We cut to the young, smiling woman who, in a sari of bright summer colours, explains that the tea company had invited her to come and talk with people. She recalls her uncertainty, asking, 'Who would want to speak to a call girl?' Cut back to the booth, and we see the two women being served tea, as they spark up a conversation and the older woman shares that she is employed by an insurance company nearby. Offering to explain how it works, she asks her young companion where she lives, and when she learns that her home is in the red light district, they fall silent.

The discomfort is palpable, and the young woman fears the insurer may walk away. Indeed, were it not for the presence and ritual of the tea (it is insulting to leave once it has been offered), the conversation may well have ended there. But the young woman asks, 'What kind of insurance should I get?' – to which the reply comes, 'You should get health insurance.' She responds, 'Why? Because of what I do?' Just as it seems that they may have hit an impasse, the young woman asks what kind of insurance she should get for her daughter and, caught off guard, the older lady's face lights up. They swap stories of their daughters and realize that, notwithstanding their apparent differences, they actually hold the hopes and fears of motherhood in common. As the video comes to a close against a stirring soundtrack, the older woman admits that under normal circumstances she would never have talked with a 'call girl' if their paths had crossed. Yet, now that tea has been shared, and stories exchanged, she understands that, 'she's also a working woman like me', a mother who 'worries about her daughter's exams the same way I do'. As the video fades, a final message appears across the screen, 'Sometimes, common ground is just a cup away'.

While this may seem like a clichéd ending for what many would consider a provocative campaign, by choosing to close on this note, Brooke Bond sends a clear and powerful message of their brand's commitment to certain social values. Although such decisions to tackle taboo subjects are not without risk, those brands that are willing to challenge entrenched views, offer alternative perspectives and engage their audiences at a deeper level, not only stand to attract greater attention, they also create the space from which a more compassionate and thoughtful dialogue can emerge.

Key takeaways

- Online, we can fall prey to the online disinhibition effect and self-disclose or act out more intensely than we would in real life.

- Apologies are most effective when we express remorse, take responsibility, promise forbearance and offer repair.
- The worse the service failure, the bigger the impact on customer satisfaction, commitment, trust and negative word of mouth.
- In the absence of resolution, consumers may take active, expressive or avoidant routes to come to terms with the issue.
- When employees show empathy during customer complaints, it can generate customer gratitude, loyalty and better chances of reaching satisfying resolutions.
- Empathic distress is our inability to tolerate the suffering of other people, and can sometimes lead to a lack of compassion towards others.
- Nonviolent communication is a powerful tool for resolving conflict, which relies on observing facts, taking responsibility for our feelings, stating our needs without judgement and making clear requests.
- Social identity theory suggests our self-concept is influenced by our social groups, and that we classify people as 'us' versus 'them' in three stages: social categorization, social identification and social comparison.

CHAPTER EIGHT

Adapting to virtual-first relationships without losing touch

Technology doesn't just do things for us. It does things to us, changing not just what we do but who we are. SHERRY TURKLE[1]

The ghost in the machine

Before the COVID-19 pandemic hit, taking air travel with it, much of my public-facing work involved giving keynotes and workshops to rooms chock-full of people. From the grand stages of San Francisco's Symphony Hall and London's Barbican, to the enclaves of Fortune 500 companies, the success (or failure) of these engagements would hinge largely on my capacity to respond in real time to the needs of the audience as each session unfolded. Whether through the gestural feedback of someone leaning away, or the waves of bobbing heads rippling through an auditorium, being able to observe and adapt to the responses of others was key to delivering a dynamic, engaging performance.

Of course, the moratorium on movement changed all of that. As we hurtled into lockdown, restrictions demanded that businesses transform themselves practically overnight, with entire sectors racing to digitize services and supply chains so as to render their workforces (and offerings) remote. In my own industry, going virtual wasn't a huge leap, and I was lucky to be able to continue working from home. At first, the thought of no longer having to contend with packed flights (and their attendant carbon footprints) was a welcome relief, but as time wore on, I became aware of new setbacks we would all have to face if we were to navigate this brave new world.

For my part, determined to offer a warm, engaging experience despite the conditions, I deployed all the skills in my possession to craft and maintain that delicate balance between professionalism and intimacy, all within the confines of the screen. From stage-setting my backgrounds and selecting the right lighting, to ensuring an emotionally expressive gaze down the barrel of the camera, I was intent upon approximating as 'real' a sense of connection as I could muster, given the limitations. While the response was positive (especially for the simulated eye contact), on a personal level I couldn't help feeling that there was something missing. Beyond the familiar eye-strain and lack of non-verbal feedback, I was also yearning for the presence of the 'other', that vibrant and energizing sense of being in physical proximity to fellow human beings. Despite my best efforts, no matter what tactics I applied I couldn't transcend the boundaries of the screen, couldn't leap the limits of my virtual stage to engage in the way I really wanted to: with my whole being.

I realized that, despite my best efforts, I had become something of a pixelated echo of myself, a proverbial *ghost in the machine*. An elegant phrase attributed to the Oxford philosopher Gilbert Ryle,[2] this idiom refers to the Cartesian idea of the body–mind relationship, a dualist perspective that still persists today. Although a good 70 years have elapsed since its inception, the concept of a mind superior to (and distinct from) the body is a fallacy we appear stubbornly unwilling to relinquish, despite mounting evidence to the contrary. As we become ever more enmeshed with our technology, the notion that we might some-day replace in-person interactions with virtual substitutes seems less far-fetched than it once did, especially as advances in avatars (robots that we can control and 'inhabit' remotely) gathers apace. Yet, for any meaningful, qualitative parity to exist between our in-person and virtual experiences, there must be what cele-brated psychoanalyst and author of *Screen Relations*,[3] Dr Gillian Isaacs Russell, refers to as **functional equivalence** – our physical and virtual experiences would have to function in a largely inter-changeable way. Of course, if you have ever shared virtual beers with friends you will know that it's a far cry from the loud and cheerful experience of gathering at the local pub, and while Gillian tells me that there is, of course, a tremendous positive in having such technologies to hand, it is also true that 'The communication is paler, it's more anaemic than it would be if we were together in person.' But why should this be?

Returning to the body–mind relationship, in recent years a particular field of science exploring this domain has thrown into question many of the binary models espoused by philosophies and religions alike. Unlike its dichotomous predecessors, this new approach, known as **embodied cognition**, suggests that just as our minds influence our bodily actions, so our bodies influence our minds. According to this perspective, everything from our judgement and reasoning, to the mental constructs we create around categories and concepts, are shaped (and even deter-mined) by our physical, bodily interaction with the world.[4] As opposed to the computational view of cognition (which asserts that our minds operate as information processing systems imple-mented by the neural activity in our brains), embodiment proposes that the brain is not the only cognitive resource available to us. Rather, we actually draw from a much richer repertoire of inputs that stems not only from our motor and perceptual systems, but also from our bodily interactions with the physical environment.

Various quirky experiments have been conducted to explore this relationship, from inducing certain physical sensations with a sound of a dentist's drill[5] (just thinking of it makes me wince), to increasing the speed with which people process pleasant sentences, by having them hold a pencil between their teeth (thus engaging many of the muscles we use to smile).[6] In the past decade alone, neuroscientists have made great strides in mapping out the connections between the physical body, specific structures in the brain and various facets of the mind – from our sense of emotion and self-awareness, to our very consciousness and will.[7] In fact, this area of research has become so hot that some scientists in the field of robotics suggest we will only be able to create true artificial intelligence if (and when) it is designed to inhabit a sensing, moving body through which to interact with its environment (more on this in Chapter 9).[8]

Given that so much of how we make sense of the world is dependent on our embeddedness within it, it makes sense that the wholesale replacement of in-person interactions with virtual ones would be unsatisfying at best, and at worst, leave us feeling dazed, exhausted and out of touch. When I ask Gillian her thoughts on this, she points towards the work of renowned neurologist Antonio Damasio, who famously suggested that as beings, we are embodied, not simply 'embrained'.[9] In Gillian's words, 'We perceive and communicate through our whole body, not just through our words, our verbal, explicit communication, and not just through what goes on in our mind.' Perhaps it is for this reason why, after the initial novelty of video conferencing wore off, lockdown headlines were awash with a new breed of ailment to add to the pandemic list – 'zoom fatigue' – a condition familiar to anyone who has spent more than a few woeful afternoons in back-to-back calls.

Ascribed by researchers at Stanford University to the increased stress of the 'non-verbal overload' caused by interminable video calls, it appears that the exhaustion we feel is in part due to the 'increased self-evaluation from staring at a video of oneself' and 'excessive amounts of close-up eye gaze', as well as our reduced mobility and the increased cognitive load (mental effort) required to send and receive non-verbal signals.[10] The effects are so pronounced, that a 'Zoom Exhaustion and Fatigue Scale' has even been developed to help organizations measure just how exhausted their people are, and how we might change the technologies we use so as to reduce stressors going forwards.[11] As data starts to roll in on what has, in effect, amounted to a massive unofficial social experiment, it looks as though science is starting to confirm what we already surmised: that sustained, technologically mediated communication takes a toll, both on body and mind.

The exact nature of this toll and why it arises is a question that has attracted many explanations, chief among them the loss of the rich, diverse environments and interactions that bring texture to our everyday lives. Where previously we might have walked to work, met in coffee shops or ambled to the gym, as pandemic restrictions encroached, we were suddenly forced to meet all of these needs within the space of four walls. All at once, the distinct locations in which we would work, rest and play folded in upon themselves, until they could all collapse origami-like within the tiny, two-dimensional surface of our screens, creating a state that Amy C Edmondson describes to me as a '"blursday" world'. She explains that when we are 'sitting in the same chair at the same laptop in the same home, taking every meeting from that same spot, it is harder, I think, to retain in memory the nuances of the experiences that we are having'. When I ask her how we might compensate for this impoverished form of relating, Amy suggests that in the absence of 'spontaneous human interactions', and 'those little bits of time when you go to a meeting and you're in the room and people are arriving at slightly different times and you're just chatting – connecting and saying, "How was your weekend?"', it is incumbent upon us 'to then work even harder at inviting, at clarifying, at connecting'.

Of course, amidst the tremendous challenges of life under lockdown, it was precisely the social (and economic) lifeline afforded by technology that enabled many of us to continue our lives in ways previous generations could only have dreamt of. In the absence of being able to meet physically, it served as a conduit to both work colleagues and loved ones alike, by creating a sense of **telepresence** (from the Greek root 'tele-', meaning 'at a distance'), which Dr Gillian Isaacs Russell describes as 'an illusion that we're present with each other... that what is going on between us is not mediated'. Although enchanting while it holds, this illusion requires the 'temporally appropriate feedback' of nods, utterances and responses exchanged in real time in order to be maintained. In a virtual world, where such feedback is dependent upon both the latency of the platform and the fluidity of the overall experience, a sense of telepresence can be fragile and fleeting. As Gillian points out, 'There are things that interfere always when you are using technology. This means that the illusion that we are together, that we have a sense of presence, gets shattered, it falls away and needs to be re-established as we go along.'

Of course, given what we know about embodied cognition, it should come as no surprise that in the absence of rich sensory cues we seek compensation for the losses incurred. From paying greater attention to the words we utter, to deciphering the minute expressions of faces suspended on our screens, we are left frantically gathering any scrap of information that might bring colour and dimension to an otherwise flattened experience. When we relate in this way, the greatest casualties are often the gestures and non-verbal cues we rely on to communicate with one another and establish rapport. Without the possibility of reading (and when in flow, unconsciously mimicking) the facial and gestural expressions of others, our capacity to internalize and mirror their emotional state[12] becomes curtailed, dampening empathic connection and making it harder to read the cadence of the conversation.

So what can we do in order to revivify what can swiftly become a rather pallid experience? I reach out to Dr Aaron Balick, a psychotherapist, author and director of the international psychology hub Stillpoint International, to find out. He tells me that we must first be able to wholeheartedly acknowledge the difference between virtual and real-life exchanges, and that we may need to 'incorporate ways of being that may differ entirely from the way that we naturally interact in face-to-face encounters. So it might mean taking the time to purposefully look inwards, to make inquiries about your body sensations, to actively be more aware. It might mean asking people to engage in some kind of ritual before and after a meeting so they have the space to check in with themselves first.'

Let's get physical

The trouble is, of course, that while these strategies are indeed useful, they cannot replace the true sense of **presence** we experience when physically interacting with someone in a shared space. Defined as a core neuropsychological phenomenon that arises from our ability to interact with (and therefore locate ourselves in) the external world, this kind of presence is something that virtual environments can only vaguely emulate, which is why it can feel so tiring and unsatisfying to spend time there.[13] As Dr Gillian Isaacs Russell tells me, real presence not only influences how we behave, but also what we attend to and how we process and remember our experiences. She explains that our experience of being present 'stems from an organism's capacity... to locate itself in an external world according to the action that you can do in it to impact it. And people experience presence if they are able to act out in an external world and successfully transform their intentions into actions. So it's not the same thing as emotional engagement; presence isn't the same thing as absorption or the degree of technological immersion.

For humans, these actions specifically include the person's capacity or even potential capacity to interact with another person in a shared external environment.' It is the potential to reach out and hold someone's hand, to share some food, to hug goodbye.

What's interesting is that this loss of presence also appears to impact the quality of our experience and memories. Drawing upon research from counselling and psychotherapy, Dr Aaron Balick explains, 'sessions that go online are more forgettable than ones that happen in real life. One of the reasons we think that is the case is because you're not engaging as much of your brain... You are not going there and coming home from it. You are not using your five senses, like the smell and feel of the room you might be in... You are just sitting on your bum in the same place you were sitting on your bum watching Netflix or doing your taxes.' But why should this experience be less vivid than any other?

When three neuroscientists (O'Keefe, an American, and the Mosers, a Norwegian husband-and-wife team) set out to better understand how we generate mental maps of our environment, none of them could have predicted where their enquiries might lead. Following several decades of independent, attentive research investigating place cells and grid cells – a system of nerves that would come to be known as the 'inner GPS' of the brain – in 2014 the trio were awarded the Nobel Prize in Physiology or Medicine. Their discovery? That the neural system that determines our perception and recall of where we are in the environment also connects to the events we have experienced there. In short, their work revealed the deep relationship that exists between our ability to physically travel through space, and our capacity to mentally travel through memory. A potential game changer for how we understand issues of spatial memory loss in conditions such as Alzheimer's, their breakthrough was heralded a 'paradigm shift' in understanding how cells work together to perform certain functions, a discovery that would open 'new avenues' to understanding how our planning, thinking and memory processes might work.[14]

How is this relevant to us, you might ask? Well, because the brain appears to respond in a dramatically different way depending on whether we are engaged in a physical setting or a virtual one. It is precisely this peculiarity that a team of neurophysicists at UCLA hoped to investigate when they placed a selection of rats in tiny harnesses to observe how they would respond when immersed in a virtual environment. The results were quite shocking – when manoeuvring through a virtual room, the pattern of activity in the hippocampus (an area associated with spatial learning) was completely different than when the rats moved through an identical physical room. Despite exhibiting similar behaviours in both, when in the virtual space, over half of the rats' hippocampal neurons shut down and the remaining fired randomly, essentially causing the internal mental map of the environment to disappear.[15] While both spaces may have elicited a similar conscious experience in the rats, at a neural level, the change in setting was yielding markedly distinct responses. Given that the hippocampus is vital to all manner of creatures in creating mental maps of our surroundings, the fact that it may operate in an entirely different way when in a virtual versus physical environment could have important implications, the likes of which we are yet to discover.

On a day-to-day level, this may be one of the reasons why, after yet another video meeting sat at the same desk, we can feel dazed or forgetful, as though the information shared didn't really sink in. It is for this reason that I will often compensate by taking hand-written notes (to improve comprehension and recall),[16] or opt for an audio call so I can go out and walk (known to increase creative ideation, both in real time and for a short while after).[17] It's also why I will sometimes stand to allow some movement, so my hands and body can **gesture** more freely as I think. What's interesting is that much of the gesture-based research bears out the benefits I've mentioned. From helping young children to learn and retain new knowledge, to conveying concepts or processes more clearly, gesturing serves many functions, and plays a vital role in embodiment-based learning even as we move through adulthood.[18] Given that gestures also help us to read and express emotions, it is a form of communication that business leaders (especially those wishing to engage with an increasingly perceptive, demanding workforce) cannot afford to overlook.

Equally vital to the transmission of emotion is **eye gaze**. Held too long or not long enough, whether it is uncomfortably intense or alluringly intermittent, the nature of our looking can reveal not only how we feel in a given moment, but also our intentions towards other people. The problem is that online, real, mutual eye gaze is not possible, which is one of the reasons why video chats actually inhibit trust.[19] Even when we try to emulate it (with one person staring directly into the camera, as I described earlier), the gaze is one-sided at best, and gives rise to another problem: the active party must forfeit their chance to observe and respond to the facial responses of the other(s). Given that avoiding eye contact even for a short while can leave us feeling ostracized and our self-esteem lowered (which can increase our desire to act out aggressively),[20] it is no wonder that we try to compensate when interacting remotely.

The problem is that in our well-meaning attempt to fake it, we run the risk of unleashing a whole new set of problems, including those demonstrated in a fascinating experiment designed by a team of psychologists at University College London. Upon collecting personality data from more than 400 volunteers, the researchers ran video clips in which actors appeared to be gazing directly at the viewer for differing lengths of time. When asked to report their level of comfort in response, participants indicated that they preferred eye contact of an average duration of 3.2 seconds (or more, if the actor seemed trustworthy). As one of the authors of the study, Alan Johnston, explained, since gaze communicates that 'you are an object of interest', and that 'interest is linked to intention', if someone is staring at you for a while (even through a screen) it doesn't take long for the brain to assume that they may have certain intentions towards you – whether good or bad.[21]

Now, managing eye gaze may be tricky enough when dealing with a single conversation partner, but add a few extra to the mix in gallery view, and other issues pop up, whack-a-mole style. As the number of floating heads increases, so our central vision comes under more strain, as it tries to parse information from a mosaic of faces too small and too numerous to meaningfully decode. Of course, a simple hack is to switch views so we are only having to deal with the speaker. Yet because so many functions are available, both within the platform (with chat, Q&A, and so on) and beyond (the countless tabs and apps we may be using), whatever interventions we make we are still at risk of falling prey to **continuous partial attention.** Coined by former Apple and Microsoft executive Linda Stone, this phrase describes our tendency to scan for activities and opportunities in a way that creates not only an 'artificial sense of constant crisis' and high alert, but also feelings of exhaustion, overwhelm, and lack of fulfilment.[22] Over time, this continuous division of attention and anticipation of connection (think social media) can result in hyper-stimulation and stress, states that ironically render us inaccessible to the present moment.

This is not to minimize the extraordinary benefits that remote work has to offer. But with virtual meetings now an established feature in the businesses firmament, it would be careless to ignore the potential complications it can bring. From problems with setting clear boundaries and safeguarding high-quality attention, to issues of collaboration arising from lack of in-person contact, it is no wonder that some of the world's largest companies have chosen to respond by 'doubling down on office space'.[23] Yet whatever our relationship to the office or shared workspace going forward, it is clear that for some scenarios at least, we would be better served relating in physical presence with one another, rather than through the cold veil of a screen. When it comes to video calls for example, research from the field of criminology suggests that we actually find it harder to discern whether others are lying when via a screen, than when judgements are made from transcripts and audio alone.[24]

In the absence of rich interpersonal cues, then, it can be hard to assess and weigh the fullness of communication that is so readily available to us in ordinary settings – a fact that is especially true when it comes to judging the trustworthiness of unfamiliar others, where merely being exposed to someone's non-verbal cues (such as leaning away or nodding one's head) can enhance how accurately we predict their economic behaviours[25] (and many more besides). Given that high-touch multi-sensory environments provide a much richer space for the flourishing of culture, collaboration and creative ideation, an organization that can meet its people's needs both for flexibility and personal contact is one that will have the upper hand when it comes to building resilience in the long term.

Discomfort, danger and psychological safety

Of the debates most alive in this moment, one of the most fascinating is that which explores our ideas around discomfort and safety. From the shadow-banning of social media users (when a person and/or their content is blocked from appearing within a community, without their awareness), to the no-platforming of controversial figures (when they are denied access to venues in which to communicate their opinions), a war of ideas is being waged at the heart of modern culture as to what speech should be deemed acceptable, and when (or if) it should be considered to have gone too far. Whatever our opinions on the matter, when it comes to the resilience of a business, and especially where innovation is concerned, it is the ability to provide **psychological safety** that can make the difference between a truly visionary organization and a mediocre one. So what exactly is psychological safety?

To understand this, let us first outline what it is not. In an era punctuated by conversations around wellbeing and mental health, it could be easy to assume that psychological safety equates blanket protection from discomfort of any kind, a feat I would wager impossible even in the most bubble-wrapped of existences. In the current context, problems arise when, as Jonathan Haidt and Greg Lukianoff describe in their book *The Coddling of the American Mind*, our idea of safety undergoes 'concept creep', extending beyond definitions of physical harm to also encompass protection from emotional discomfort (a process that all too often results in the conflation of both).[26]

It is these divergent concepts around safety and the unintended consequences they may lead to that CNN's Van Jones illustrated eloquently when, in 2017, he addressed the students of Chicago University about two competing ideas of safe spaces.[27] The first idea, that of being physically safe, protected from sexual or physical abuse and harassment, he was all for (understandably so). But the second idea, one that stipulated the 'need to be safe ideologically', he opined as a 'horrible view'. Why, you might ask? The answer comes in the entreaty he made to his audience. Rather than want for their ideological safety, he wished for these students to be strong, to be encouraged to cultivate that robust, resilient quality that comes from encounters with cognitive friction, from having one's cherished ideas and ideals challenged by those around us.

If you have ever experimented with mindfulness practices, you will likely have a sense of the discipline and courage it takes to sit with discomfort, especially in the face of distractions. Yet it is precisely this skill that, when developed over time, can enable us to unhook from our emotional rollercoasters long enough to observe and judge our inner landscape and outer context with greater clarity. It is also this ability that can empower individuals within supportive teams to challenge and push one another, so that they can take the kinds of risks that really move the needle. Since it is at our very edges that we tend to encounter the greatest leaps in creativity, perhaps it is not *safety from discomfort* we should be seeking, but rather the *safety to take risks*, the likes of which can result in breakthroughs of all kinds.

It is this sense of psychological safety that Amy C Edmondson brought to prominence in her influential article in 1999,[28] and more widely through her book, *The Fearless Organization*.[29] It is the experience of feeling secure enough to communicate and express ourselves without the fear of incurring negative consequences to our status, self-image or professional career. From facilitating learning and organizational change, to boosting employee engagement, psychological safety has all manner of benefits, especially when it comes to successfully navigating uncertain, interdependent and rapidly evolving environments. Not only can it boost team innovation and the amount we learn from our mistakes, it can also increase the likelihood of successful process innovation (by which I mean new, deliberate organizational attempts to change service and product processes).

Yet creating contexts of psychological safety can raise its own challenges. When I ask Amy about what goals we might set in order for organizations to move in this direction, she replies, 'It takes deliberate effort to create a climate of candour... because the natural instinct for human beings is to hold back, to wait and see, to read the tea leaves and figure out what will make me look good in the eyes of my peers or my managers. In subtle ways, people are always aware of what might or might not be "welcome around here". We're so good at sizing situations up that we do it without thinking; we do it spontaneously.' Since this instinct for self-preservation is such a powerful one, it also requires more than just a mission statement and good intentions to displace. Rather, if we are to change the pattern, Amy suggests one must 'override natural instincts, and if you want to override natural instincts, it has to be done with effort and deliberate intent... it starts with being clear and explicit about why. If people don't appreciate why their voice might be welcomed by others, then the easiest thing to do, the safest thing to do, is to hold back. But if they are getting message after message after message that says, "We need you, we're dependent on you. You might see something that I miss. Your ideas have been great in the past. Your perspective on what customers want is unique", then they will feel able to speak up. Hearing those kinds of messages all the time helps us take them seriously.'

When it comes to team settings, it is about holding the shared belief that no one will be blamed, humiliated or punished for speaking up, and committing to generosity of spirit when interpreting other's intentions, so that feedback is received as helpful rather than critical. Ultimately, it requires that we intentionally create an environment that supports learning and growth, in which team members feel respected, accepted and safe enough to take risks – especially when the outcome to those risks is uncertain.[30] In Amy's words, it is about putting in the work so as to make 'our differences discussable', a cultivatable skill that 'starts with curiosity, with a reminder that we should be interested in each other'. Whether in person or online, if we wish to foster an 'orientation towards collaboration' we must first be able to 'approach each other across a boundary – whether that boundary involves nations, or functions, or expertise – with curiosity, a genuine sense that the person on the other side of this boundary is a treasure, is a person who brings something I don't have'.

While psychological safety is vital in motivating us to speak up and improve our team within the physical workplace,[31] it is of particular importance when interacting with one another remotely, especially since virtual teams tend to report higher levels of conflict.[32] Beyond the everyday issues inherent in collaboration, when it comes to virtual teamwork the sense of safety that is so crucial for effective knowledge-sharing can be undermined by self-consciousness (think the little self-view video in the corner of the screen), which in turn limits the degree to which we will contribute to the conversation.[33] In fearing that we might be judged harshly, our desire to protect our self-esteem, reputation or wellbeing (and even opportunities for promotion) can result in silence, an outcome that robs us of personal growth, and the organization of feedback that could prove essential to its success.

One way to reduce these problems is to host a kick-off meeting in which team members are encouraged to get to know one another informally before starting their work.[34] Not only can these virtual off-task gatherings help improve levels of cooperation and trust,[35] but unplanned interactions can even help smooth out and prevent conflicts before they arise.[36] Another route to minimizing conflict in virtual teams is to reduce the structure of the task itself. While this may sound counterintuitive, by allowing the task to be less regimented, inflexible and tightly defined, we create space for team members to spend more time relating with one another and forming bonds that, in the longer term, can lead to better outcomes all round.[37] Whatever approach you take, if you are working with dispersed teams it is this opportunity for spontaneous interaction that is most often lacking, and it's also one of the most important aspects of a relationship we must consciously build back in.

Of course, if we wish to nurture psychological safety, we must also turn our attention to building trust. Although conceptually related, psychological safety refers to our beliefs about existing group norms, whereas trust is the foundational structure that exists in a relationship between two individuals, and relates to the expectations we hold about another person's motives and future behaviours. If we believe that the other person will behave towards us in a predictable and benevolent way, our willingness to be vulnerable with them (to trust them) will tend to increase. This is why, when working with established teams, psychological safety can be augmented by supporting strong relationships between individual members (cultivating interpersonal trust), and encouraging mutual respect, shared knowledge and goals so that they may better engage in and learn from failures.[38]

For self-managed teams that are dealing with stable tasks, having a clear, formalized team structure (with a defined hierarchy and levels of specialization) can help to reduce conflict and promote information sharing, thus encouraging learning and a more continuous pace of improvement.[39] Yet whatever your team's structure or purpose, if you want its members to develop their own social and psychological resources, then creating the conditions in which trust, curiosity, inspiration and confidence can flourish is essential. Of course, the more heavily a team relies on virtual communications to function, the more important team trust becomes to their performance,[40] which can be problematic when you consider that trust generally takes longer to build online than when face to face.[41] So what are some of the techniques we can employ to optimize virtual communication, develop trust and support the performance and wellbeing of our teams?

Making the most of it

A good place to start is to understand the traps and limitations of virtual communications so that we can avoid some of the most pernicious pitfalls. Despite the ubiquity of email, as a tool for self-expression it happens to be particularly mendacious. Perhaps because of its simplicity and convenience, when it comes to text-based communication we tend to overestimate our level of persuasiveness while at the same time underestimating the power of face-to-face interactions. While we may feel equally confident making requests through either means, a recent study found that those who made face-to-face interactions were 34 times more effective than requests solicited via email, meaning that to obtain the same results you would achieve by asking six people in person, you would have to blast out a whopping 200 emails.[42] In a follow-up study, the same researchers pinpointed a potential reason for this, namely that the non-verbal cues present in face-to-face exchanges can serve to add legitimacy to our requests (a dynamic to which the participants were completely oblivious).[43]

However advanced our technology may be, it seems that we consistently overlook and undervalue the richness of in-person interaction, the nuances of which we have elegantly evolved to respond to. In the absence of contextual cues and non-verbal feedback, text is easily misinterpreted and its tone of voice lost, resulting in recipients misinterpreting work emails as more neutral or emotionally negative than intended by the sender.[44] When employed as the primary channel for communication, this can lead us to perceive our relationships with co-workers as impersonal and even cold, a trend that does not bode well for reducing conflict.[45] Given that even the erroneous spelling error or misuse of capitals can set people off,[46] if it's persuasiveness you're after, you're more likely to get the results you want by meeting in person, or at least opting for the marginally richer medium of audio or video calls.

We consistently overlook and undervalue the richness of in-person interaction, the nuances of which we have elegantly evolved to respond to.

It's partly for these reasons that many businesses will intentionally create periodic opportunities to gather in person, whether at conferences, meetings or events, but in the absence of longer-term operational changes, the same old issues will tend to reappear when everyone reverts to their inboxes.[47] Instead, a more lasting solution to enhancing communication can be to provide team training exercises specifically designed to cultivate group trust.[48] By giving team members the opportunity to practise working together and receiving constructive feedback for improved interactions, leaders can help foster a greater sense of trust and understanding, which in turn can build team resilience against future challenges. Such training can also provide valuable windows within which to teach employees the interpersonal skills, attitudes and culture the business wishes to promote, with one-to-one coaching around performance and their team's mission lending additional support.[49]

But what about when teams and colleagues are dispersed, and in-person meetings are not possible? Well, if the team in question comprises individuals who are highly specialized in their respective fields (and their expertise doesn't overlap), team trust appears to be relatively unaffected by an increase in virtual communications.[50] But for everyone else, when it comes to video calls, there are several interventions I have found to be useful. Perhaps the most important of these is explicitly stating the rules of engagement in advance (such as maintaining confidentiality and the permission to speak freely) as a means of laying the groundwork for trust and collaboration, whether in team settings or when working one-to-one. By outlining the parameters beforehand, it allows for questions and concerns to be addressed in a more personal setting, free from peer pressure or stressful time constraints.

With virtual workshops I have conducted, for instance, there have been occasions where the organizers have wanted to record sessions for internal purposes, whether to learn from or improve upon the structure of the event, or to create ongoing resources. In such cases, reaching out to participants to request informed consent a couple of weeks prior has proven invaluable, not only for the respect it communicates to those involved, but for the agency it grants to those wishing to opt out or suggest workarounds. In practical terms, I have found it rare that anyone opt out entirely, and where discussions have arisen they have served to highlight ways in which we could improve the overall experience for everyone, resulting in better outcomes and a more candid environment within which creativity and collaboration can flourish.

Beyond the setting of clear boundaries and expectations, there are also things that leaders can do to create a psychologically safe team. The first is to actively invite and appreciate the contribution of others, both in word and action. This kind of **leader inclusiveness** not only encourages greater collaboration between team members, it can also reduce some of the negative effects of status, such as our tendency to ignore the contributions from those junior to us, or the temptation to withhold important information from our superiors for fear of attracting reprisals.[51] As well as actively soliciting and appreciating the contributions of others, leaders can also increase the performance of their teams by explicitly welcoming a diversity of thinking, especially if they are working with heterogenous (or divergent) information. In these scenarios, teams that are 'persuaded of the value of diversity' tend to outperform those that value similarity,[52] meaning that the beliefs one instils as a leader (whether pro-similarity or pro-diversity) can have a significant impact on the performance of a team and, by extension, the organization.

Perhaps one of the most notorious case studies exploring how to boost performance was that of Google's Project Aristotle, a piece of research designed to identify the key dynamics of effective teams. Of the factors that were considered important (including dependability, meaning, impact, structure and clarity), psychological safety was the one that came out on top, and by a long shot. Not only were Googlers on teams with high psychological safety less likely to jump ship, they also brought in more revenue, were more likely to 'harness the power of diverse ideas from their teammates', and were rated as effective by executives twice as often as their peers.[53] In their State of DevOps annual report, Google credited a culture of psychological safety as 'predictive of software delivery performance, organizational performance, and productivity',[54] an assertion that has not gone unnoticed by those at the forefront of organizational performance, nor by the hundreds of thousands of people who have gone on to view Amy C Edmondson's TED talk on the subject.

Titled *Building a Psychologically Safe Workplace*,[55] Amy's talk outlines three distinct scenarios in which a nurse, a junior pilot and a newly appointed executive, each afraid to voice their concerns to their superiors or peers, fall prey to workplace silence. Rather than appear incompetent, ignorant, negative or intrusive, each professional chooses to hold their tongue, a decision that leads to dire outcomes, the likes of which you can probably imagine. While the decisions we make at work may not entail life-or-death consequences, nevertheless our attempts to ward off any negative attention can result in withholding questions and ideas, denying mistakes and weaknesses, and generally attempting not to rock the boat. While this kind of strategy can work in terms of impression management (sure, we may not lose face in the moment), Amy argues that it robs us of the precious opportunity to learn, innovate and grow.

In order to combat this problem, she outlines three simple steps we can take to foster psychological safety within our teams. The first is to frame the work as a *learning problem* rather than an execution problem, which means being explicit in naming high levels of uncertainty and interdependence where these arise (as in the three scenarios mentioned earlier, with the nurse, the pilot and the executive). By creating a 'rationale for speaking up', this framing sets the tone for what behaviour is acceptable and even encouraged within the context. The second step is to openly accept your *own fallibility* to your team, by acknowledging, in Amy's words, 'I may miss something, I need to hear from you.' In recognizing that to err is human, you essentially place yourself on an equal footing with the rest of your team, thereby making it safe for any member, regardless of their status, to also speak up. The third and final step Amy offers is to *model curiosity* by asking a lot of questions, thus leading by example and creating a dynamic that invites more questions, contributing to a greater sense of safety for others to speak up.

Of course, this makes sense when operating with others in a shared physical space (whether in the ER, the cockpit or a board meeting), but what about when our work is primarily remote? When I ask Amy about this, she points out that while technology-mediated communication may not be as rich or nuanced as in real life, nonetheless, 'it can be helpful to use some of technology's compensatory features. For instance, you can invite people to express reactions with the emoticons, you can use polls to get a sense of the room's views on an issue, you can ask people to check the yes/no button to get a quick vote on something, to see whether more discussion is needed, for example.' When it comes to these tools, she points out that 'even though they are somewhat artificial or clunky, they are participation forcers' that act as 'scaffolding to help us connect and engage in a different way, because we're not connecting and engaging in the usual way'.

So how can we use these features to better encourage engagement? First, let's look at the lowly poll function. Although a simple tool, when employed as a linear rating scale it can be useful for assessing the extent to which people agree or disagree with the statement you are putting forward, thus yielding qualitatively richer responses. For instance, if you wanted to ascertain the success of your company's inclusion initiatives, you could ask 'On a scale of 1 to 5, please rate the level to which you feel included in this company.' By offering a clear statement and a range against which to respond, you can obtain more accurate results from which to build generative conversations and potential interventions. If it is binary answers you're looking for, then the simple yes/no function will invite more rapid input, as well as provide a quick way of noting and welcoming missing respondents to join in. Of course, by virtue of its anonymity, this function can also provide a compelling way to elicit more honest feedback than when attached to a name or specific individual. Yet while this may help us to identify grievances, it really only circumvents the issue of psychological safety in the long term (no one knows who shared what, so the risk of feeling humiliated remains low). Despite its uses then, to really provide value this approach must be deployed within a context of candour in which constructive feedback is welcomed and embraced.

When it comes to the qualitative, most of us will instinctively turn to the chat function, which although useful in allowing people to contribute in their own time (often all at once), can result in a torrent of text in which gems are overlooked and crucial feedback lost. Quite aside from the additional splintering of attention this can cause, when chat gets overloaded in this way it can lead to frustration and overwhelm, resulting in a percentage of participants disengaging altogether. In such instances, having a dedicated facilitator or team on hand to manage the flow can be helpful, failing which one can simply turn the chat off, so as to turn attention entirely to the conversation at hand. Again, setting instructions or parameters at the outset of how this function will (or should) be used, can help to create clear boundaries and expectations, thus ensuring a more contained, fluent experience overall.

On the occasion that groups are large and the issues complex, the best way to create an environment of psychological safety can be to provide smaller breakout rooms. By enabling people to meet virtually in groups of three or four, the virtual dynamic becomes more natural, with participants free to talk without having to mute and unmute themselves intermittently. Within this more conversational context, each group can be assigned a specific task or issue to discuss and brainstorm, before selecting a spokesperson to share their ideas or solutions with the wider group. Not only does this approach create a space within which quieter voices can be heard, it also allows for a greater breadth of opinions to be raised and shared with the whole. Whether achieved via a straightforward, automated breakout chat, or by using software through which participants can gather at virtual roundtables, this kind of configuration can be a great way of reducing the fear and peer pressure that can arise when engaging in large groups online.

Finally, a word on good old-fashioned video and audio. As we have already explored, the use of video conferencing can have all manner of unintended consequences on our attention and subjective experience, which is why hiding self-view and placing the speaker full-screen are generally good rules of thumb to follow. If you are working with a small group (for me, three people is the maximum number for comfort), then switching to audio only can allow for greater attention to be paid to the speaker, and to the content and tone of their speech. By stripping away visual cues and distractions (along with eye-strain and self-surveillance), moving to audio-only conversations can prove not only more intimate and relational, but also more enriching and easeful. Ultimately, whatever the approach or technology you are using, if it's a high-performing, innovative and mutually supportive team you're looking to foster, then establishing the right conditions for psychological safety, both online and offline, should be one of your greatest priorities.

Key takeaways

- Virtual and in-person interactions are not functionally equivalent, interchangeable experiences.
- Research in embodied cognition suggests that our minds and bodily actions influence one another.
- Sustained technologically mediated communication takes a toll on body and mind, and strips us of vital non-verbal cues we rely on to infer meaning.
- Under the right conditions, virtual interactions can create the illusion that we are present with each other, a phenomenon known as telepresence.
- In physical contexts, presence is a core neuropsychological phenomenon that arises from our ability to interact with and locate ourselves in the environment.

- The loss of real eye-gaze in virtual interactions can lead to discomfort, inhibition of trust and psychological strain.
- When online, we constantly scan for opportunities to connect, which can leave us feeling alert, exhausted, overwhelmed and inaccessible to the present moment. This is known as continuous partial attention.
- Psychological safety means feeling secure enough to speak up without the fear of incurring negative consequences, and it is vital for facilitating learning, employee engagement, innovation and learning from mistakes. It requires deliberate effort to cultivate.
- Boosting psychological safety requires leader inclusiveness and the welcoming of diverse contributions from team members.
- In virtual interactions, tools such as polls, chat functions, emoticons and Q&As can be employed as participation forcers that scaffold more meaningful connection.

CHAPTER NINE

Business, unusual

*There is nothing like a dream
to create the future.* VICTOR HUGO[1]

The great reset

As spring 2020 rolled in, and the waves of lockdown with it, few could have predicted the transformation that would unfold as the world shuttered its doors. From the unimaginably rapid adoption of remote working practices, to the swallowing up of brick-and-mortar stores and services by massive, scalable platforms, the pandemic forced the acceleration of many trends that would otherwise have taken years to coalesce. Whether our access to education and healthcare provisions, or the means through which we consumed entertainment and food, in a few short months the systems upon which we relied had become unrecognizable to those of the decade before.

Of the changes foisted upon us, many were heart-breaking and painful. From the grief of losing loved ones and livelihoods, to the mental health toll of prolonged isolation, no life was left untouched by the upheaval of the pandemic. Where people were lucky enough to work remotely, fresh challenges surfaced around the use of shared spaces, competing demands of family life, and access to material resources – issues that, unless carefully addressed, will likely persist as we move into a more fluid, blended model of business. Under good conditions, working remotely can of course provide the cherished autonomy and flexibility so many of us crave, when matched with concerted effort and effective self-management. But if the lockdowns taught us anything, it is that the wholesale replacement of office-based work with its dispersed, virtual substitute, can be challenging even in the most equipped of set-ups.

Despite the many benefits of remote working, preliminary research suggests that it may not be as good a fit for everyone as we might have hoped. An initial study of 3,200 British workers by Chidiebere Ogbonnaya, senior lecturer at the University of Sussex Business School, suggests that the degree to which we are suited to remote work may be contingent upon our personality. On the positive side, when asked to rate themselves across different personality traits, people who scored high for openness, agreeableness or extroversion reported less worry and depression when working from home. Those with higher scores in neuroticism, however, were more likely to report feeling gloomy and worried, alongside those with low scores in conscientiousness (who also reported greater difficulties in planning and organizing things carefully).[2] So while remote and flexible work practices undoubtedly have their perks, they are unlikely to replace the need for physical spaces within which we might gather, organize and support one another to do our best work. It is precisely this theme that I reach out to Chris Kane, author, adviser and advocate, to explore.

Place and purpose

Having started his professional life as a chartered surveyor, Chris's 30-year career in corporate real estate and workplace strategy has seen him operate as Vice President of International Corporate Real Estate for The Walt Disney Company, and oversee the BBC's decade-long, £2 billion 'analogue to digital' property portfolio regeneration. Having recently published a fascinating book, *Where is My Office?: Reimagining the workplace for the 21st century*,[3] he is one of those rare people whose breadth and depth of experience grant him a unique vantage point from which to envision the workplace(s) of the future.

When we speak, he explains, 'What has happened in the last year is that us human beings have gone through a very, very big behavioural shift. For those who work in the traditional offices, they are asking themselves, "What is the purpose of the office?"' As we emerge from restrictions, Chris tells me that 'there are some existential questions for the real-estate industry, but also for business', and that 'Business leaders are very aware of the fact that they have been living in an environment where the war for talent has raged. It is going to get even more challenging post-COVID-19, because the talented people they wish to hire and keep are thinking "Do you know what, I'm not sure I want to do commuting" – and that is happening across the world.'

Of course, for such transitions to work, not only must we undergo massive structural and logistical shifts, but also shifts in mindset. 'We've all been in the 20th century accustomed to homogenized thinking', Chris explains, and 'whereas the 21st century is truly the century of digital… it is also where a one-size-fits-all mindset just doesn't work. Because if you look at this shift in consumer preferences over the last 20 years, we have moved very much into customization and on-demand, so the workplace is also going to have to shift from fixed to fluid.' When I ask him what the office of the future might look like, Chris is quick to outline that while we cannot simply point in one particular direction (no two businesses are alike, after all), offices will likely be 'more of a social hub, rather than a place where people go to sit at desks. It'll be somewhere where people congregate to do joint work, to solve problems, to be creative.'

Whether and how this change materializes, however, will depend on the context of the business, 'The office, I think, is going to be distributed for some companies, not all, because certain financial services companies cannot be as distributed as they may like.' He points towards the example of Standard Chartered Bank which, in November 2020, announced that it would be offering flexible work options (both in terms of time and location) to over 90 per cent of its 85,000 employees by 2023.[4] Whether its workforce opts to work from home, near-home workspaces or the bank's premises, this fluid, distributed model is one we are likely to see a lot more of as other businesses follow suit, a trend that, as Chris suggests, 'goes back to choice'.

While some businesses may have been quick to extol the virtues of working from home, others have swiftly realized that it is hard to maintain the 'soul' of an organization if its many limbs are scattered across the globe. When I ask occupational psychologist Lewis Garrad how we might mitigate the downsides of such a set-up while fostering a sense of community, he tells me that businesses are investing heavily in the concept of *organization network analysis*, a system of 'looking at the connections between people in a community group organization based on their digital interactions, which are fairly easy to track'. From emails and calendar invites, to the use of geolocation badges, companies can extract reliable signals of relationship strength between co-workers, so as to better identify strong and weak relationship ties that might otherwise be invisible to the hierarchical structures of the organization. By mapping out the frequency, strength and nature of interactions, these patterns of influence and collaboration can provide valuable insights around information flow, levels of trust and inclusion, and which partnerships or teams are proving the most productive. As our reliance on technology increases, these kinds of processes will become ever more valuable in helping business leaders to make better, more informed decisions that will benefit the resilience of the organization.

Of course, the adoption of such strategies also raises fundamental questions around trust, surveillance and autonomy, and when I ask Dan Pink about how businesses might better motivate and engage a remote workforce, his response rings as clearly as a bell: 'Start with the premise that you can trust the people you work with. If you begin with the opposite premise – as many organizations do – the best you'll get will be compliance. You'll never get excellence.' It is a theme that resonates across many of the interviews I conduct, and it crops up again when I ask John Featherby about the qualities most vital to the long-term success of a business. He answers, 'High-quality relationships. Trust, basically. If you can't trust that you are seriously in it for one another and for the bigger purpose, you're always going to run aground in some way. Almost all problems stem from a lack of willingness to trust that we care for one another and the greater good that we're in pursuit of.'

The problem, as psychoanalyst Dr Gillian Isaacs Russell explains, is that trust tends to be harder to cultivate in virtual settings – harder, but not impossible. Pointing towards a study conducted by Rocco back in 1998,[5] she explains that 'trust breaks down in technologically mediated contacts, but can be repaired by some initial face-to-face contact', which is why 'something as simple and essential as trust needs to be promoted for people working together by having face-to-face meetings from time to time'. To

Trust tends to be harder to cultivate in virtual settings – harder, but not impossible.

illustrate her point, she explains, 'There's that really common exercise that people do to build trust, where someone falls backwards and the group catches them. Of course that isn't physically possible when you are online. There is no risk online, and if there is no potential to be dropped, then you cannot truly be held.' As Gillian suggests, while 'regularly coming back together as a community is essential for a safe and productive business practice', it also serves another, deeper function. 'One of the things that helps people to be resilient is being part of the community and to be able to feel that you have *shared* traditions: cultural traditions, faith traditions, "takes-a-village" traditions, working as a community together.'

It is this sense of community that crops up again when I speak with Octavius Black, CEO of MindGym, a company whose mission is to 'use the latest psychology and behavioural science to transform how people think, feel and behave and so improve the performance of companies and the lives of people who work in them'.[6] He warns, 'If we can't find a way of being co-located for two or three days a week, it will have a negative impact on belonging, corporate culture, loyalty, and all sorts of factors.' As our dependence on technology deepens, we must remember that our ability to adapt to new ways of working will not rest solely in our use of AI, machine intelligence and automation. Rather, it will depend on our ability to use the technologies available to us, in concert with the human qualities that allow us to create, relate and innovate – which may be why, as Octavius suggests, 'behavioural science will become the mainstay of how businesses make the most of their people'.

The war for talent

Among the many ways in which organizations can build resilience in the face of uncertainty, there is one that has surfaced more than any other in all the conversations, articles and journals I have drawn upon to write this book. Whether looking through the lens of sustainability, human resources or technology, it is the golden thread of *talent* that weaves the other themes together. From how we can attract and retain the best people, to the means through which we might develop and support them, it is how we make the most of our human potential that sits at the heart of great business.

It is how we make the most of our human potential that sits at the heart of great business.

As we ride this boom of technology and emerge into what will undoubtedly be a new way of working, collaborating and organizing, it is this ability to manage talent and build high-quality, trusting relationships that will set one business apart from the next – especially as the pool of talent to which we have access expands ever wider. With diminished concerns around employees' physical locations, and the challenges we are seeing to cultures of (in-person) presenteeism, access to high-quality talent will continue to grow, and the battle for the best, intensify. When I ask Dr Tomas Chamorro-Premuzic what organizations can do to thrive in the long term, he replies that for any given business, 'what matters is what they are doing in the realm of human capital, and whether they can produce and nurture talented people and great leaders'.

We have long understood the value and power of crafting great customer experiences, to the extent that entire industries have blossomed in dedication to the subject – yet when it comes to those we employ, it appears that we still have a lot to learn. When I speak with Brian Solis, digital anthropologist, futurist, author, and global innovation evangelist at Salesforce, he suggests, 'There is this notion of wellness that we have long ignored in business. The concept of, to give it a word or a term, employee experience.' As we look ahead, 'The future of work that I think we are going to have to contend with is reprogramming a society to be healthier, happier and more creative as we become more and more digital.' Whether that means offering wellbeing packages, designing green environments that are self-sustaining, or rooting one's business in a deeper sense of purpose, it is clear that whatever emerges next will be shaped by the expectations of the workforce.

It is a theme I hear echoed by David Rowan, former editor of WIRED UK, when he tells me, 'I think we are in an era where it is very dangerous to rely on hierarchies with bosses at the top deciding... what should happen. I think it's much more exciting now seeing companies where they trust the front-line workers to decide where the future lies.' He continues, 'Organizations that are able to accept that the real creative force is the workforce – not necessarily senior people, but people at every level, people who are talking to the customer, people who are spotting day-to-day how demand is changing – if you give power to these people, to have a say in how they work, what the product should be, what the company should be doing, then this can be transformative.' Ultimately, for an organization to thrive, David suggests, 'It needs to be declarative about what it stands for and what it will not do.'

But doing (and being) good is not just about attracting the best people and boosting potential gains – it is also about avoiding hefty costs. As Rita Clifton poignantly explains, 'Businesses that are not sustainable have got a risk and also, frankly, a talent risk. If you don't look after your employees, for example, if you are not good at looking after the environment and being socially responsible in the main, you will not attract the best type of employees, and particularly not very able and talented young people who want to work for an organization that makes them feel proud and is doing the right thing.' Of course, for such changes to take place, there must also be a shift in values, a point that Dan Pink speaks to when he explains that, 'especially in leadership, there is a premium on taking care of your employees... All these things that were once dismissed as touchy feely – empathy, belonging, purpose – are becoming hard-headed forces in business success.'

Somewhat of a misnomer, these complex, misleadingly titled 'soft skills' are not only becoming more valuable in a world of evolving expectations and progressive automation, they are also some of the most vital qualities we are failing to teach those entering the workforce. Brian Solis puts it succinctly when he tells me, 'We're essentially grooming a generation of students, and have been actually, for a world that doesn't exist when they are ready to work. And it is actually happening to today's workforce, where they are becoming irrelevant in real time.' He explains,

'These soft skills that are critical, become rather hard skills that we have. They are not easy. Empathy is actually another skill that is going to need to be much more important, especially at the leadership level. Collaboration, working with people, self-management, self-government, self-drive, self-determination, these things are going to be much, much more critical moving forward.' As the march of technology picks up speed, then, as Brian points out, we will need people to train and program the robots, for which a whole new suite of skills will become necessary, 'So things like analytical thinking and innovation, creativity, active learning and learning strategies, complex problem-solving, critical thinking and analysis, originality, initiative, grit, leadership, this concept of social capital, technology literacy, digital literacy, resilience, stress tolerance… these things [that] are not taught in school today.' But as the education system struggles to catch up, the burden of 'pushing these soft/hard skills into our employees, and training them for the future that is actually unfolding now' will fall to business leaders and those of us in human resources. So where to begin?

To boldly go…

Occupational psychologist Lewis Garrad suggests that technology may yield an answer. When we speak, he tells me, 'What to invest your time in is a huge problem for many people right now, they just don't even know where to start.' He points towards AI technologies that are currently being developed 'to predict skills that are going to be valuable for the next phase', technologies that would enable businesses to pay for skills models that identify capabilities likely to be in demand. Lewis explains that such services could prove invaluable in defining how people are paid and trained, providing another asset for the ongoing reskilling of an ever-changing workforce. While the use of technology to enhance latent human capabilities is not new, as our world multiplies in complexity, it is precisely these kinds of applications that could help us navigate towards a more humane future.

This possibility is one that reverberates throughout the conversations I have around virtual and augmented reality, and while this broad and complex category has inspired both hope and hype over the years, it may be that we are finally reaching a point at which the resources exist to create truly immersive, naturalistic experiences, the likes of which could profoundly change the ways in which we live. When I speak to Jeremy Dalton, Head of XR at PwC UK, and author of *Reality Check*,[7] he predicts that 'virtual reality and augmented reality will become a core technology that is used within organizations, regardless of their industry. As a result of that, the technology will become so widespread that it will form another device for us alongside our laptops and smartphones.' He describes a day in the near future in which we will simply put on a headset and be transported into a shared virtual environment with anyone, anywhere (technology and bandwidth permitting). 'We already do that with clients from all over the world, we send headsets out to them and we engage with them in creative workshops, but it will become even easier as the technology advances.'

A far cry from the high-latency, nausea-inducing arcade experiences of the 1990s, this rapidly evolving breed of virtual reality (VR) (in its various permutations) looks set to fulfil many of the visions of its earliest proponents, not least due to its promise of a more naturalistic form of communication, one in which we are free again to move, gesticulate and interact with a broader range of senses than afforded by our screens. Yet while its use for collaboration and communication is clear, the real power of VR may lay in its ability to effect profound emotional change in those that experience it. As Jeremy explains, 'The strength of virtual reality comes from the fact that you are able to feel completely immersed in a different environment. It helps you to create an emotional connection to the content, provides a distraction-free environment and, in a lot of ways, it removes the constraints of the physical world.' Of course, this may not be useful in all scenarios, and while VR may have a powerful use case in the realm of learning and development, for instance, Jeremy is swift to reflect, 'For the objective you are trying to achieve, is the technology helpful? Do you want to create an emotional connection with your content? Maybe you do when you are talking about diversity and inclusion, but if you are talking about, let's say, regulatory risk, maybe you are not so bothered about the emotional connection to the content there.' The trick, he suggests, is to use the technology where it most makes sense.

Yet for many of the most complex and pressing challenges of our time, it is precisely the ability to cultivate empathy – the kind that we feel, rather than the kind that we think – that may help us to bridge the distance between competing perspectives, and find common ground towards resolving the intractable crises we face. It is a topic I have the privilege of exploring with Nell Watson, a tech ethicist, machine intelligence researcher and AI faculty member at Singularity University. She tells me that although 'VR has a bit of a problem, in that it needs to be experienced to be truly understood', nonetheless, 'immersive experiences like games, particularly virtual reality games, can provide so many opportunities for increased empathy'. From releases such as Mafia III, which sheds light on the racism you would endure as a Black protagonist in 1968 Louisiana, to the war and refugee camp situations created by researcher Nonny de la Peña, Nell explains that VR can give us 'a very strongly vicarious experience of what it is like to be in those situations'. By placing ourselves so immersively in the shoes of others, VR 'sidesteps our cognitive processes and gets right to the emotional core of how something feels'.

The ability to cultivate empathy may help us to bridge the distance between competing perspectives, and find common ground towards resolving the intractable crises we face.

When I ask Nell about the future she envisions, she says, 'I think working in tandem with machine intelligence is going to be a key skill in the 2020s and beyond, the same way that people had to learn how to type in the 1980s through 90s.' As we come to terms with remote work and reduced possibilities for travel, she predicts a wave of avatar technologies, 'basically like a robot that you can directly control, that will mirror your own movements'. Once available widely enough, these will provide us with 'the ultimate way of telecommuting from any corner of the planet, especially because of satellite networks like Starlink, which have very high bandwidth, very low latency connections'. In such scenarios, 'an engineer might inhabit a robot in a remote location in Alaska to fix an airplane, or something like that, without physically needing to go there'. While this might sound fantastical to some, Nell explains, 'These technologies are advancing at an incredible rate, I'm continually blown away by just how sophisticated and how relatively affordable – we're talking US $5,000 or so – many of these systems are becoming.' For the price of a souped-up Mac, it's no wonder that Nell believes these technologies might well have geopolitical ramifications.

Although the human embodiment of machines may read like science fiction, this possible future could be closer than we think. After all, we already have driverless cars, and, as Nell points out, 'just the same way that self-driving vehicles recorded millions of hours of human driving in order to learn from those experiences, robots will learn from human-piloted avatars'. If this feels too shocking a prediction, she suggests there is going to be a learning curve, 'where most people will learn how to work in tandem with machine intelligence, and some people won't. Just the same way that some people missed the computerization wave and ended up kind of locked out of career advancement, I think a similar thing might happen in the 2020s if we don't encourage people at an early stage to become more familiar with working in concert with AI, and to understand the benefits of why they should do so.' Yet as we employ machine intelligence and algorithmic solutions to help us optimize processes, manage people and automate tasks, Nell believes that we must do so with a focus on finding 'ways to improve people's autonomy, to respect the dignity of the person'.

Whatever our desires and apprehensions, it is clear that we cannot hold back the tide of technological advancement, nor can we deny the complexity of the task that lies ahead. As we stand on the cusp of deep societal change, I believe that we must grasp this rare and precious moment to determine what we might yet become. Amidst the tumult and uncertainty, as our old systems splinter beneath the weight of new challenges, it is our human capacity for creativity, ingenuity and reinvention that will determine our resilience, both as individuals and as a species. And it is those with the greatest courage to dream boldly, to whom the brightest future will belong.

Endnotes and references

Author website: nathalienahai.com
Book website: businessunusualthebook.com
The Hive Podcast: nathalienahai.com/the-hive-podcast
The Values Map: thevaluesmap.com

Chapter 1

1 Nin, A (1992) *Delta of Venus*, Penguin Books, London
2 Taylor, S E, Lerner, J S, Sherman, D K, Sage, R M and McDowell, N K (2003) Are self-enhancing cognitions associated with healthy or unhealthy biological profiles? *Journal of Personality and Social Psychology*, **85** (4), p 605
3 Koole, S L, Smeets, K, Van Knippenberg, A and Dijksterhuis, A (1999) The cessation of rumination through self-affirmation, *Journal of Personality and Social Psychology*, **77** (1), p 111
4 Creswell, J D, Welch, W T, Taylor, S E, Sherman, D K, Gruenewald, T L and Mann, T (2005) Affirmation of personal values buffers neuroendocrine and psychological stress responses, *Psychological Science*, **16** (11), pp 846–51
5 Grotberg, E H (ed.) (2003) *Resilience for Today: Gaining strength from adversity*, Greenwood Publishing Group, Westport CT
6 Frankl, V E (1985) *Man's Search for Meaning*, Simon and Schuster, New York
7 Tedeschi, R G and Calhoun, L G (2004) Posttraumatic growth: conceptual foundations and empirical evidence, *Psychological Inquiry*, **15** (1), pp 1–18
8 Sutcliffe, K M and Vogus, T J (2003) Organizing for resilience, in Cameron, K, Dutton, J E and Quinn R E (eds) *Positive Organizational Scholarship*, Berrett-Koehler, San Francisco CA

9 Accenture (28 April 2020) COVID-19: How consumer behavior will be changed, https://www.accenture.com/us-en/insights/consumer-goods-services/coronavirus-consumer-behavior-research (archived at https://perma.cc/85QD-2J7G)

10 EY (2020) Future Consumer Index: How COVID-19 is changing consumer behaviors, https://www.ey.com/en_uk/consumer-products-retail/how-covid-19-could-change-consumer-behavior (archived at https://perma.cc/RKP9-8ZS9)

11 Plant Based Foods Association (2020) Retail Sales Data, https://www.plantbasedfoods.org/retail-sales-data/ (archived at https://perma.cc/VLA9-8T4V)

12 Guardian (2020) UK Demand For New Vegan Food Products Soars in Lockdown, https://www.theguardian.com/lifeandstyle/2020/jul/25/uk-demand-for-new-vegan-food-products-soars-in-lockdown#:~:text=Latest%20figures%20reveal%20that%20companies,vegan%20alternatives%20continued%20to%20soar (archived at https://perma.cc/4AWL-UDSX)

13 News.com.au (2019) More Australians Taking Up Vegan and Vegetarian Diets, https://www.news.com.au/lifestyle/health/diet/more-australians-taking-up-vegan-and-vegetarian-diet/news-story/0676836c8695a0e53c24aac4d47d9106 (archived at https://perma.cc/PKY4-JSAS)

14 Statista (2019) Meat Consumption and Vegetarianism in Europe – Statistics and Facts, https://www.statista.com/topics/3345/meat-consumption-and-vegetarianism-in-europe/ (archived at https://perma.cc/DW8Y-DLRS)

15 Bloomberg Green (2020) Pandemic to Spark Biggest Retreat for Meat Eating in Decades, https://www.bloomberg.com/news/articles/2020-07-07/pandemic-set-to-spark-biggest-retreat-for-meat-eating-in-decades#:~:text=The%20pandemic%20is%20poised%20to,data%20from%20the%20United%20Nations (archived at https://perma.cc/KH5L-5QJF)

16 Kantar's COVID-19 Barometer, https://www.kantar.com/uki/campaigns/covid-19-barometer (archived at https://perma.cc/5HW2-YKXQ)

17 SunStar, Bacolod (2020) Urban Farming Gaining Ground Amid Pandemic, https://www.sunstar.com.ph/article/1862275/Bacolod/Business/Urban-farming-gaining-ground-amid-pandemic (archived at https://perma.cc/7NEX-BQEA)

18 The New York Times (2020) How This N.Y. Island Went From Tourist Hot Spot to Emergency Garden, https://www.nytimes.com/2020/07/23/nyregion/governors-island-nyc-urban-farm.html (archived at https://perma.cc/Y7ND-UAMC)

19 History.com (2018) America's Patriotic Victory Gardens, https://www.history.com/news/americas-patriotic-victory-gardens (archived at https://perma.cc/PP8J-B9PM)

20 The Guardian (2020) Ban SUV Adverts to Meet UK Climate Goals, Report Urges, https://www.theguardian.com/environment/2020/aug/03/ban-suv-adverts-to-meet-uk-climate-goals-report-urges (archived at https://perma.cc/G3FL-NVKP)

21 International Energy Agency (2019) Growing Preference for SUVs Challenges Emissions Reductions in Passenger Car Market, https://www.iea.org/commentaries/growing-preference-for-suvs-challenges-emissions-reductions-in-passenger-car-market (archived at https://perma.cc/9P4H-W988)

22 Vice (2020) The New Ford Bronco is an Obscene Monument to Climate Denialism, https://www.vice.com/en/article/akzj4p/the-new-ford-bronco-is-an-obscene-monument-to-climate-denialism (archived at https://perma.cc/GZV9-XK9M)

23 Auto Evolution (2018) Ford Announces 'Business Transformation', https://www.autoevolution.com/news/ford-announces-business-transformation-130562.html (archived at https://perma.cc/MX2G-P4BZ)

24 CNBC (2021) Biden Plans To Replace Government Fleet With Electric Vehicles, https://www.cnbc.com/2021/01/25/biden-plans-to-replace-government-fleet-with-electric-vehicles.html (archived at https://perma.cc/S95Q-GZVY)

25 BBC (2020) US Farmers' Beef With Burger King Over Cow Fart Ad, https://www.bbc.co.uk/news/business-53435857#:~:text=Fast%20food%20chain%20Burger%20King,to%20reduce%20

greenhouse%20gas%20emissions.&text=Burger%20King%20
claims%20adding%20lemongrass,and%20dramatically%20
reduce%20methane%20emissions (archived at https://perma.cc/
T7MZ-5DP7)

26 Medium (2019) New Study Shows Employees Seek and Stay Loyal to
Greener Companies, https://medium.com/swytch/new-study-shows-
employees-seek-and-stay-loyal-to-greener-companies-f485889f9a7f
(archived at https://perma.cc/X4RA-D3PJ)

27 Weber Shandwick (2019) Employee Activism in the Age of Purpose:
Employees (Up)Rising, https://www.webershandwick.com/news/
employee-activism-age-of-purpose/ (archived at https://perma.
cc/5J2D-SJJM)

28 Global Climate Strike (2019) 7.6 Million People Demand Action After
Week of Climate Strikes, https://350.org/press-release/6-6-million-
people-demand-action-after-week-of-climate-strikes/ (archived at
https://perma.cc/8KA7-WDUE)

29 World Economic Forum (2020) COVID-19 is a Litmus Test for
Stakeholder Capitalism, https://www.weforum.org/agenda/2020/03/
covid-19-is-a-litmus-test-for-stakeholder-capitalism/ (archived at
https://perma.cc/QAX4-4SUK)

30 Kantar's COVID-19 Barometer (nd) (canvased over 30,000 people's
opinion in over 50 markets), https://www.kantar.com/uki/campaigns/
covid-19-barometer (archived at https://perma.cc/5HW2-YKXQ)

31 The Guardian (2020) Why the Covid-19 Financial Crisis Will Leave
Lasting Scars on Gen Z, https://www.theguardian.com/us-news/2020/
jul/06/gen-z-covid-19-financial-crisis-lasting-scars (archived at https://
perma.cc/MFC2-E5X5)

32 Law.com (2020) Pressure's On: Big Law targeted by student activists,
https://www.law.com/2020/03/13/pressures-on-big-law-targeted-by-
student-activists/?slreturn=20210314090752 (archived at https://
perma.cc/YWZ3-GK5S)

33 The New York Times (2021) We Built Google: This is not the
company we want to work for, https://www.nytimes.com/2021/01/04/
opinion/google-union.html (archived at https://perma.cc/VC8K-7CU3)

34 Marsh & McLennan (nd) ESG as a Workforce Strategy, https://www.mmc.com/insights/publications/2020/may/esg-as-a-workforce-strategy.html (archived at https://perma.cc/N4KV-CF7J)

35 BCG (2017) Total Societal Impact: A new lens for strategy, https://www.bcg.com/en-gb/publications/2017/total-societal-impact-new-lens-strategy (archived at https://perma.cc/7FHX-3H7B)

36 Financial Times (2021) Bank of England Given New Mandate To Buy 'Green' Bonds, https://www.ft.com/content/f436d69b-2bf0-48cd-bb34-644856fba17f (archived at https://perma.cc/3GUY-CXDN)

37 FT Adviser (2019) FCA Moves To Protect Investors From 'Greenwashing', https://www.ftadviser.com/regulation/2019/10/16/fca-moves-to-protect-investors-from-greenwashing/#:~:text=The%20Financial%20Conduct%20Authority%20has,the%20sustainability%20of%20their%20investments (archived at https://perma.cc/5AUW-YPMB)

38 CityWire (2020) Are You Ready? New Mifid II rules will make IFAs have ESG process, https://citywire.co.uk/new-model-adviser/news/are-you-ready-new-mifid-ii-rules-will-make-ifas-have-esg-process/a1321630 (archived at https://perma.cc/8H82-W6FE)

39 Marsh & McLennan (nd) ESG as a Workforce Strategy; Analysis uses ILOSTAT data from Q4 2019. Generation definitions are from Pew Research Center, https://www.mmc.com/insights/publications/2020/may/esg-as-a-workforce-strategy.html (archived at https://perma.cc/N4KV-CF7J)

40 Mercer (nd) 2020 Global Talent Trends Study, https://www.mercer.com/our-thinking/career/global-talent-hr-trends.html (archived at https://perma.cc/XF57-XTTU)

41 Kantar's COVID-19 Barometer: Generational differences, https://www.pressreleasepoint.com/global-covid-19-barometer-more-half-millennials-and-genzs-household-incomes-impacted-covid-19 (archived at https://perma.cc/H4DY-DRAQ)

42 World Economic Forum (2020) The Global Risks Report 2020, https://www.weforum.org/reports/the-global-risks-report-2020 (archived at https://perma.cc/X7D8-YPSQ)

43 McKinsey Research (2020) How COVID-19 Is Impacting Consumer Behavior: Now and forever, https://www.mckinsey.com/~/media/mckinsey/industries/retail/our%20insights/how%20covid%2019%20is%20changing%20consumer%20behavior%20now%20and%20forever/how-covid-19-is-changing-consumer-behaviornow-and-forever.pdf (archived at https://perma.cc/PH2G-ER2K)

44 Bloomreach (nd) The State of Commerce Experience, https://www.bloomreach.com/en/resources/whitepapers/state-of-commerce-experience-study.html (archived at https://perma.cc/6ZD9-75RQ)

45 McKinsey (nd) Consumer Sentiment and Behavior Continue to Reflect the Uncertainty of the COVID-19 Crisis, https://blog.adobe.com/en/2020/04/01/mckinsey-research-how-covid-19-is-impacting-consumer-behavior (archived at https://perma.cc/B4E4-2MTX)

46 Global Web Index (2020) CBE: Consumer Behavior Evolution Through Sixty Days of COVID-19, https://www.globalwebindex.com/webinars/coronavirus-gwipress (archived at https://perma.cc/EX3Y-QSSA)

47 Deadline (2020) Tom Hanks-Starrer 'Greyhound' Torpedoes Apple TV+ Opening-Weekend Records, https://deadline.com/2020/07/tom-hanks-greyhound-apple-tv-opening-weekend-record-breaker-1202985492/ (archived at https://perma.cc/LJ3N-WQCW)

48 PC Mag (2020) AMC Strikes Deal with Universal to Release Blockbuster Films Online Much Sooner, https://uk.pcmag.com/digital-life/127954/amc-strikes-deal-with-universal-to-release-blockbuster-films-online-much-sooner (archived at https://perma.cc/H4SF-RD9Y)

49 Adobe Blog (2020) Adobe Unveils Comprehensive Report Analyzing Effectiveness of Premium Versus Non-Premium Media, https://blog.adobe.com/en/publish/2020/01/07/adobe-unveils-comprehensive-report-analyzing-effectiveness-of-premium-versus-non-premium-media.html#gs.yr4qxt (archived at https://perma.cc/P5EL-4NSN)

50 Edelman (2020) Edelman Trust Barometer, https://www.edelman.com/trust/2020-trust-barometer (archived at https://perma.cc/RNM3-DPF9)

51 BCG (2017) Creating Value from Disruption (While Others Disappear), https://www.bcg.com/en-gb/publications/2017/value-creation-strategy-transformation-creating-value-disruption-others-disappear (archived at https://perma.cc/H77J-C9CP)

52 BCG (2020) Managing the Cyber Risks of Remote Work, https://www.bcg.com/en-gb/publications/2020/covid-remote-work-cyber-security (archived at https://perma.cc/T239-CMMK)

53 BCG (2020) The Digital Path to Business Resilience, https://www.bcg.com/publications/2020/digital-path-to-business-resilience (archived at https://perma.cc/7HGJ-3BH8)

54 BCG (2019) The Bionic Company, https://www.bcg.com/publications/2019/bionic-company (archived at https://perma.cc/P4ZM-VLPC)

Chapter 2

1 Grazia (2015) 132 Years of Chanel: Her best quotes, https://graziadaily.co.uk/fashion/news/132-years-chanel-best-quotes/ (archived at https://perma.cc/H3JS-N6UB)

2 Simpson, J A (2007) Foundations of interpersonal trust, in Kruglanski, A W and Higgins, E T (eds) *Social Psychology: Handbook of basic principles*, 2nd edn, Guilford Press, New York, pp. 587–607

3 Certified B Corporation (nd) COVID-19 Resource Center, https://bcorporation.net/ (archived at https://perma.cc/PN5G-UXC4)

4 Landrum, S (2017) Millennials Driving Brands To Practice Socially Responsible Marketing, *Forbes*, https://www.forbes.com/sites/sarahlandrum/2017/03/17/millennials-driving-brands-to-practice-socially-responsible-marketing/#5bca8e984990 (archived at https://perma.cc/R7U9-APZJ)

5 Huffington Post (2016) Corporate Social Responsibility Matters: Ignore Millennials at your peril, https://www.huffpost.com/entry/corporate-social-responsi_9_b_9155670 (archived at https://perma.cc/Z7W5-LVPH)

6   RepTrak (nd) 2020 Global RepTrak: Ranking the brands, https://
    www.reptrak.com/rankings/ (archived at https://perma.cc/GYS3-BFBP)

7   Reputation Institute (2018) What It Takes To Be a Top 10 Most
    Reputable Company in 2018, https://www.reputationinstitute.com/
    blog/what-it-takes-be-top-10-most-reputable-company-2018 (archived
    at https://perma.cc/2TG3-SS2E)

8   Edelman Trust Barometer (2020) https://www.edelman.com/
    trust/2020-trust-barometer (archived at https://perma.cc/RNM3-
    DPF9)

9   Bozic, B (2017) Consumer trust repair: a critical literature review,
    European Management Journal, 35 (4), pp 538–47

10 The Guardian (2009) Singer Gets His Revenge on United Airlines and
    Soars To Fame, https://www.theguardian.com/news/blog/2009/jul/23/
    youtube-united-breaks-guitars-video (archived at https://perma.cc/
    CPC6-WHC4)

11 CBS News (2017) Teenage Girls Barred From United Flight Over
    Leggings, https://www.cbsnews.com/news/girls-barred-united-flight-
    leggings/ (archived at https://perma.cc/E6QJ-Z3PM)

12 Inc (2017) United Airlines Forcibly Drags Bloodied Passenger Off
    Flight and Doesn't Apologize (No, He Wasn't Wearing Leggings),
    https://www.inc.com/chris-matyszczyk/united-forcibly-drags-
    passenger-off-flight-and-doesnt-apologize-no-he-wasnt-wear.html
    (archived at https://perma.cc/F8R3-SRMA)

13 Independent (2020) Dragged Off: The new book from Dr David Dao,
    who was forcibly removed from a united flight, https://www.
    independent.co.uk/travel/news-and-advice/united-airlines-
    overbooking-david-dao-chicago-b1776123.html (archived at https://
    perma.cc/973B-QJ99)

14 Dao, D (2021) *Dragged Off: Refusing to give up my seat on the way
    to the American dream*, Mango Media, Miami FL

15 Knight, J G, Mather, D and Mathieson, B (2015) The key role of
    sincerity in restoring trust in a brand with a corporate apology, in
    Leroy Jr Robinson (ed) *Marketing Dynamism & Sustainability:
    Things Change, Things Stay the Same...* Springer, Cham, Switzerland,
    pp 192–5

16 Utz, S, Matzat, U and Snijders, C (2009) On-line reputation systems: the effects of feedback comments and reactions on building and rebuilding trust in on-line auctions, *International Journal of Electronic Commerce*, **13** (3), pp 95–118

17 Xie, Y and Peng, S (2009) How to repair customer trust after negative publicity: the roles of competence, integrity, benevolence, and forgiveness, *Psychology & Marketing*, **26** (7), pp 572–89

18 BBC (2020) Simpsons Ends Use of White Actors to Voice People of Colour, https://www.bbc.co.uk/news/entertainment-arts-53201667 (archived at https://perma.cc/H4BU-NQ9E)

19 Beverland, M B and Farrelly, F J (2010) The quest for authenticity in consumption: consumers' purposive choice of authentic cues to shape experienced outcomes, *Journal of Consumer Research*, **36** (5), pp 838–56

20 Emerson, R W (2014) *Essays: 'To be yourself in a world that is constantly trying to make you something else is the greatest accomplishment'*, A Word To The Wise, Exton

21 Netflix (2019) *Queer Eye: We're in Japan!*, https://www.netflix.com/ title/81075744 (archived at https://perma.cc/65FB-7UK7)

22 Instagram – Naomi Watanabe (2020) https://www.instagram. com/p/B-RYrv-Abxq/ (archived at https://perma.cc/7PYJ-NLL7)

23 Labrecque, L I, Markos, E and Milne, G R (2011) Online personal branding: processes, challenges, and implications, *Journal of Interactive Marketing*, **25** (1), pp 37–50

24 Schallehn, M, Burmann, C and Riley, N (2014) Brand authenticity: model development and empirical testing, *Journal of Product & Brand Management*, **23** (3), pp 192–9

25 Moulard, J G, Raggio, R D and Folse, J A G (2016) Brand authenticity: testing the antecedents and outcomes of brand management's passion for its products, *Psychology & Marketing*, **33** (6), pp 421–36

26 Festinger, L (1957) *A Theory of Cognitive Dissonance*, vol. 2, Stanford University Press, Palo Alto, CA

27 Beverland, M B and Farrelly, F J (2010) The quest for authenticity in consumption: consumers' purposive choice of authentic cues to shape experienced outcomes, *Journal of Consumer Research*, **36** (5), 838–56

28 Fritz, K, Schoenmueller, V and Bruhn, M (2017) Authenticity in branding: exploring antecedents and consequences of brand authenticity, *European Journal of Marketing*, **51** (2), pp 324–48

29 Beverland, M B, Lindgreen, A and Vink, M W (2008) Projecting authenticity through advertising: consumer judgments of advertisers' claims, *Journal of Advertising*, **37** (1), pp 5–15

30 Turner, C and Manning, P (1988) Placing authenticity – on being a tourist: a reply to Pearce and Moscardo, *The Australian and New Zealand Journal of Sociology*, **24** (1), pp 136–9

31 Matlin, M W and Gawron, V J (1979) Individual differences in Pollyannaism, *Journal of Personality Assessment*, **43** (4), pp 411–12

32 Cheung, W Y, Wildschut, T, Sedikides, C, Hepper, E G, Arndt, J and Vingerhoets, A J (2013) Back to the future: nostalgia increases optimism, *Personality and Social Psychology Bulletin*, **39** (11), pp 1484–96

33 Matlin, M W and Stang, D J (1978) *The Pollyanna Principle: Selectivity in language, memory, and thought*, Schenkman Pub. Co, Cambridge Mass.

34 Routledge, C, Wildschut, T, Sedikides, C, Juhl, J and Arndt, J (2012) The power of the past: nostalgia as a meaning-making resource, *Memory*, **20** (5), pp 452–60

35 Feed the Frontlines (nd) https://www.feedthefrontlinesnyc.org/ (archived at https://perma.cc/MTZ7-HNE4)

36 Bloomberg Quicktake (2020) *Twitter*, https://twitter.com/QuickTake/status/1289579001837576202 (archived at https://perma.cc/XWK6-LJML)

37 Morhart, F, Malär, L, Guèvremont, A, Girardin, F and Grohmann, B (2015) Brand authenticity: an integrative framework and measurement scale, *Journal of Consumer Psychology*, **25** (2), pp 200–18

38 Morhart, F, Malär, L, Guèvremont, A, Girardin, F and Grohmann, B (2015) Brand authenticity: an integrative framework and measurement scale, *Journal of Consumer Psychology*, **25** (2), pp 200–18

39 Fritz, K, Schoenmueller, V and Bruhn, M (2017) Authenticity in branding: exploring antecedents and consequences of brand authenticity, *European Journal of Marketing*, **51** (2), pp 324–48

Chapter 3

1 Frankl, V E (1985) *Man's Search for Meaning*, Simon and Schuster, New York

2 Kasser, T and Ryan, R M (1996) Further examining the American dream: differential correlates of intrinsic and extrinsic goals, *Personality and Social Psychology Bulletin*, **22** (3), pp 280–7

3 Kasser, T and Ahuvia, A (2002) Materialistic values and well-being in business students, *European Journal of Social Psychology*, **32** (1), pp 137–46

4 Kasser, T and Ryan, R M (2001) Be careful what you wish for: optimal functioning and the relative attainment of intrinsic and extrinsic goals, in P Schmuck and K M Sheldon (eds), *Life Goals and Well-Being: Towards a positive psychology of human striving*, Hogrefe & Huber Publishers, Seattle WA, pp 116–31

5 Bauer, M A, Wilkie, J E, Kim, J K and Bodenhausen, G V (2012) Cuing consumerism: situational materialism undermines personal and social well-being, *Psychological Science*, **23** (5), pp 517–23

6 Teague, M V, Storr, V H and Fike, R (2020) Economic freedom and materialism: an empirical analysis, *Constitutional Political Economy*, **8**, pp 1-44.

7 Esposto, A G and Zaleski, P A (1999) Economic freedom and the quality of life: an empirical analysis, *Constitutional Political Economy*, **10** (2), pp 185–97

8 De Soysa, I and Vadlammanati, K C (2013) Do pro-market economic reforms drive human rights violations? An empirical assessment, 1981–2006, *Public Choice*, **155** (1–2), pp 163–87

9 Krieger, T and Meierrieks, D (2016) Political capitalism: the interaction between income inequality, economic freedom and democracy, *European Journal of Political Economy*, **45**, pp 115–32

10 Gehring, K (2013) Who benefits from economic freedom? Unraveling the effect of economic freedom on subjective well-being, *World Development*, **50**, pp 74–90

11 Kahneman, D and Deaton, A (2010) High income improves evaluation of life but not emotional well-being, *Proceedings of the National Academy of Sciences*, **107** (38), pp 16489–93

12 Twenge, J M and Cooper, A B (2020) The expanding class divide in happiness in the United States, 1972–2016. *Emotion*, doi: https://doi.org/10.1037/emo0000774 (archived at https://perma.cc/W4YN-6Q6B)

13 Aknin, L B, Wiwad, D and Hanniball, K B (2018) Buying well-being: spending behavior and happiness, *Social and Personality Psychology Compass*, **12** (5), p e12386

14 Matz, S C, Gladstone, J J and Stillwell, D (2016) Money buys happiness when spending fits our personality, *Psychological Science*, **27** (5), pp 715–25

15 Aristotle [4th Century BCE] (1985) *Nicomachean Ethics*, trans. T Irwin, Hackett, Indianapolis, IN

16 Kahneman, D (2011) *Thinking, Fast and Slow*, Macmillan, New York

17 Gupta, A (2019) Meaningful Consumption: A eudaimonic perspective on the consumer pursuit of happiness and well-being, https://digitalcommons.unl.edu/businessdiss/57/ (archived at https://perma.cc/L5BJ-PLH2)

18 Ryff, C D and Singer, B H (2008) Know thyself and become what you are: a eudaimonic approach to psychological well-being, *Journal of Happiness Studies*, **9** (1), pp 13–39

19 Ryff, C D (1989) Happiness is everything, or is it? Explorations on the meaning of psychological well-being, *Journal of Personality and Social Psychology*, **57** (6), p 1069

20 Maslow, A H (1951) Resistance to acculturation, *Journal of Social Issues*, **7** (4), pp 26–9

21 Ryff, C D and Singer, B (1998) The contours of positive human health, *Psychological Inquiry*, **9** (1), pp 1–28

22 Allport, G W (1937) Personality: A psychological interpretation.

23 Gupta, A. (2019). Meaningful Consumption: A eudaimonic perspective on the consumer pursuit of happiness and well-being (Dissertation), https://digitalcommons.unl.edu/businessdiss/57/ (archived at https://perma.cc/L5BJ-PLH2)

24 Patagonia, https://www.patagonia.com/activism/ (archived at https://perma.cc/S7P3-QAFS)

25 Fernando, M and Chowdhury, R (2016) Cultivation of virtuousness and self-actualization in the workplace, in A J G Sison (ed), *The Handbook of Virtue Ethics in Business and Management*, Springer, Dordrecht, pp 1–13

26 Maslow, A H, Stephens, D C and Heil, G (1998) *Maslow on Management*, John Wiley, New York

27 Hoffman, E (1988) *The Right To Be Human: A biography of Abraham Maslow*, Jeremy P. Tarcher, Inc., New York, p 42

28 Morin, E M (2004) The meaning of work in modern times, in *10th World Congress on Human Resources Management, Rio de Janeiro, Brazil*, vol 20, p 2004

29 Maslow, A H (1968) *Toward a Psychology of Being*, Van Nostrand, New York

Chapter 4

1 Hoda Kotb (2020) *This Just Speaks to Me: Words to Live By Every Day*, Putnam, New York

2 Mind The Product, Joe Tinston (2020) How Bloom & Wild Made Customer Experience More Thoughtful: A case study, https://www.mindtheproduct.com/how-bloom-wild-made-customer-experience-more-thoughtful-a-case-study/ (archived at https://perma.cc/K8MF-HND5)

3 Essential Retail (nd) Behind Bloom & Wild's 'Thoughtful Marketing' – Using Tech to Give Online a Human Touch, https://www.essentialretail.com/features/bloom-and-wild-thoughtful/

4 Bloom & Wild (nd) Meet Our Thoughtful Marketing Community, https://www.bloomandwild.com/thoughtful-marketing-community (archived at https://perma.cc/E2SU-LPA6)

5 Ryan, R M and Deci, E L (2000) Self-determination theory and the facilitation of intrinsic motivation, social development, and well-being, *American Psychologist*, **55** (1), p 68

6 Waterman, A S (1993) Two conceptions of happiness: contrasts of personal expressiveness (eudaimonia) and hedonic enjoyment, *Journal of Personality and Social Psychology*, **64** (4), p 678

7 Kim, Y, Butzel, J S and Ryan, R M (1998) Interdependence and well-being: a function of culture and relatedness needs, *International Society for the Study of Personal Relationships*, Saratoga Spring, NY

8 Sheldon, K M, Ryan, R and Reis, H T (1996) What makes for a good day? Competence and autonomy in the day and in the person, *Personality and Social Psychology Bulletin*, **22** (12), pp 1270–9

9 Carver, C S and Scheier, M (1990) *Principles of Self-Regulation: Action and emotion*, The Guilford Press, New York

10 Patrick, H, Knee, C R, Canevello, A and Lonsbary, C (2007) The role of need fulfillment in relationship functioning and well-being: a self-determination theory perspective, *Journal of Personality and Social Psychology*, **92** (3), p 434

11 Ryan, R M and Deci, E L (2000) Self-determination theory and the facilitation of intrinsic motivation, social development, and well-being, *American Psychologist*, **55** (1), p 68

12 Kasser, T and Ryan, R M (1996) Further examining the American dream: differential correlates of intrinsic and extrinsic goals, *Personality and Social Psychology Bulletin*, **22** (3), pp 280–7

13 Certified B Corporation (nd) About B Corps, https://bcorporation.net/about-b-corps (archived at https://perma.cc/9PJA-JTUD)

14 Bowlby, J (1969) *Attachment and Loss*, Basic Books, New York

15 Thomson, M, MacInnis, D J and Whan Park, C (2005) The ties that bind: measuring the strength of consumers' emotional attachments to brands, *Journal of Consumer Psychology*, **15** (1), pp 77–91

16 Bowlby, J (1980) *Loss: Sadness and depression*, Basic Books, New York

17 Richins, M L (1994) Special possessions and the expression of material values, *Journal of Consumer Research*, **21** (3), pp 522–33

18 Mikulincer, M, Hirschberger, G, Nachmias, O and Gillath, O (2001) The affective component of the secure base schema: affective priming with representations of attachment security, *Journal of Personality and Social Psychology*, **81** (2), p 305

19 Bretherton, I (1992) The origins of attachment theory: John Bowlby and Mary Ainsworth, *Developmental Psychology*, **28** (5), p 759

20 Veloutsou, C and Moutinho, L (2009) Brand relationships through brand reputation and brand tribalism, *Journal of Business Research*, **62** (3), pp 314–22

21 Grisaffe, D B and Nguyen, H P (2011) Antecedents of emotional attachment to brands, *Journal of Business Research*, **64** (10), pp 1052–9

22 Oliver, R L (1999) Whence consumer loyalty?, *Journal of Marketing*, **63** (4_suppl1), pp 33–44

23 Park, C W, MacInnis, D J, Priester, J, Eisingerich, A B and Iacobucci, D (2010) Brand attachment and brand attitude strength: conceptual and empirical differentiation of two critical brand equity drivers, *Journal of Marketing*, **74** (6), pp 1–17

24 Fedorikhin, A, Park, C W and Thomson, M (2008) Beyond fit and attitude: the effect of emotional attachment on consumer responses to brand extensions, *Journal of Consumer Psychology*, **18** (4), pp 281–91

25 Thomson, M, MacInnis, D J and Whan Park, C (2005) The ties that bind: measuring the strength of consumers' emotional attachments to brands, *Journal of Consumer Psychology*, **15** (1), pp 77–91

26 Park, C W, MacInnis, D J, Priester, J, Eisingerich, A B and Iacobucci, D (2010) Brand attachment and brand attitude strength: conceptual and empirical differentiation of two critical brand equity drivers, *Journal of Marketing*, **74** (6), pp 1–17

27 Schmalz, S and Orth, U R (2012) Brand attachment and consumer emotional response to unethical firm behavior, *Psychology & Marketing*, **29** (11), pp 869–84

28 Hazan, C and Shaver, P R (1994) Attachment as an organizational framework for research on close relationships, *Psychological Inquiry*, **5** (1), pp 1–22

29 Patrick, H, Knee, C R, Canevello, A and Lonsbary, C (2007) The role of need fulfillment in relationship functioning and well-being: a self-determination theory perspective, *Journal of Personality and Social Psychology*, **92** (3), p 434

30 Thomson, M (2006) Human brands: investigating antecedents to consumers' strong attachments to celebrities, *Journal of Marketing*, **70** (3), pp 104–19

31 Sirgy, M J (1982) Self-concept in consumer behavior: a critical review, *Journal of Consumer Research*, **9** (3), pp 287–300

32 Fritz, K, Schoenmueller, V and Bruhn, M (2017) Authenticity in branding: exploring antecedents and consequences of brand authenticity, *European Journal of Marketing*, **51** (2), pp 324–48

33 Festinger, L (1957) *A Theory of Cognitive Dissonance*, vol. 2, Stanford University Press, Palo Alto, CA

34 Fritz, K, Schoenmueller, V and Bruhn, M (2017) Authenticity in branding: exploring antecedents and consequences of brand authenticity, *European Journal of Marketing*, **51** (2), pp 324–48

35 Japutra, A, Ekinci, Y and Simkin (2018) Tie the knot: building stronger consumers' attachment toward a brand, *Journal of Strategic Marketing*, **26** (3), pp 223–40

36 Malär, L, Krohmer, H, Hoyer, W D and Nyffenegger, B (2011) Emotional brand attachment and brand personality: the relative importance of the actual and the ideal self, *Journal of Marketing*, **75** (4), pp 35–52

37 Forbes (2020) BrewDog is Officially the First Carbon Negative Beer Business, https://www.forbes.com/sites/emanuelabarbiroglio/2020/08/25/brewdog-is-officially-the-first-carbon-negative-beer-business/ (archived at https://perma.cc/2NUF-NN5U)

38 Aaker, J L (1999) The malleable self: the role of self-expression in persuasion, *Journal of Marketing Research*, **36** (1), pp 45–57

39 Kim, H R, Lee, M and Ulgado, F M (2005) Brand Personality, Self-Congruity and the Consumer–Brand Relationship, *ACR Asia-Pacific Advances*, https://www.acrwebsite.org/volumes/11876/volumes/ap06/AP-06/full (archived at https://perma.cc/26R4-7EGT)

40 Fournier, S (1998) Consumers and their brands: developing relationship theory in consumer research, *Journal of Consumer Research*, **24** (4), pp 343–73

41 Kelly Wynne (2020) On This Date In 1985 Coca-Cola Became New Coke But Not For Long — Here's What Happened, *Newsweek*, https://www.newsweek.com/this-date-1985-coca-cola-became-new-coke-not-long-heres-what-happened-1499579 (archived at https://perma.cc/Z968-KT2B)

42 Kuehlwein, J P and Schaefer, W (2017) Ueber-branding: how modern prestige brands create meaning through mission and myth – part 1, *Journal of Brand Strategy*, **5** (4), pp 395–409

43 Brakus, J J, Schmitt, B H and Zarantonello, L (2009) Brand experience: what is it? How is it measured? Does it affect loyalty?, *Journal of Marketing*, **73** (3), pp 52–68

44 Stokburger-Sauer, N, Ratneshwar, S and Sen, S (2012) Drivers of consumer–brand identification, *International Journal of Research in Marketing*, **29** (4), pp 406–18

45 Brown, T J and Dacin, P A (1997) The company and the product: corporate associations and consumer product responses, *Journal of Marketing*, **61** (1), pp 68–84

46 Vlachos, P A and Vrechopoulos, A P (2012) Consumer–retailer love and attachment: antecedents and personality moderators, *Journal of Retailing and Consumer Services*, **19** (2), pp 218–28

47 Vlachos, P A and Vrechopoulos, A P (2012) Consumer–retailer love and attachment: antecedents and personality moderators, *Journal of Retailing and Consumer Services*, **19** (2), pp 218–28

48 Eccles, R G, Ioannou, I and Serafeim, G (2014) The impact of corporate sustainability on organizational processes and performance, *Management Science*, **60** (11), pp 2835–57

49 Khan, M, Serafeim, G and Yoon, A (2016) Corporate sustainability: first evidence on materiality, *The Accounting Review*, **91** (6), pp 1697–724

50 Hyde, J S (2005) The gender similarities hypothesis, *American Psychologist*, **60** (6), p 581

51 Follett, M P (1924) *Creative Experience*, Longmans, Green and Company, New York

52 Penta, L J (1996) Hannah Arendt: on power, *The Journal of Speculative Philosophy*, **10** (3), pp 210–29

53 Collins, M A and Amabile, T M (1999) Motivation and creativity, in R J Sternberg (ed.) *Handbook of Creativity*, Cambridge University Press, Cambridge, pp 1051–7

54 Kaufman, S B (2020) *Transcend: The new science of self-actualization*, TarcherPerigee, New York

55 Steinmann, B, Klug, H J and Maier, G W (2018) The path is the goal: how transformational leaders enhance followers' job attitudes and proactive behavior, *Frontiers in Psychology*, **9**, 2338

56 Mercado Libre (2018) Great place to work, https://www. greatplacetowork.com/best-workplaces/worldsbest/2018/mercado-libre (archived at https://perma.cc/QPR6-WAF4)

57 BBC (2020) The Boss Who Put Everyone on 70K, https://www.bbc. co.uk/news/stories-51332811 (archived at https://perma.cc/VK9U-8UNV)

58 The New York Times (2015) Praise and Skepticism as One Executive Sets Minimum Wage to $70,000 a Year, https://www.nytimes. com/2015/04/20/business/praise-and-skepticism-as-one-executive-sets-minimum-wage-to-70000-a-year.html (archived at https://perma.cc/S28U-ZNUW)

59 Weiss, M, Norton, M I, Norris, M and McAra, S (2015) The $70 K CEO at Gravity Payments, https://hbsp.harvard.edu/product/816010-PDF-ENG (archived at https://perma.cc/PY9V-EAPF)

60 Market Watch (2020) This Company Pays Its Workers a $70,000 Minimum Salary, and That's Helping It Weather the Coronavirus Crisis, https://www.marketwatch.com/story/how-giving-employees-a-70k-minimum-salary-is-helping-this-company-weather-the-coronavirus-crisis-2020-04-07 (archived at https://perma.cc/MFH8-3B89)

61 Kraft, A G, Vashishtha, R and Venkatachalam, M (2018) Frequent financial reporting and managerial myopia, *The Accounting Review*, **93** (2), pp 249–75

62 Polman, P (2014) Business, Society, and the Future of Capitalism, *McKinsey*, https://www.mckinsey.com/business-functions/sustainability/ our-insights/business-society-and-the-future-of-capitalism (archived at https://perma.cc/YQU5-8KFM)

63 Department for Business, Energy and Industrial Strategy (2019) Corporate Governance: The Companies (Directors' Remuneration Policy and Directors' Remuneration Report) Regulations 2019 – Frequently Asked Questions, https://www.gov.uk/government/ publications/companies-directors-remuneration-policy-and-directors-remuneration-report-regulations-2019 (archived at https://perma. cc/6MMR-26RR)

64 Aitken, M J, Harris, F H D B and Ji, S (2015) A worldwide examination of exchange market quality: greater integrity increases market efficiency, *Journal of Business Ethics*, **132** (1), pp 147–70

65 McFall, L (1987) Integrity, *Ethics*, **98** (1), pp 5–20

66 Murphy, P E, Laczniak, G R and Wood, G (2007) An ethical basis for relationship marketing: a virtue ethics perspective, *European Journal of Marketing*, **41** (1/2), pp 37–57

67 Brown, M T (2006) Corporate integrity and public interest: a relational approach to business ethics and leadership, *Journal of Business Ethics*, **66** (1), pp 11–18

68 Davis, A L and Rothstein, H R (2006) The effects of the perceived behavioral integrity of managers on employee attitudes: a meta-analysis, *Journal of Business Ethics*, **67** (4), pp 407–19

69 Nahai, N (2017) *Webs of Influence: The psychology of online persuasion: the psychology of online persuasion*, Pearson, Harlow

Chapter 5

1 Roosevelt, E (1983) *You Learn By Living*, John Knox Press London

2 Forbes (2020) #BlackOutTuesday Brings Music Industry to a Pause, But Some Artists Warn Against Obscuring Black Lives Matter Posts, https://www.forbes.com/sites/isabeltogoh/2020/06/02/

blackouttuesday-brings-music-industry-to-a-pause-but-some-artists-warn-against-obscuring-black-lives-matter-posts/ (archived at https://perma.cc/9GHF-BDUK)

3 Marketing Week (2020) If 'Black Lives Matter' to Brands, Where Are Your Black Board Members?, https://www.marketingweek.com/mark-ritson-black-lives-matter-brands/ (archived at https://perma.cc/DKZ3-V7Q6)

4 Bartholomew, J (2018) The awful rise of 'virtue signalling', *The Spectator*, https://www.spectator.co.uk/article/the-awful-rise-of-virtue-signalling (archived at https://perma.cc/4ALF-VCHC)

5 Wills, M (2020) Abolitionist 'Wide Awakes' Were Woke Before 'Woke', *JSTOR Daily*, https://daily.jstor.org/abolitionist-wide-awakes-were-woke-before-woke/ (archived at https://perma.cc/UJS6-5R5C)

6 Wallace, E, Buil, I and De Chernatony, L (2020) 'Consuming good' on social media: what can conspicuous virtue signalling on Facebook tell us about prosocial and unethical intentions?, *Journal of Business Ethics*, **162** (3), pp 577–92

7 Vogel, E A, Rose, J P, Roberts, L R and Eckles, K (2014) Social comparison, social media, and self-esteem, *Psychology of Popular Media Culture*, **3** (4), p 206

8 Hawes, T, Zimmer-Gembeck, M J and Campbell, S M (2020) Unique associations of social media use and online appearance preoccupation with depression, anxiety, and appearance rejection sensitivity, *Body Image*, **33**, pp 66–76

9 Dexerto.com (2020) TikTok & Instagram Influencers Exposed For Renting Fake Private Jet Set, https://www.dexerto.com/entertainment/tiktok-instagram-influencers-exposed-for-renting-fake-private-jet-set-1424440/ (archived at https://perma.cc/5XT6-UNL4)

10 Jezebel (2020) 'Fake Private Plane Girls': The Deceptive Genius of the Influencer Backdrop Economy, https://jezebel.com/fake-private-plane-girls-the-deceptive-genius-of-the-i-1845203013 (archived at https://perma.cc/4WLZ-D4GB)

11 Youyou, W, Kosinski, M and Stillwell, D (2015) Computer-based personality judgments are more accurate than those made by humans, *Proceedings of the National Academy of Sciences*, **112** (4), pp 1036–40

12 Verplanken, B and Herabadi, A (2001) Individual differences in impulse buying tendency: feeling and no thinking, *European Journal of Personality*, **15** (S1), pp S71–S83

13 Leutner, F (2016) Profiling Consumers: The role of personal values in consumer preferences. Submitted for the degree of PhD, Department of Psychology and Language Sciences, University College London

14 Barrick, M R, Mount, M K and Judge, T A (2001) Personality and performance at the beginning of the new millennium: what do we know and where do we go next?, *International Journal of Selection and assessment*, **9** (1–2), pp 9–30

15 Chamorro-Premuzic, T (2007) BPS textbooks in psychology, *Personality and Individual Differences*, Blackwell Publishing, Malden

16 Caprara, G V, Barbaranelli, C and Guido, G (2001) Brand personality: how to make the metaphor fit?, *Journal of Economic Psychology*, **22** (3), pp 377–95

17 Siguaw, J A, Mattila, A and Austin, J R (1999) The brand-personality scale: an application for restaurants, *Cornell Hotel and Restaurant Administration Quarterly*, **40** (3), pp 48–55

18 Bouchard Jr, T J and McGue, M (2003) Genetic and environmental influences on human psychological differences, *Journal of Neurobiology*, **54** (1), pp 4–45

19 Dikcius, V, Seimiene, E and Zaliene, E (2013) Congruence between brand and consumer personalities, *Economics and Management*, **18** (3), pp 526–36

20 Edwards, J R and Cable, D M (2009) The value of value congruence, *Journal of Applied Psychology*, **94** (3), p 654

21 Sihvonen, J (2019) Understanding the drivers of consumer–brand identification, *Journal of Brand Management*, **26** (5), pp 583–94

22 Lee, J and Cho, M (2019) New insights into socially responsible consumers: the role of personal values, *International Journal of Consumer Studies*, **43** (2), pp 123–33

23 Parks-Leduc, L, Feldman, G and Bardi, A (2015) Personality traits and personal values: a meta-analysis, *Personality and Social Psychology Review*, **19** (1), pp 3–29

24 Schwartz, S H (2012) An overview of the Schwartz theory of basic values, *Online Readings in Psychology and Culture*, **2** (1), pp 2307–0919, http://dx.doi.org/10.9707/2307-0919.1116 (archived at https://perma.cc/8PB6-AYYV)

25 Caplan, B (2003) Stigler–Becker versus Myers–Briggs: why preference-based explanations are scientifically meaningful and empirically important, *Journal of Economic Behavior & Organization*, **50** (4), pp 391-405

26 Sandy, C J, Gosling, S D and Durant, J (2013) Predicting consumer behavior and media preferences: the comparative validity of personality traits and demographic variables, *Psychology & Marketing*, **30** (11), pp 937–49

27 Edelman (2018) Two-thirds of Consumers Worldwide Now Buy On Beliefs, https://www.edelman.com/news-awards/two-thirds-consumers-worldwide-now-buy-beliefs (archived at https://perma.cc/AS2P-L9ZU)

28 Jonsen, K, Galunic, C, Weeks, J and Braga, T (2015) Evaluating espoused values: does articulating values pay off?, *European Management Journal*, **33** (5), pp 332–40

29 Accenture (2018) To Affinity and Beyond: From Me to We: The Rise of the Purpose-Led Brand, https://www.accenture.com/us-en/insights/strategy/brand-purpose (archived at https://perma.cc/U3X2-9AM9)

30 Allen, M W (2002) Human values and product symbolism: do consumers form product preference by comparing the human values symbolized by a product to the human values that they endorse?, *Journal of Applied Social Psychology*, **32** (12), pp 2475–501

31 Baumgartner, H (2002) Toward a personology of the consumer, *Journal of Consumer Research*, **29** (2), pp 286–92

32 Allen, M W (2001) A practical method for uncovering the direct and indirect relationships between human values and consumer purchases, *Journal of Consumer Marketing*, **18** (2), pp 102–20

33 Schwartz, S H and Melech, G (2000) National differences in micro and macro worry: social, economic, and cultural explanations, in E Diener and E M Suh (eds) *Culture and Subjective Well-Being*, MIT Press, Cambridge MA, pp 219–56

34 Davidov, E (2010) Testing for comparability of human values across countries and time with the third round of the European Social Survey, *International Journal of Comparative Sociology*, **51** (3), pp 171–91

35 Milberg, S J, Park, C W and McCarthy, M S (1997) Managing negative feedback effects associated with brand extensions: the impact of alternative branding strategies, *Journal of Consumer Psychology*, **6** (2), pp 119–40

36 Schermer, J A, Vernon, P A, Maio, G R and Jang, K L (2011) A behavior genetic study of the connection between social values and personality, *Twin Research and Human Genetics*, **14** (3), pp 233–9

37 Rokeach, M (1968) *Beliefs, Attitudes, and Values*, Josey-Bass, San Francisco CA

38 Schwartz, S H (1992) Universals in the content and structure of values: theoretical advances and empirical tests in 20 countries, *Advances in Experimental Social Psychology*, **25** (1), pp 1–65

39 Roberts, B W, Walton, K E and Viechtbauer, W (2006) Patterns of mean-level change in personality traits across the life course: a meta-analysis of longitudinal studies, *Psychological Bulletin*, **132** (1), p 1

40 Bardi, A, Lee, J A, Hofmann-Towfigh, N and Soutar, G (2009) The structure of intraindividual value change, *Journal of Personality and Social Psychology*, **97** (5), p 913

41 Schwartz, S H (2006) Basic Human Values: An Overview, http://www.yourmorals.org/schwartz

42 Besley, J C (2008) Media use and human values, *Journalism & Mass Communication Quarterly*, **85** (2), pp 311–30

43 Schwartz, S H and Bardi, A (1997) Influences of adaptation to communist rule on value priorities in Eastern Europe, *Political Psychology*, **18** (2), pp 385–410

44 Kohn, M L and Schooler, C (1983) *Work and Personality: An inquiry into the impact of social stratification*, Ablex Pub., Norwood NJ

45 Bilsky, W and Schwartz, S H (1994) Values and personality, *European Journal of Personality*, **8** (3), pp 163–81

46 Inglehart, R (2020) *Modernization and Postmodernization: Cultural, economic, and political change in 43 societies*, Princeton University Press, Princeton NJ

47 Schwartz, S H (1994) Beyond individualism/collectivism: new cultural dimensions of values, in U Kim, H C Triandis, C Kâğitçibaşi, S-C Choi and G Yoon (eds), *Cross-Cultural Research and Methodology Series, Vol 18: Individualism and collectivism: theory, method, and applications*, Sage Publications, Thousand Oaks CA, pp 85–119

48 Just Capital (nd) Mission & Impact, https://justcapital.com/mission-impact/ (archived at https://perma.cc/QBZ5-FRBG)

49 Rogers, E M and Bhowmik, D K (1970) Homophily-heterophily: relational concepts for communication research, *Public Opinion Quarterly*, **34** (4), pp 523–38

50 Gilly, M C, Graham, J L, Wolfinbarger, M F and Yale, L J (1998) A dyadic study of interpersonal information search, *Journal of the Academy of Marketing Science*, **26** (2), pp 83–100

51 Zhang, J and Bloemer, J M (2008) The impact of value congruence on consumer-service brand relationships, *Journal of Service Research*, **11** (2), pp 161–78

Chapter 6

1 Carnegie, C (2010) *How To Win Friends and Influence People*, Simon & Schuster, New York

2 Weizenbaum, J (1976) *Computer Power and Human Reason: From judgment to calculation*, W H Freeman, New York

3 Corydon Ireland (2012) Alan Turing at 100, *Harvard Gazette*, https://news.harvard.edu/gazette/story/2012/09/alan-turing-at-100/ (archived at https://perma.cc/6JVR-2STV)

4 Goleman, D (2005) *Emotional Intelligence: Why it can matter more than IQ*, Bantam, New York

5 Salovey, P and Mayer, J D (1990) Emotional intelligence, *Imagination, cognition and personality*, **9** (3), pp 185–211

6 Salovey, P and Grewal, D (2005) The science of emotional intelligence, *Current Directions in Psychological Science*, **14** (6), pp 281–5

7 Salovey, P and Grewal, D (2005) The science of emotional intelligence, *Current Directions in Psychological Science*, **14** (6), pp 281–5

8 Isen, A M, Johnson, M M, Mertz, E and Robinson, G F (1985) The influence of positive affect on the unusualness of word associations, *Journal of Personality and Social Psychology*, **48** (6), p 1413

9 Bodie, G D, Vickery, A J, Cannava, K and Jones, S M (2015) The role of 'active listening' in informal helping conversations: impact on perceptions of listener helpfulness, sensitivity, and supportiveness and discloser emotional improvement, *Western Journal of Communication*, **79** (2), pp 151–73

10 Topornycky, J and Golparian, S (2016) Balancing openness and interpretation in active listening, *Collected Essays on Learning and Teaching*, **9**, pp 175–84

11 Bove, L L (2019) Empathy for service: benefits, unintended consequences, and future research agenda, *Journal of Services Marketing*, **33** (1), pp 31–43

12 Windahl, C (2017) Market sense-making in design practice: exploring curiosity, creativity and courage, *Journal of Marketing Management*, **33** (3–4), pp 280–91

13 Saxby, C, Celuch, K and Walz, A (2015) How employee trustworthy behaviors interact to emotionally bond service customers, *Journal of Consumer Satisfaction, Dissatisfaction and Complaining Behavior*, **28**, p 75

14 Giacobbe, R W, Jackson Jr, D W, Crosby, L A and Bridges, C M (2006) A contingency approach to adaptive selling behavior and sales performance: selling situations and salesperson characteristics, *Journal of Personal Selling & Sales Management*, **26** (2), pp 115–42

15 Baron-Cohen, S, Richler, J, Bisarya, D, Gurunathan, N and Wheelwright, S (2003) The systemizing quotient: an investigation of adults with Asperger syndrome or high-functioning autism, and normal sex differences, *Philosophical Transactions of the Royal Society of London. Series B: Biological Sciences*, **358** (1430), pp 361–74

16 Huang, M H and Rust, R T (2018) Artificial intelligence in service, *Journal of Service Research*, **21** (2), pp 155–72

17 Reynolds, W J and Scott, B (2000) Do nurses and other professional helpers normally display much empathy?, *Journal of Advanced Nursing*, **31** (1), pp 226–34

18 Polani, D (2017) Emotionless Chatbots are Taking Over Customer Service – and it's Bad News for Consumers, https://theconversation.com/emotionless-chatbots-are-taking-over-customer-service-and-its-bad-news-for-consumers-82962 (archived at https://perma.cc/22AE-FRP7)

19 Batt-Rawden, S A, Chisolm, M S, Anton, B and Flickinger, T E (2013) Teaching empathy to medical students: an updated, systematic review, *Academic Medicine*, **88** (8), pp 1171–7

20 Davis, M H (1983) Measuring individual differences in empathy: evidence for a multidimensional approach, *Journal of Personality and Social Psychology*, **44** (1), p 113

21 Kanske, P, Böckler, A, Trautwein, F M, Parianen Lesemann, F H and Singer, T (2016) Are strong empathizers better mentalizers? Evidence for independence and interaction between the routes of social cognition, *Social Cognitive and Affective Neuroscience*, **11** (9), pp 1383–92

22 Van Boven, L, Loewenstein, G, Dunning, D and Nordgren, L F (2013) Changing places: a dual judgment model of empathy gaps in emotional perspective taking, in J M Olson and M P Zanna (eds) *Advances in Experimental Social Psychology*, vol. 48, Academic Press, New York, pp 117–71

23 Loewenstein, G (1996) Out of control: visceral influences on behavior, *Organizational Behavior and Human Decision Processes*, **65** (3), pp 272–92

24 Taylor, S E (2006) Tend and befriend: biobehavioral bases of affiliation under stress, *Current Directions in Psychological Science*, **15** (6), pp 273–7

25 Hatfield, E, Cacioppo, J T and Rapson, R L (1994) *Emotional Contagion, Studies in Emotion and Social Interaction,* Cambridge University Press, Cambridge

26 Levy, D A and Nail, P R (1993) Contagion: a theoretical and empirical review and reconceptualization, *Genetic, Social, and General Psychology Monographs*, **119** (2), pp 233–84

27 Delvaux, E, Meeussen, L and Mesquita, B (2016) Emotions are not always contagious: longitudinal spreading of self-pride and group pride in homogeneous and status-differentiated groups, *Cognition and Emotion*, **30** (1), pp 101–16

28 Goldenberg, A, Garcia, D, Halperin, E, Zaki, J, Kong, D, Golarai, G and Gross, J J (2020) Beyond emotional similarity: the role of situation-specific motives, *Journal of Experimental Psychology: General*, **149** (1), p 138

29 Lomanowska, A M and Guitton, M J (2016) Online intimacy and well-being in the digital age, *Internet Interventions*, **4**, pp 138–44

30 Goldenberg, A, Garcia, D, Halperin, E, Zaki, J, Kong, D, Golarai, G and Gross, J J (2020) Beyond emotional similarity: the role of situation-specific motives, *Journal of Experimental Psychology: General*, **149** (1), p 138

31 Kramer, A D, Guillory, J E and Hancock, J T (2014) Experimental evidence of massive-scale emotional contagion through social networks, *Proceedings of the National Academy of Sciences*, **111** (24), pp 8788–90

32 Kramer, A D, Guillory, J E and Hancock, J T (2014) Experimental evidence of massive-scale emotional contagion through social networks, *Proceedings of the National Academy of Sciences*, **111** (24), pp 8788–90

33 Panger, G (2016) Reassessing the Facebook experiment: critical thinking about the validity of Big Data research, *Information, Communication & Society*, **19** (8), pp 1108–26

34 Hill, K (2014) Facebook Doesn't Understand the Fuss about its Emotion Manipulation Study, *Forbes*, https://www.forbes.com/sites/kashmirhill/2014/06/29/facebook-doesnt-understand-the-fuss-about-its-emotion-manipulation-study/?sh=64c61a9366db (archived at https://perma.cc/32BA-S9FP)

35 Goldenberg, A and Gross, J J (2020) Digital emotion contagion, *Trends in Cognitive Sciences*, **24** (4), pp 316–28

36 Brady, W J, Crockett, M J and Van Bavel, J J (2020) The MAD model of moral contagion: the role of motivation, attention, and design in the spread of moralized content online, *Perspectives on Psychological Science*, **15** (4), pp 978–1010

37 Carter, R (1999) *Mapping the Mind*, University of California Press, Berkeley, Los Angeles, London

38 Buechel, S and Hahn, U (2018) Emotion Representation Mapping for Automatic Lexicon Construction (Mostly) Performs on Human Level, https://arxiv.org/abs/1806.08890 (archived at https://perma.cc/3FM4-8LLK)

39 Guerini, M and Staiano, J (2015) Deep Feelings: A massive cross-lingual study on the relation between emotions and virality, *Proceedings of the 24th International Conference on World Wide Web*, pp 299–305, https://doi.org/10.1145/2740908.2743058 (archived at https://perma.cc/3EZY-LZAD)

40 Cacioppo, J T, Gardner, W L and Berntson, G G (1997) Beyond bipolar conceptualizations and measures: the case of attitudes and evaluative space, *Personality and Social Psychology Review*, **1** (1), pp 3–25

41 BBC (2018) Vote Leave's Targeted Brexit Ads Released By Facebook, https://www.bbc.com/news/uk-politics-44966969 (archived at https://perma.cc/TKE2-CTH2)

42 The Independent (2016) Donald Trump's 'Celebrity-Style' Tweets Helped Him Win US Presidential Election, Says Data Scientist, https://www.independent.co.uk/news/world/americas/donald-trump-twitter-account-election-victory-president-elect-david-robinson-statistical-analysis-data-scientist-a7443071.html (archived at https://perma.cc/Q5NX-NT2R)

43 Brady, W J, Wills, J A, Jost, J T, Tucker, J A and Van Bavel, J J (2017) Emotion shapes the diffusion of moralized content in social networks, *Proceedings of the National Academy of Sciences*, **114** (28), pp 7313–8

44 Variety (2020) Twitter, Facebook Slap Warning Labels on Trump's Tweet Charging Democrats With Trying to 'Steal' Election', https://variety.com/2020/digital/news/twitter-facebook-trump-warning-label-steal-election-1234822899/#! (archived at https://perma.cc/39VS-BMBW)

45 Guerini, M and Staiano, J (2015) Deep Feelings: A massive cross-lingual study on the relation between emotions and virality, *Proceedings of the 24th International Conference on World Wide Web*, pp 299–305, https://doi.org/10.1145/2740908.2743058 (archived at https://perma.cc/3EZY-LZAD)

46 TikTok (nd) *Washington Post*, https://www.tiktok.com/@washingtonpost (archived at https://perma.cc/QW8X-ZUFJ)

47 George, J M (1991) State or trait: effects of positive mood on prosocial behaviors at work, *Journal of Applied Psychology*, **76** (2), p 299

48 Forgas, J P (1998) On feeling good and getting your way: mood effects on negotiator cognition and bargaining strategies, *Journal of Personality and Social Psychology*, **74** (3), p 565

49 Baron, R A (1990) Environmentally induced positive affect: its impact on self-efficacy, task performance, negotiation, and conflict, *Journal of Applied Social Psychology*, **20** (5), pp 368–84

50 Sullivan, M J and Conway, M (1989) Negative affect leads to low-effort cognition: attributional processing for observed social behavior, *Social Cognition*, **7** (4), pp 315–37

51 George, J M (1991) State or trait: effects of positive mood on prosocial behaviors at work, *Journal of Applied Psychology*, **76** (2), p 299

52 Carver, C S, Kus, L A and Scheier, M F (1994) Effects of good versus bad mood and optimistic versus pessimistic outlook on social acceptance versus rejection, *Journal of Social and Clinical Psychology*, **13** (2), pp 138–51

53 Barsade, S G (2002) The ripple effect: emotional contagion and its influence on group behavior, *Administrative Science Quarterly*, **47** (4), pp 644–75

54 Sullins, E S (1991) Emotional contagion revisited: effects of social comparison and expressive style on mood convergence, *Personality and Social Psychology Bulletin*, **17** (2), pp 166–74

55 Friedman, H S and Riggio, R E (1981) Effect of individual differences in nonverbal expressiveness on transmission of emotion, *Journal of Nonverbal Behavior*, **6** (2), pp 96–104

56 Buck, R (1984) *The Communication of Emotion*, Guilford Press, New York

57 Gerson, A C and Perlman, D (1979) Loneliness and expressive communication, *Journal of Abnormal Psychology*, **88** (3), p 258

58 Barsade, S G (2002) The ripple effect: emotional contagion and its influence on group behavior, *Administrative Science Quarterly*, **47** (4), pp 644–75

Chapter 7

1 Schopenhauer, A (2014) *Schopenhauer: Parerga and paralipomena: volume 1: short philosophical essays*, Cambridge University Press, Cambridge

2 Hardaker, C (2010) Trolling in asynchronous computer-mediated communication: from user discussions to academic definitions, *Journal of Politeness Research*, **6** (2), pp 215–42

3 Suler, J (2004) The online disinhibition effect, *Cyberpsychology & Behavior*, **7** (3), pp 321–6

4 Nadler, A and Liviatan, I (2006) Intergroup reconciliation: effects of adversary's expressions of empathy, responsibility, and recipients' trust, *Personality and Social Psychology Bulletin*, **32** (4), pp 459–70

5 Scher, S J and Darley, J M (1997) How effective are the things people say to apologize? Effects of the realization of the apology speech act, *Journal of Psycholinguistic Research*, **26** (1), pp 127–40

6 Tweet, 23 February, 2018, https://twitter.com/AndrewBloch/status/966957339981918208 (archived at https://perma.cc/UP8L-AJ4P)

7 Keaveney, S M (1995) Customer switching behavior in service industries: an exploratory study, *Journal of Marketing*, **59** (2), pp 71–82

8 Weun, S, Beatty, S E and Jones, M A (2004) The impact of service failure severity on service recovery evaluations and post-recovery relationships, *Journal of Services Marketing*, **18** (2), pp 133–46

9 Kahneman, D and Tversky, A (1979) Prospect theory: an analysis of decision under risk, *Econometrica*, **47** (2), pp 263–92

10 Tversky, A and Kahneman, D (1992) Advances in prospect theory: cumulative representation of uncertainty, *Journal of Risk and Uncertainty*, **5** (4), pp 297–323

11 Smith, A K, Bolton, R N and Wagner, J (1999) A model of customer satisfaction with service encounters involving failure and recovery, *Journal of Marketing Research*, **36** (3), pp 356–72

12 Tax, S S, Brown, S W and Chandrashekaran, M (1998) Customer evaluations of service complaint experiences: implications for relationship marketing, *Journal of Marketing*, **62** (2), pp 60–76

13 Blodgett, J G, Hill, D J and Tax, S S (1997) The effects of distributive, procedural, and interactional justice on postcomplaint behavior, *Journal of Retailing*, **73** (2), pp 185–210

14 Duhachek, A (2005) Coping: a multidimensional, hierarchical framework of responses to stressful consumption episodes, *Journal of Consumer Research*, **32** (1), pp 41–53

15 Joireman, J, Grégoire, Y, Devezer, B and Tripp, T M (2013) When do customers offer firms a 'second chance' following a double deviation? The impact of inferred firm motives on customer revenge and reconciliation, *Journal of Retailing*, **89** (3), pp 315–37

16 Huefner, J and Hunt, H K (2000) Consumer retaliation as a response to dissatisfaction, *Journal of Consumer Satisfaction, Dissatisfaction and Complaining Behavior*, **13**, pp 61–82

17 Simon, F (2013) The influence of empathy in complaint handling: evidence of gratitudinal and transactional routes to loyalty, *Journal of Retailing and Consumer Services*, **20** (6), pp 599–608

18 Wacker, R and Dziobek, I (2018) Preventing empathic distress and social stressors at work through nonviolent communication training: a field study with health professionals, *Journal of Occupational Health Psychology*, **23** (1), p 141

19 Michie, S and Williams, S (2003) Reducing work-related psychological ill health and sickness absence: a systematic literature review, *Occupational and Environmental Medicine*, **60** (1), pp 3–9

20 Singer, T and Lamm, C (2009) The social neuroscience of empathy, *Annals of the New York Academy of Sciences*, **1156** (1), pp 81–96

21 Batson, C D, Fultz, J and Schoenrade, P A (1987) Distress and empathy: two qualitatively distinct vicarious emotions with different motivational consequences, *Journal of Personality*, **55** (1), pp 19–39

22 Tang, Y Y, Tang, R and Posner, M I (2016) Mindfulness meditation improves emotion regulation and reduces drug abuse, *Drug and Alcohol Dependence*, **163**, pp S13–S18

23 Uchino, B N, Bowen, K, de Grey, R G K, Smith, T W, Baucom, B R, Light, K C and Ray, S (2016) Loving-kindness meditation improves relationship negativity and psychological well-being: a pilot study, *Psychology*, **7** (01), p 6

24 O'Connor, L E, Rangan, R K, Berry, J W, Stiver, D J, Ark, W and Li, T (2015) Empathy, compassionate altruism and psychological well-being in contemplative practitioners across five traditions, *Psychology*, **6** (08), p 989

25 Rosenberg, M B and Chopra, D (2015) *Nonviolent Communication: A language of life: life-changing tools for healthy relationships*, PuddleDancer Press

26 Rosenberg, M B and Chopra, D (2015) *Nonviolent Communication: A language of life: life-changing tools for healthy relationships*, PuddleDancer Press

27 Rosenberg, M B and Chopra, D (2015) *Nonviolent Communication: A language of life: life-changing tools for healthy relationships*, PuddleDancer Press

28 Denham, S A (1986) Social cognition, prosocial behavior, and emotion in preschoolers: contextual validation, *Child Development*, **57** (1), pp 194–201

29 Cox, E and Dannahy, P (2005) The value of openness in e-relationships: using nonviolent communication to guide online coaching and mentoring, *International Journal of Evidence Based Coaching and Mentoring*, **3** (1), pp 39–51

30 The Conversation (2018) Nike's Courageous New Ad Campaign Mixing Racial Politics With Sport Will Be Vindicated, https://theconversation.com/nikes-courageous-new-ad-campaign-mixing-racial-politics-with-sport-will-be-vindicated-102707 (archived at https://perma.cc/TV4G-ZPCE)

31 The Guardian (2018) Nike's Colin Kaepernick Ad Campaign Sends 'Terrible Message', Says Donald Trump, https://www.theguardian.com/sport/2018/sep/04/donald-trump-colin-kaepernick-nike-ad-campaign-response (archived at https://perma.cc/684N-GRN4)

32 CNBC (2018) Nike Shares Fall As Backlash Erupts Over New Ad Campaign Featuring Colin Kaepernick, https://www.cnbc.com/2018/09/04/nike-shares-tumble-after-company-reveals-new-ad-campaign-featuring-colin-kaepernick.html (archived at https://perma.cc/J53U-TRVR)

33 New York Times (2018) Nike Nearly Dropped Colin Kaepernick Before Embracing Him, https://www.nytimes.com/2018/09/26/sports/nike-colin-kaepernick.html (archived at https://perma.cc/TX8L-EL3R)

34 FiveThirtyEight.com (2017) Colin Kaepernick is Not Supposed To Be Unemployed, https://fivethirtyeight.com/features/colin-kaepernick-is-not-supposed-to-be-unemployed/ (archived at https://perma.cc/WJ3F-P25Q)

35 Brian Schaffner (2018) *Twitter*, https://twitter.com/b_schaffner/status/1036987938008166405 (archived at https://perma.cc/XQ6D-KU4R)

36 Washington Post (2020) Most Americans Support Athletes Speaking Out, Say Anthem Protests Are Appropriate, Post Poll Finds, https://www.washingtonpost.com/sports/2020/09/10/poll-nfl-anthem-protests/ (archived at https://perma.cc/767U-VNXV)

37 NBC News (2020) Poll: More Voters Acknowledge Symptoms of Racism But Disagree About Its Causes, https://www.nbcnews.com/politics/meet-the-press/poll-more-voters-acknowledge-symptoms-racism-disagree-about-its-causes-n1234363 (archived at https://perma.cc/Q5CV-AQ64)

38 Tajfel, H, Turner, J C, Austin, W G and Worchel, S (1979) An integrative theory of intergroup conflict, *Organizational Identity: A reader*, **56**, p 65

39 Tajfel, H, Turner, J C, Austin, W G and Worchel, S (1979) An integrative theory of intergroup conflict, *Organizational Identity: A reader*, **56**, p 65

40 Smith, E R (1999) Affective and cognitive implications of a group becoming a part of the self: new models of prejudice and of the self-concept, in D Abrams and M A Hogg (eds) *Social Identity and Social Cognition*, Blackwell Publishing, Oxford, pp 183–96

41 Jamieson, J P, Koslov, K, Nock, M K and Mendes, W B (2013) Experiencing discrimination increases risk taking, *Psychological Science*, **24** (2), pp 131–9

42 Brown, J J and Reingen, P H (1987) Social ties and word-of-mouth referral behavior, *Journal of Consumer Research*, **14** (3), pp 350–62

43 YouTube (2016) Brooke Bond Red Label – Taste of Togetherness | That Kind Of A Woman, https://www.youtube.com/watch?v=AEqL-kZUxwY&feature=emb_logo (archived at https://perma.cc/6W74-KN8D)

Chapter 8

1 The New York Times (2013) The Documented Life – Sherry Turkle, https://www.nytimes.com/2013/12/16/opinion/the-documented-life.html (archived at https://perma.cc/EX2Q-3Y6N)

2 Ryle, G (2009) *The Concept of Mind*. Routledge, Abingdon

3 Russell, G I (2018) *Screen Relations: The limits of computer-mediated psychoanalysis and psychotherapy*, Routledge, Abingdon

4 Kemmerer, D, Miller, L, MacPherson, M K, Huber, J and Tranel, D (2013) An investigation of semantic similarity judgments about action and non-action verbs in Parkinson's disease: implications for the embodied cognition framework, *Frontiers in Human Neuroscience*, **7**, p 146

5 Thompson, J J, Ritenbaugh, C and Nichter, M (2009) Reconsidering the placebo response from a broad anthropological perspective, *Culture, Medicine, and Psychiatry*, **33** (1), pp 112–52

6 Pecher, D and Zwaan, R A (eds) (2005) *Grounding Cognition: The role of perception and action in memory, language, and thinking*, Cambridge University Press, Cambridge

7 Damasio, A R (1999) *The Feeling of What Happens: Body and emotion in the making of consciousness*, Houghton Mifflin Harcourt, New York. See also Edelman, G M (2004) *Wider Than the Sky: The phenomenal gift of consciousness*, Yale University Press, New Haven CT

8 Pfeifer, R and Scheier, C (2001) *Understanding Intelligence*, MIT Press, Cambridge MA

9 Damasio, A R (1994) *Descartes' Error: Emotion, reason and the human brain*, Picador, London

10 Bailenson, J N (2021) Nonverbal overload: a theoretical argument for the causes of zoom fatigue, *Technology, Mind, and Behavior*, **2** (1), doi.org/10.1037/tmb0000030

11 Fauville, G, Luo, M, Muller Queiroz, A C, Bailenson, J N and Hancock, J (2021) Zoom Exhaustion & Fatigue Scale, https://ssrn. com/abstract=3786329 (archived at https://perma.cc/694M-3U9G)

12 Dimberg, U, Thunberg, M and Elmehed, K (2000) Unconscious facial reactions to emotional facial expressions, *Psychological Science*, **11** (1), pp 86–9

13 Isaacs Russell, G (2020) Remote working during the pandemic: a Q&A with Gillian Isaacs Russell: questions from the editor and editorial board of the BJP, *British Journal of Psychotherapy*, **36** (3), pp 364–74

14 The Nobel Prize, press release, 6 October 2014, https://www. nobelprize.org/prizes/medicine/2014/press-release/ (archived at https://perma.cc/JYT7-6KDT)

15 Aghajan, Z M, Acharya, L, Moore, J J, Cushman, J D, Vuong, C and Mehta, M R (2015) Impaired spatial selectivity and intact phase precession in two-dimensional virtual reality, *Nature Neuroscience*, **18** (1), pp 121–8

16 Mueller, P A and Oppenheimer, D M (2014) The pen is mightier than the keyboard: advantages of longhand over laptop note taking, *Psychological Science*, **25** (6), pp 1159–68

17 Oppezzo, M and Schwartz, D L (2014) Give your ideas some legs: the positive effect of walking on creative thinking, *Journal of Experimental Psychology: Learning, Memory, and Cognition*, **40** (4), p 1142

18 Kontra, C, Goldin-Meadow, S and Beilock, S L (2012) Embodied learning across the life span, *Topics in Cognitive Science*, **4** (4), pp 731–9

19 Nguyen, D T and Canny, J (2007) Multiview: Improving trust in group video conferencing through spatial faithfulness, *Proceedings of the SIGCHI Conference on Human Factors in Computing Systems*, pp 1465–74, https://doi.org/10.1145/1240624.1240846 (archived at https://perma.cc/23DV-D87Q)

20 Wirth, J H, Sacco, D F, Hugenberg, K and Williams, K D (2010) Eye gaze as relational evaluation: averted eye gaze leads to feelings of ostracism and relational devaluation, *Personality and Social Psychology Bulletin*, **36** (7), pp 869–82

21 Melinda Wenner Moyer (2016) Eye Contact: How Long Is Too Long?, *Scientific American*, https://www.scientificamerican.com/article/eye-contact-how-long-is-too-long/ (archived at https://perma.cc/FP7T-T6DK)

22 Linda Stone (nd) FAQ, https://lindastone.net/faq/ (archived at https://perma.cc/WX2H-N4YD)

23 Pallavi Gogoi (2020) Time To Ditch Those Awful Zoom Calls, CEOs Say, *NPR*, https://www.npr.org/2020/10/14/923428794/from-the-folks-who-brought-you-boring-meetings-ceos-want-to-ditch-sterile-zoom-c?t=1602963864075&t=16033 (archived at https://perma.cc/K9GA-C8B5)

24 Bradford, D, Goodman-Delahunty, J and Brooks, K R (2013) The impact of presentation modality on perceptions of truthful and deceptive confessions, *Journal of Criminology*, 2013, pp 1–10

25 DeSteno, D, Breazeal, C, Frank, R H, Pizarro, D, Baumann, J, Dickens, L and Lee, J J (2012) Detecting the trustworthiness of novel partners in economic exchange, *Psychological Science*, **23** (12), pp 1549–56

26 Haidt, J and Lukianoff, G (2018) *The Coddling of the American Mind: How good intentions and bad ideas are setting up a generation for failure*, Penguin, New York

27 UChicago Institute of Politics (2017) CLIP: Van Jones On Safe Spaces On College Campuses, *YouTube*, https://www.youtube.com/watch?v=Zms3EqGbFOk&feature=emb_logo (archived at https://perma.cc/9CD8-AEK2)

28 Edmondson, A (1999) Psychological safety and learning behavior in work teams, *Administrative Science Quarterly*, **44** (2), pp 350–83

29 Edmondson, A C (2018) *The Fearless Organization: Creating psychological safety in the workplace for learning, innovation, and growth*, John Wiley & Sons, Hoboken NJ

30 Edmondson, A (1999) Psychological safety and learning behavior in work teams, *Administrative Science Quarterly*, **44** (2), pp 350–83

31 Detert, J R and Treviño, L K (2010) Speaking up to higher-ups: how supervisors and skip-level leaders influence employee voice, *Organization Science*, **21** (1), pp 249–70

32 Cramton, C D (2001) The mutual knowledge problem and its consequences for dispersed collaboration, *Organization Science*, **12** (3), pp 346–71

33 Zhang, Y, Fang, Y, Wei, K K and Chen, H (2010) Exploring the role of psychological safety in promoting the intention to continue sharing knowledge in virtual communities, *International Journal of Information Management*, **30** (5), pp 425–36

34 Gibson, C B and Cohen, S G (eds) (2003) *Virtual Teams That Work: Creating conditions for virtual team effectiveness*, John Wiley & Sons, Hoboken NJ

35 Moore, D A, Kurtzberg, T R, Thompson, L L and Morris, M W (1999) Long and short routes to success in electronically mediated negotiations: group affiliations and good vibrations, *Organizational Behavior and Human Decision Processes*, 77 (1), pp 22–43

36 Hinds, P J and Mortensen, M (2005) Understanding conflict in geographically distributed teams: the moderating effects of shared identity, shared context, and spontaneous communication, *Organization Science*, **16** (3), pp 290–307

37 Devine, D J (2002) A review and integration of classification systems relevant to teams in organizations, *Group Dynamics: Theory, research, and practice*, **6** (4), p 291

38 Carmeli, A and Gittell, J H (2009) High-quality relationships, psychological safety, and learning from failures in work organizations, *Journal of Organizational Behavior: The international journal of industrial, occupational and organizational psychology and behavior*, **30** (6), pp 709–29

39 Bunderson, J S and Boumgarden, P (2010) Structure and learning in self-managed teams: why 'bureaucratic' teams can be better learners, *Organization Science*, **21** (3), pp 609–24

40 Breuer, C, Hüffmeier, J and Hertel, G (2016) Does trust matter more in virtual teams? A meta-analysis of trust and team effectiveness considering virtuality and documentation as moderators, *Journal of Applied Psychology*, **101** (8), p 1151

41 Wilson, J M, Straus, S G and McEvily, B (2006) All in due time: the development of trust in computer-mediated and face-to-face teams, *Organizational Behavior and Human Decision Processes*, **99** (1), pp 16–33

42 Roghanizad, M M and Bohns, V K (2017) Ask in person: you're less persuasive than you think over email, *Journal of Experimental Social Psychology*, **69**, pp 223–6

43 Bohns, V K (2017) A Face-to-Face Request is 34 Times More Successful Than an Email, *Harvard Business Review,* https://hbr.org/2017/04/a-face-to-face-request-is-34-times-more-successful-than-an-email (archived at https://perma.cc/G9X2-RA46)

44 Byron, K (2008) Carrying Too Heavy a Load? The communication and miscommunication of emotion by email, https://doi.org/10.5465/amr.2008.31193163 (archived at https://perma.cc/266R-CAL2)

45 Markus, M L (1994) Electronic mail as the medium of managerial choice, *Organization Science*, **5** (4), pp 502–27

46 Byron, K and Baldridge, D C (2005) Toward a model of nonverbal cues and emotion in email, *Academy of Management Proceedings*, **2005** (1), pp B1–B6, Briarcliff Manor, NY 10510: Academy of Management

47 Breuer, C, Hüffmeier, J and Hertel, G (2016) Does trust matter more in virtual teams? A meta-analysis of trust and team effectiveness considering virtuality and documentation as moderators, *Journal of Applied Psychology*, **101** (8), p 1151

48 Lukić, J M and Vračar, M M (2018) Building and nurturing trust among members in virtual project teams, *Strategic Management*, **23** (3), pp 10–16

49 Watkins, M (2013) Making Virtual Teams Work: Ten Basic Principles, *Harvard Business Review*, https://hbr.org/2013/06/making-virtual-teams-work-ten (archived at https://perma.cc/3JCK-HQXR)

50 Li, M and Prewett, M (2020) Building Trust in Modern Teams, https://fisher.osu.edu/blogs/leadreadtoday/blog/building-trust-in-modern-teams-2#_edn5 (archived at https://perma.cc/84DV-A4V4)

51 Nembhard, I M and Edmondson, A C (2006) Making it safe: the effects of leader inclusiveness and professional status on psychological safety and improvement efforts in health care teams, *Journal of Organizational Behavior: The international journal of industrial, occupational and organizational psychology and behavior*, **27** (7), pp 941–66

52 Homan, A C, Van Knippenberg, D, Van Kleef, G A and De Dreu, C K (2007) Bridging faultlines by valuing diversity: diversity beliefs, information elaboration, and performance in diverse work groups, *Journal of Applied Psychology*, **92** (5), p 1189

53 re:Work, rework.withgoogle.com

54 DORA State of DevOps (2020) Accelerate State of DevOps Report 2019, https://services.google.com/fh/files/misc/state-of-devops-2019.pdf (archived at https://perma.cc/A5CR-FH8C)

55 Amy Edmondson (2014) Building a Psychologically Safe Workplace | Amy Edmondson | TEDxHGSE, *YouTube*, https://www.youtube.com/watch?v=LhoLuui9gX8&feature=youtu.be (archived at https://perma.cc/9MK7-8X7Q)

Chapter 9

1 Hugo, V (1862) *Les Misérables, 1,* vol. 2, Thomas Nelson & Sons, New York

2 Chidiebere Ogbonnaya (2020) Remote Working Is Good for Mental Health... But For Whom and At What Cost?, *LSE,* https://blogs.lse. ac.uk/businessreview/2020/04/24/remote-working-is-good-for-mental-health-but-for-whom-and-at-what-cost/ (archived at https://perma. cc/9L5G-MWTR)

3 Kane, C (2020) *Where is My Office?: Reimagining the workplace for the 21st century,* Bloomsbury Publishing, London

4 Raconteur (2021) Why It Pays to Get to Know Your Employees, https://www.raconteur.net/hr/employee-engagement/covid-workforce-personalities/ (archived at https://perma.cc/QS5B-ZNGJ)

5 Rocco, E (1998) Trust Breaks Down In Electronic Contexts But Can Be Repaired By Some Initial Face-To-Face Contact, *Proceedings of the SIGCHI Conference on Human Factors in Computing Systems,* pp 496–502, https://doi.org/10.1145/274644.274711 (archived at https:// perma.cc/2GXM-SLJC)

6 MindGym (nd) About Us, https://uk.themindgym.com/about-us/ (archived at https://perma.cc/Y6PH-RST7)

7 Dalton, J (2021) *Reality Check: How immersive technologies can transform your business,* Kogan Page, London

Index

Inspire series